THE DISCOVERY
OF FREEDOM

Man's Struggle
Against Authority

Rose Wilder Lane

THE DISCOVERY
OF FREEDOM

*Man's Struggle
Against Authority*

ROSE WILDER LANE

Fiftieth Anniversary Edition

With New Forewords by
Roger Lea MacBride
and Hans F. Sennholz

Fox &
Wilkes
San Francisco, 1993

Cover Designed by Deanne Hollinger

This edition reprinted 1993 by Fox & Wilkes

ISBN 0-930073-00-2
Printed in the United States of America

FOREWORD TO THE FIFTIETH ANNIVERSARY OF THE FIRST PUBLICATION OF
THE DISCOVERY OF FREEDOM

Gramma. That's what she wanted me to call her, and I did. It is still a little strange for me to refer to that extraordinary person—the author of this book—in any other manner.

I met her about 1946 through my father, who had worked on one of her novels for the *Reader's Digest*. I hitchhiked often from our Westchester County, New York, home to her house and small acreage in nearby Danbury, Connecticut. I would toil in her garden on a Saturday afternoon. When the light failed she would cook us her famous Missouri chicken pie; afterwards we watched the flames in her fireplace while I asked—and she answered—all the questions a seventeen-year-old would pose to a sixty-ish person who had known Everybody, and thought all the thoughts possible about Everything.

I do not exaggerate. Before I met her she had met, and was on good terms with, Jack London, Charlie Chaplin, Henry Ford, Herbert Hoover, Leon Trotsky, King Zog (of Albania), Dorothy Thompson, Sinclair Lewis . . .

And Jack Reed, who almost got her to join the Communist Party in New York in 1918. Gramma had picked up socialist ideas from her aunt Eliza Jane in 1904, with whom she spent a year in Crowley, Louisiana. Aunt Eliza was a thinker of New Ideas, a suffragette, and amazingly for a woman at that time, a street-corner campaigner for Eugene Debs.

But also from Eliza Jane, she became committed to rigorous intellectual honesty and critical analysis.

So when Rose went to Europe as a writer for the Red Cross after World War I she observed at first hand the application and results of socialist/communist ideas. And observed the disastrous results.

She figured it all out. Of course there were a few classical liberal scholars of the late nineteenth and early twentieth centuries who knew the score, and tried to make it known. They failed and faded. Gramma may have been—and I think she was—one of the first modern writers who reached out successfully to general opinion.

She was doubtful that she had been successful. The book in your hands was first published at the very zenith of collectivist thought here and abroad. Remember: Hayek's *The Road To Serfdom* appeared after this work.

So she and a very few close friends and individualist thinkers set out to grab the minds of promising young people. They were (in the entirety as Rose told me) Albert Jay Nock, Isabel Paterson, H. L. Mencken, George Schuyler, and herself.

What they accomplished for what we now call the libertarian revolution of thought is a wholly different story. But, as Gramma confessed to me around 1960, she cast her net for just that reason, and fished me out.

Readers will know the public story of the heritage I have devotedly carried out. Readers will discover from this small memoir, and from this seminal individualist work, what a magnificent person can be.

I cannot end this without writing—

With love, Gramma.

Roger Lea MacBride

Miami, Florida
Fall, 1993

FOREWORD BY HANS F. SENNHOLZ

For a young immigrant it was highly complimentary and stirring that Rose Wilder Lane, this nationally known author, should show any interest in him at all. She was curious from the first moment my articles appeared in the opinion journals and D. Van Nostrand published my book on European unification and pacification. In the early nineteen-fifties I was one of a handful of young academicians who showed any interest in Austrian economics and its social and political ramifications. Lonely and curious, she frequently invited me and my family to her charming country home near Danbury, Connecticut. Our visits to Rose in a family plane, flying in all kinds of weather, at first from Irvington and Tarrytown, New York, and later from Grove City, Pennsylvania, to Danbury, and our long discussions well into the night, are some of the most cherished memories in my life.

Her great interest in my humble efforts probably sprang from several considerations. Surely, she, the great author who had published hundreds of short stories and articles and whose novels were high on the best-seller list, eagerly sought to guide and direct this fledgling writer. She probably viewed it as her task to rear and guide this young mind, to teach him how to write, to pour fresh ideas over his mind, and to fix a noble purpose in his heart. But there may also have been a great measure of curiosity about this young immigrant from the Old World who began to espouse ideas about individual freedom and the private property order. To her, the Old World was part of a vast pagan world that is ruled by ancient superstition and baleful tradition. In her mind, I came from the heartland of that pagan world.

In our heated discussions about both worlds, the Old and the New, Rose would summarily indict Old World thinkers for holding to the ancient belief that some authority always controls the individual. I was stunned by this summary rejection of European thought which, as I viewed it, had given birth to the

New World and continued to leave its mark on contemporary American thought. I would hold forth on the glory of ancient Greece and the power and might of the Roman Empire. She would wax eloquent about Moses and the ancient Israelites, about Mohammed and the Saracens, and especially about the American settlers who rose against their English masters. For Rose Wilder Lane the history of mankind could be understood only as the theater of two diverse forces, the authoritarians and the revolutionists, locked in an unending struggle for supremacy.

If Rose were still alive today, she undoubtedly would point with joy to the disintegration of the Evil Empire, the Soviet Union, as another glorious example of the triumphant spread of the American Revolution. She was convinced that the change had merely begun and no one could know when it would end. But she knew precisely why it would end: for the very reason man had always descended into paganism and barbarism during some six thousand years: his submission to Authority, to Government.

And she would rejoice about the emerging countries in Asia, Latin America, and Africa which look upon the U.S. as their beacon in the night and their leader in an unsettled world, even though this leader presently is pointing in the wrong direction. I now wonder how Rose would explain this leader's deviation from the straight and narrow. Would she lay the blame on Old World thinkers casting their evil spells over the hearts and minds of the American people? Or would she conclude that the present deviation is merely a temporary aberration which will be corrected shortly?

There never appear more than a few great individuals in an age, spirits of discovery and intellect, great minds in advance of their time, and pioneers for generations to come. Rose Wilder Lane was such an individual.

Hans F. Sennholz

Fall, 1993

INTRODUCTION TO THE 1984 EDITION

This is a revolutionary work. It picks up and develops the individualistic aspects of the American political thought of Thomas Paine, Thomas Jefferson, James Madison, George Mason and others, which so strangely dropped into neglect in the aftermath of the French Revolution in the 1790s. Disregarding a few intellectuals who failed to excite the imaginations of their fellows, let alone any significant number of Americans, nothing of the originality and power of the American revolutionaries has appeared until the publication of this book.

The Discovery of Freedom was first published during the Second World War. Rose Wilder Lane told me that the publishers made no effort to promote the book. Its total sales were tiny even for that period, and doubly so for a book written by a nationally known literary figure whose career had encompassed investigative journalism, the publication of hundreds of short stories and articles, and a number of recent novels that had placed high on the best seller lists.

Nonetheless, the book *did* circulate, often dog-eared copies passed from hand to hand and *did* influence many people. Along with Ayn Rand's different approach to the basis of freedom, it was the seminal force creating the current wide trend toward individualistic views in America. Henry Grady Weaver produced an adaptation and popularization of the book, which appeared under the title *The Mainspring of Human Progress*, which subsequently sold hundreds of thousands of copies.

When the Declaration of Independence was written, a way of thinking about individuals appeared which completely reversed all the old ideas. The individual would be master of his own fate. Kings were just ordinary mortals. Government would be the servant and not the master of men. *Discovery* renewed the thinking of the Declaration. In 1962, Jasper Crane, a vice president of DuPont, said that the government established as the fruit of the American Revolution, though fashioned after the nature of man, ". . . wasn't appreciated. The meaning of liberty was unknown and our heritage was almost wasted away. Then, a book appeared called *The Discovery of Freedom*. A new literature developed and has now reached great and influential volume." He meant that this book laid the conceptual groundwork for virtually the entire libertarian school of thought, as well as for much of the then (and now moribund) post-war "conservative" movement.

These ideas are spreading ever more rapidly. They have led directly and indirectly to the creation of centers of study and dispersion of individualist ideas such as the Foundation for Economic Education, the Institute for Humane Studies, the Cato Institute, and Laissez Faire Books, to name but a few. And thousands of intellectuals and academics have applied and refined her ideas in their own works, yet remain only dimly aware of their debt to Rose Lane. But that debt can now be acknowledged.

Mrs. Lane would not agree with all of the developments of her concepts by today's partisans of individualist thought. But the relationship is very much comparable to the impact of Karl Marx's *Das Capital* on later exponents of socialist ideas. *The Discovery of Freedom* may be as far-reaching in its grasp and celebration of the idea of human freedom as Marx's work was in creating the major threat to that very freedom.

Rose Wilder Lane was not the sort of person to distill her ideas from dusty old books. As an impecunious writer in new York, she fell in with the Greenwich Village radicalism of Emma Goldman and John Reed that was then cheering the Bolshevik Revolution and, like so many others who hunger for human freedom, she became sympathetic to the stated ideals of communism. A trip to the Soviet Union, and her experiences with the communist system and the miseries it produced, soon convinced her that communism would increase, rather than decrease, the exploitation of man by man. She came to know personally and well many of the major actors on the world stage, from Leon Trotsky to Herbert Hoover, whose first biography she wrote. These experiences, as well as travels to and immersion in Moslem cultures, created in her an understanding of the dynamics of human societies, of what makes them run. Her wide reading served to extend and refine an understanding gained through extensive personal experience with politics and the operation of complex human systems.

The author's work on the principles and historical relationships set out in *Discovery* didn't stop with this book. *Discovery* was rather the beginning; she devoted a large part of the next twenty-five years to testing and expanding her thought. Over the years she carried on extensive correspondence with Orval Watts, Ludwig von Mises, Jasper Crane, Bob LeFevre, Hans Sennholz and Frank Meyer, to mention but a few, sharpening her ideas, trying out her understandings on their minds. Jasper Crane kept all of her letters and carbons of his own between 1945 and 1968. This immensely stimulating exchange between two splendid human beings was published in 1972 by Caxton under the title *The Lady and the Tycoon*, which I edited. And during the last decade of her life she made great strides in the preparation of a sequel to this present book. Her working title was *The Discovery of Liberty*; I am preparing part of that material for possible publication.

As the years went by, Rose told me many times that she found more and more "mistakes" in *The Discovery of Freedom*. She recalled: "I said that ownership is a civil right, without seeing that I was contradicting myself." There aren't many errors of that order of importance; most of those she deplored are minor indeed. For example, the book says: "Mohammed had invented trench warfare." Well, strictly speaking, he hadn't; Julius Caesar and others had previously made use of it; Mohammed, not knowing that, really "re-invented" it, and her failure so to say pained so exacting a person as Rose Wilder Lane.

The scholarly and literary figure Albert Jay Nock said, I think, all that need be said of this aspect of the book in a review shortly after its first publication: "She makes . . . statements which, to say the least, are questionable. The curious thing, however, is that all these, without exception, are *obiter dicta*. None of them has any bearing on the actual substance of her work. When it comes to anything fundamental, Mrs. Lane never makes a mistake. She is always right. In this respect the book is really remarkable."

The last word I can say is that Rose Wilder Lane was as skillful a user of our language as anyone yet born. Even if this book were not great in content, which it is, its narrative and illustrative appeal would still make it great reading.

Roger Lea MacBride

Charlottesville, Virginia
July, 1984

CONTENTS

Contents

THE DISCOVERY
OF FREEDOM

Man's Struggle
Against Authority

The Situation

—1—

HERE is a planet, whirling in sunlit space.

This planet is energy. Every apparent substance composing it is energy. The envelop of gases surrounding it is energy. Energy pours from the sun upon this air and earth.

On this earth are living creatures. Life is energy.

Every living creature has consciousness and desires. The imperative desire is to continue to live, and living is not easy. Life struggles to exist, among not-living energies that destroy it.

The energy of heat, cold, storms, floods, drought, is the deadly enemy of every human being. His second enemy is the living energy of other creatures, the animals, the plants, that kill him and that he kills for his food and other uses.

Everyone must constantly be defended against these enemies. Farmers and sailors and doctors always know this. Linemen know it, and engineers, chemists, truck drivers and railroad men and oil drillers and sand-hogs and construction workers and airplane pilots and weather forecasters—all the fighters who protect human lives in modern civilization, and keep this civilization in existence.

These men, who know the human situation on this earth and stand the brunt of it, enable others to forget it.

The thinkers—scholars, teachers, writers, politicians—fed and warmed and lulled like babies, can forget their real situation. But their acts recognize it. They live in houses, they use electric lights, they pay someone to stoke the furnace. They are thrifty of water when a drought threatens their city water

The Situation

supply, and their lives. And, as men never were able to do before, they take precautions against the microbes that kill more people than wars.

Men are alive on this earth, only because the imperative human desire is to attack the enemies of human life. Today many Americans may not know this—unless fire, flood, hurricane, epidemic, breaks through the thin defences built around them.

But how are they using their energy? How have Americans been using their energies for a hundred years? What is the meaning of this Republic in history, but an unprecedented fury of human energy, attacking the non-human world, and making this earth more habitable for human beings?

Swiftly, in seventy years, Americans have built defences against darkness—from pine-knots and candles to kerosene lamps, gas jets, electric bulbs, neon lights, fluorescent tubes. In my lifetime, Americans have created astounding defences against weather—from fireplace and stove to furnaces, radiators, automatic oil-burners, insulation, air-conditioning.

Americans make the stupendous attack on Space: steamboats, railroads, subways, automobiles, planes, stratosphere flying, inter-planetary rockets. And on Time: telegraph, transoceanic cables, telephones, radio, television.

In less than one century, human energy—*only in these States and on the western rim of Europe*—has made such a terrific attack on the enemies of human life that it has created the whole modern world.

Why was such an attack never made before?

For sixty known centuries, multitudes of men have lived on this earth. Their situation has been the everlasting human situation. Their desire to live has been as strong as ours. Their energy has always been enough to make this earth at least habitable for human beings. Their intelligence has been great.

Yet for six thousand years, most men have been hungry. Famines have always killed multitudes, and still do over most of this earth. Ninety-five years ago, the Irish were starving to

The Situation

death; no one was surprised. Europeans had never expected to get from this earth enough food to keep them all alive.

Why did men die of hunger, for six thousand years?

Why did they walk, and carry goods and other men on their backs, for six thousand years, and suddenly, in one century, only on a sixth of this earth's surface, they make steamships, railroads, motors, airplanes, and now are flying around the earth in its utmost heights of air?

Why did families live six thousand years in floorless hovels, without windows or chimneys, then, in eighty years and only in these United States, they are taking floors, chimneys, glass windows for granted, and regarding electric lights, porcelain toilets, and window screens as minimum necessities?

Why did workers walk barefoot, in rags, with lousy hair and unwashed teeth, and workingmen wear no pants, for six thousand years, and here, in less than a century—silk stockings, lip sticks, permanent waves, sweaters, overcoats, shaving cream, safety razors. It's incredible.

For thousands of years, human beings use their energies in unsuccessful efforts to get wretched shelter and meager food. Then on one small part of the earth, a few men use their energies so effectively that three generations create a completely new world.

What explains this?

The human situation on this earth is not changed; it can not be changed.

The quality of human energy does not vary greatly. A baby born in Kentucky in 1820 had no physical or mental energy superior to that of a baby born anywhere else at any other time.

The amount of human energy here is much less than anywhere else.

The physical earth has not changed in historical time. So raw materials do not explain what has been done with them here; the raw materials were here when the Mound Builders were. Vast quantities of iron, coal, oil, rubber, have always been available to human beings. Two thousand years ago when Caesar went west into Gaul, Europe was a rich and virgin wilderness inhabited by a few wandering savages, as this continent was a century ago. Not raw materials, but *the uses that human energy makes of raw materials,* create this rich new world.

The plain fact is that human energy operates more effectively in these United States than it has ever operated before, and more effectively than it operates today anywhere else on this planet.

It operates to make human lives safer, healthier, longer, more comfortable and more enjoyable.

Since life itself, and health and comfort and pleasure, are what all men have always wanted, obviously some obstacle has kept them from using their energies effectively, until now.

And since nothing is changed in the human situation on this earth, nor in human desires, this obstacle must have been in the nature of human energy itself.

— 2 —

Consider the nature of human energy.

A human being is a dynamo, generating energy. You are reading a book; you want to turn a page. You generate the energy that moves the muscles of your arm and hand, and turns the page.

This same energy has created the book. From the first stroke of an ax that a woodsman sinks into the living tree, to the printed pages bound and cut, every act of innumerable hands and minds that make the book and deliver it to you, is an operation of human energy generated by an individual's desire to act.

This individual energy, that you use to turn a page, is the only energy operating in the human world.

The ceaseless operation of this energy, ceaselessly attacking

The Situation

the non-human world and from it creating the necessities of human life, keeps men alive on this earth, and creates all the conditions in which human beings live.

Individual energy, constantly generated and constantly acting, creates the physical necessities of human existence, and creates societies, civilizations, nations, kingdoms, principalities and powers, all human relationships, all forms of human association.

Each living person is a source of this energy. There is no other source. Only an individual human being can generate human energy.

All energy operates under control. Whether it be the energy of an electron, a hurricane, or a man, energy is controlled.

This fact makes scientific knowledge possible. Not-living energy—electricity, for example—always operates in the same way in the same conditions. No one knows what controls it, but because it is controlled, men who have observed how it acts can predict, with sufficient accuracy, how it always will act.

Living energy is different; it is creative, and variable. It changes, and it changes the conditions in which it acts. It is unpredictable, because it never acts twice in precisely the same way. Not even two blades of grass in a lawn are identical. No two children of the same parents are alike; not even two quintuplets.

Yet living energy is controlled. Everyone knows what controls human energy. Your desire to turn a page generates the energy that turns the page; you control that energy. No one else, and nothing else, can control it.

Many forces can kill you. Many, perhaps, can frighten you. But no force outside yourself can *compel* you to turn that page. Nothing but your desire, your will, can generate and control your energy. You alone are responsible for your every act; no one else can be.

This is the nature of human energy; individuals generate it, and control it. Each person is self-controlling, and therefore

The Situation

responsible for his acts. Every human being, *by his nature,* is free.

But one person can not generate enough energy. A solitary man on this earth could hardly survive. His enemies are too numerous and too strong; his energy is too weak. To save his bare existence, he must have allies of his own kind.

The brotherhood of man is not a pretty phrase nor a beautiful ideal; it is a fact. It is one of the brutal realities of human life on this inhuman planet.

All men *are* brothers, of one blood, of one human race. They are brothers in one imperative desire to live, in one desperate necessity to combine their energies in order to live. Any man who injures another, injures himself, for human welfare is necessary to his own existence.

Many men do not know this fact. It is not the first fact that men have not known, nor the only one that they do not know now. There are still people who believe that the earth is flat. Because it is *not* flat, because it holds them to its surface by the attraction of its spherical mass, they can behave, within limits and for short distances, as if it were flat.

Men who behave as if the brotherhood of man were not a fact, are alive to do so only because it is a fact.

Imperative human brotherhood creates the individual's relationship with other individuals.

This relationship is always a struggle for control of their combined energies. All friends, all lovers, know that each is constantly trying to control the other's acts, or yielding to the other's effort to control his acts. Shall we stay at home, or go to a movie? Which movie?

The uses of human energy are innumerable; therefore everyone's life is a continuous succession of choices. Since no two persons are alike, they rarely choose to act in precisely the same way at the same time.

This is the human dilemma. Each individual is the source and control of human energy, but one individual can not

The Situation

generate enough energy. To live at all, and then to get the values that he wants in living, he must combine his energy with the energies of others. But in doing this, he always encounters an obstacle to the direct use of his energy to achieve his own desires.

This obstacle is the problem of *controlling* the combined energies.

This is a fact of common experience. Everyone knows, too, that the larger the number of individuals, the more difficult the problem. Two persons can solve it in a moment, but just try to get a dozen families started to a picnic!

When this problem of control extends over millions of units of varying, unpredictable human energy, obviously no effort to control them all can possibly succeed.

Yet human beings always have combined their energies in order to survive on this earth, and energy operates only under control. What, then, does control the energies of men in groups?

— 3 —

The control of human energy is individual control. An individual's desire to achieve some aim is the stimulus that generates human energy. The individual controls that energy.

He always controls it in accordance with his personal view of the desirable, the good.

In other words: Every person acts on a basis of his religious faith.

(I am not discussing religions. My interest is wholly in the unprecedented effectiveness of human energy in protecting and enriching human life, in these United States during the past century.)

Consciousness itself is an act of faith. No one can prove that he exists. No evidence of the senses, and no effort of logic, can demonstrate the existence of the element that everyone means when he says "I." I simply know that I exist.

In the same way, by faith, everyone knows that a standard

The Situation

of values exists. You can not know that you are cold, without having a standard of temperature. You can not like or dislike, or want or not want, anything, without having a standard of good. You can not generate energy to act, without desiring something that (to you) is good. You can not think, without faith that you exist and faith that a standard of value, a God, exists in the universe.

Of course, millions do not believe that Jehovah exists, or Jupiter or Brahma or Allah or Christ. It is always possible not to believe in any God in whom other men believe. But it is impossible not to believe in God. The human mind will not work without a standard of value.

Anyone who imagines that he has no religious basis of thought and action is merely using another name for his god.

Hitler truly says that no Nazi can be a Jew or a Christian. He persecutes Jews and Christians, and they say that he attacks religion. Actually he has a pagan faith that he is the Savior, the mystic Leader ordained by superhuman Powers to establish on earth the rule of the Master Race, the Millennium.

Lenin hated "religion, the opiate of the people." His devoted disciples destroyed the icons, persecuted the priests, defiled the churches—and ardently preached and practiced an utterly self-sacrificing faith in The Party. History (they have faith to believe) mystically ordains The Party to establish on the whole earth the millennial peace, plenty and justice of The Communist Commonwealth.

Read any so-called attack on religion. Listen to any man who claims to be an atheist. He bases his argument on faith in The Truth; he has a standard of good, a God. He must have one; the human mind will not work without it.

Since every individual is self-controlling, he acts in accordance with the standard of values in which he believes.

This is true, whether his God is the God of Abraham and Christ, or Reason or Destiny or History or Astrology or Economic Determinism or the Survival of the Fittest, or any other

The Situation

god by any other name. The majority of men have always believed in innumerable pagan gods. They still do.

Since the actual control of human energy is individual control, and individuals control their energy in accordance with their religious faith, the actual control of the combined energies of any large group of persons, at any time, is the religious faith prevailing among them at that time.

This faith is whatever a majority of individuals believe to be the nature of the universe and of human beings.

Part One

THE OLD WORLD

I. The Pagan Faith

VERY few men have ever known that men are free. Among this earth's population now, few know that fact.

For six thousand years at least, a majority has generally believed in pagan gods. A pagan god, whatever it is called, is an Authority which (men believe) controls the energy, the acts, and therefore the fate of all individuals.

The pagan view of the universe is that it is static, motionless, limited, and controlled by an Authority. The pagan view of man is that all individuals are, and by their nature should and must be, controlled by some Authority outside themselves.

Everyone has this belief when he is very young. A chick can scratch as soon as it is dry from the shell, and a fish emerging from the egg can swim, but a baby must be spanked before he can breathe, and then he can not control the little energy that he has. For a long time, he will kick himself in the eye when he is only trying to taste his toes to find out what they are.

He is hungry, and he can not get food. He is uncomfortable, and he can not turn over. Food, warmth, comfort, cleanliness, everything he wants and must have, come from a power outside himself, enormously stronger than he. And this power actually does control the conditions of his life.

It does not control his energy—did you ever try to stop a baby's squawling when he merely wanted to squawl?—but doubtless he feels that it does. He wants food; it feeds him. He tries to lift himself up, and it lifts him. When this great power outside himself coincides with his own energy, and

3

does what he wants to do, it must seem to him that it controls his energy. When it does with him what he does not want done, he knows that he is powerless to resist it.

If a baby were able to control his energy in thinking and speaking, any baby would say that experience proves the existence of a Great Power that controls babies.

Men do not remain babies all their lives. They grow up. A time comes when every normal man is a responsible human being. His energy creates a part of the whole human world of his time. He is free; he is self-controlling and responsible, because he generates his energy and controls it. No one and nothing else can control it.

Nevertheless, during some six thousand years of the Old World's history, a majority of men have believed that some Authority controlled them.

In all that time, human energies have never worked efficiently enough to get from this earth a reliable food supply.

II. Communism

MANY kinds of insects and some animals seem actually to be controlled by an Authority outside themselves.

A honey bee, for instance, behaves as a cell behaves in a human body. A bee apparently has no desires and makes no choices; a Will of the Masses seems to control it. A bee is ruthlessly exhausted, discarded, replaced by another to be worn out in the same changeless labor for the Swarm, just as cells are worn out and replaced. It appears that a bee has no individual life; the Swarm is the living creature.

The nearest human approach to the bee-swarm is communism.

Some sociologists say that Society began in savage communism and developed through barbarism to civilization; others expect Society to reach its final perfection in future world-communism.

To think of human society as an organism, developing, progressing or retrograding, is to think like a bee—if a bee thinks. It is to think as a pagan thinks. It is to imagine a fantasy.

In the human world there is no entity but the individual person. There is no force but individual energy. In actual human life the only real Society is every living person's contact with everyone he meets.

So far as Society has any real existence, it exists when boy meets girl, when Mrs. Jones telephones Mrs. Smith, when Robinson buys a cigar, when the motorist stops for gasoline, when a lobbyist tips a bellboy and when he meets a Congress-

The Discovery of Freedom

man, and when the Congressman votes on a bill; when the postman delivers the mail and the labor bosses discuss a strike and the milliner brings another hat and the dentist says, "Wider, please." Human relationships are so infinitely numerous and varying every moment, that no human mind can begin to grasp them.

To call all these relationships Society, and then discuss the progress or welfare of Society, as if it existed as a bee-swarm does, is simply to escape from reality to fairyland.

No one knows, or can sensibly guess, how or when or where human life began. If it began in communism, it is beginning now. Plenty of groups of all kinds of persons are living in communism. Groups of American communists have always lived in these United States.

The first thing that European intellectuals did, when the thirteen colonies were free of England, was to establish communism here. Hancock, Harvard, Shirley, Tyringham, in Massachusetts; Alfred and New Gloucester in Maine; Mount Lebanon, Watervliet, Groveland, Oneida (Community silver) in New York; South Union and Pleasant Hill in Kentucky; Bethlehem and Economy in Pennsylvania; Union Village, North Union, Watervliet, Whitewater, and Zoar in Ohio; Enfield and Wallingford, Connecticut; Bishop Hill, Illinois; Corning and Bethel, Missouri; Cedarvale, Kansas; Aurora, Oregon, and scores of other American towns and cities, were communist settlements. In the flowering of New England, Emerson's friends created the communist blossom of Brook Farm. Mr. Upton Sinclair, recently almost elected Governor of California, first established his world-wide renown as a revolutionist by founding the communist settlement of Halicon Hall in New Jersey. The American Indians were communists; so, apparently, were the Mound Builders.

Sparta was a barbarian instance of communism. Plutarch describes the Spartans: "Their discipline continued still, after they were grown men. No one was allowed to live after his own fancy, but the city was a sort of camp, in which every

6

man had his share of provisions and business set out. (Lycurgus) bred up his citizens in such a way that they neither would, nor could, live by themselves; they were to make themselves one with the public good and, clustering like bees around their commander, be by their zeal and public spirit all but carried out of themselves."

That "all but" is the stubborn difference between a man and a bee. A bee is wholly carried out of itself. So (the Spartans believed) was Lycurgus. In history, Lycurgus is a legend. The legend is that, like a bee, he poured his whole life-energy into the public good until, growing old, he killed himself to end a life that had no other value.

For five hundred years the Spartans lived in a changeless commune. King Agis IV tried to raise the standard of living; the Spartans killed him. They continued to live as cells of Sparta until less-communistic Greeks defeated them in war and destroyed the commune.

Twenty years ago the Dukhagini in the Dinaric Alps were living in the same obedience to their Law of Lek. I tried for hours to convince some of them that a man can own a house.

A dangerously radical woman of the village was demanding a house. She had helped her husband build it; now she was a childless widow, but she wanted to keep that house. It was an ordinary house; a small, stone-walled, stone-roofed hovel, without floor, window, or chimney.

Obstinately anti-social, she doggedly repeated, "With these hands, my hands, I built up the walls. I laid the roof-stones with my hands. It is my house. I want my house."

The villagers said, "It is a madness. A spirit of the rocks, not human, has entered into her."

They were intelligent. My plea for the woman astounded them, but upon reflection they produced most of the sound arguments for communism: economic equality, economic security, social order.

I said that in America a man owns a house. They could not believe it; they admired America. They had heard of its mar-

The Discovery of Freedom

vels; during the recent world war they had seen with their eyes the airplanes from that fabulous land.

They questioned me shrewdly. I staggered myself by mentioning taxes; I had to admit that an American pays the tribe for possession of a house. This seemed to concede that the American tribe does own the house. I was routed; their high opinion of my country was restored.

They were unable to imagine that any security, order, or justice could exist among men who were not controlled by some intangible Authority, which could not permit an individual to own a house.

In precisely the same way, Rousseau could not imagine any civilization if Authority did not control individuals. Twenty-five hundred years after Sparta, only two lifetimes ago, all those brilliant European intellectuals were fighting for the Rights of Man, and expecting human rights to destroy Civilization. They could not imagine any free man but the untutored, noble Red Man, naked and solitary in the American wilderness. (They did not bother to learn that the American Indians, though noble and naked, were communists.)

In 1776, these French thinkers had the freest minds in Europe. They could not imagine that an exercise of natural human rights could create a new kind of civilization. They could not imagine actual human rights; they assumed that some Authority must control individuals.

This false assumption underlies all the thought of the Old World, through its whole history, to this day. It underlies a great deal of American thinking.

This delusion has prevailed so long, and it still lures so many honest minds into escaping from facts, because it seems to solve the human problem. The problem is real; it is the problem of controlling the *combined* energies of many individuals.

Individuals must combine their energies, to survive on this planet. Their combined energies must work under some control. The question is, What controls them?

8

Communism

The Old World answer is, Authority.

This answer is the basis of human life in the Old World. No Old World thinker has ever questioned it. The question that has always engaged Old World minds is, *What* Authority?

To find The Authority, men's minds have struggled for thousands of years. To find it, active men, century after century, have revolted against their governments, killed their rulers, slaughtered each other in untold millions, and set up form after form, every imaginable form, of living Authority.

From Lycurgus to Lenin, communists reject every form of human Authority. To the question, What Authority controls human beings? the honest communist answers, No living man; no King, no Czar, no despot, no dictator, no majority, no group, no class.

A communist makes this answer because he recognizes a fact, the fact of human brotherhood. He truly says that all men are united in one common effort to survive on this earth. All men share a common human necessity, a common human aim. All men are equally entitled to life, and therefore to the necessities of life.

But from this point, a communist reasons on the ancient, pagan assumption that some Authority controls all men. He does not question this pagan superstition; he takes it for granted.

His reasoning therefore continues: Since all men are humanly equal, no man is an Authority controlling other men. If this Authority is no living man, it must be a superhuman, intangible Authority. To find out what this Authority is, observe how men behave. Their first effort is to get food, clothing, shelter. Economic Necessity controls them.

Here is the fallacy that comes from superstitious belief in Authority.

A naked man alone in the woods can flee in circles until he dies of exhaustion, or he can build a shelter of branches, kill and eat a rabbit, and make a garment of rabbit skins. His-

9

The Discovery of Freedom

torically, men have not run in circles and died; they have survived. The fact is that human life is a struggle between the man's energy, which he controls, and the non-human energies of weather and trees and rabbits.

But the communist is looking for the Authority that controls men, and taking it for granted that the man does not control himself, then the Authority that controls him must be his situation, the sum-total of trees and rabbits and weather. That is, the hunter is controlled by what he hunts. A woman does not control her gas-range, it controls her. Does it?

Since a communist does not know that individuals control themselves, he sees them as cells in Society, which (he believes) has a Great Spirit that is to the individual what the swarm is to the bee.

So far as I know, only the American Indians called this intangible Authority, The Great Spirit. Savages call it tabu. Spartans called it Sparta. My Dukhagin friends called it the Law of Lek. Many groups of communists living in these States call it God. Marx called it The Will of the Masses, and The Proletarian State. Communists in this country now call their Authority, The Party Line, and it lives in Moscow.

In theory, communism is the total self-surrender of the individual to the will of this intangible Authority, which of course is always The Good.

The theory and practice of communism are as old as history. They persist, because the theory is partly based on fact. It recognizes the equality and the brotherhood of man.

In practice, no effort to make this theory work has ever permitted human energy to work effectively, because the theory does not recognize the fact that individuals control their own energy.

Communism succeeds in controlling combined human energies, because individuals control their energies in accordance with their view (whether true or false) of the universe, of Reality, of God; and if they believe that an intangible Authority controls them, they act *as if* such an Authority did control them. If they do not believe this, they do not attempt communism.

All history proves that communism is a feasible way of living. Men have lived, and are living, in communism at every level of culture and at every economic level ever reached in the Old World.

In order to live in communism, it is necessary only that a number of men and women believe two facts and one fallacy; that all men are equal, that all men are brothers—and that an intangible Authority controls individuals.

III. The Living Authorities

THE great majority of human beings on earth believe today that a superhuman Authority controls human beings.

Italians call this pagan god Immortal Italy. Germans call it The German Race. Communists begin to believe that History is its name; that history is not a mere record of men's acts, but a Power that controls men's acts. The god has many names: Society ("Society is responsible." "Society must provide—"); The Industrial Revolution ("The Industrial Revolution creates the Capitalist System."); The Machines ("Man is the slave of The Machines." "This is a war of The Machines.") Some Americans lament the death of the god that created these United States and once made Americans strong and self-reliant. Its name is The Frontier.

Experience contradicts this pagan superstition. Whatever the intangible Authority is called, it can not be seen nor felt nor smelled nor heard. When a man musters courage to act against or without its control, it does not strike him dead. It does nothing whatever.

From this experience, the believer rarely concludes that his god does not exist. He merely changes its name, or his idea of how it works. (Or, he supposes that it controls everyone but himself. For instance, Mr. Gallup believes that a man's income dictates his opinions. He uses this discovery to make a great change in his own income. Does he find his opinions altering as his income increases?)

Since history began, men in the Old World have never doubted that some Authority controls them. But ordinary ex-

The Living Authorities

perience makes it hard to believe that this superhuman Power is wholly intangible. Most men have believed that it creates a superior *kind* of man to act as its agent.

The Japanese today believe that their Mikado is a living God. The Tibetans believe that God incarnates Himself in their Great Lama. The Pharaohs of Egypt, and the Emperors of Rome, were believed to be Gods. Until 1911, the Empress of China was sacred.

In 1776, all continental Europeans and the descendants of Europeans living in South America and most of North America believed that a King was God's agent on earth and ruled inferior men by that Divine Right.

After the first world war, all continental Europeans except the French were obeying Kings, and still believing that anyone of Royal ancestry—though crippled, diseased, imbecile or insane—was, by his birth and nature, a superior *kind* of human being.

Anyone who believes that Authority controls human beings, and who does not believe that this superhuman Authority is wholly intangible, must believe that it resides in a few living men whose *nature* is superior to the nature of most men.

Excepting communists, men in the Old World have always believed, and still believe, that superhuman Authority gives some men—by their birth, their race, their color, or by a direct act of God upon an individual—a superior nature and a right to control their inferiors.

Therefore they obey these men, supposed to be superior, who are the Government.

Whenever and wherever any large number of persons believe that Government controls them, they always break the changeless routine of communism. Their energies work, a little, to improve their living conditions.

For instance: During some sixty centuries, human energy (already having the wheel) got a cart onto two wheels, and attached knives to these wheels, to kill men. After a lapse that

13

The Discovery of Freedom

almost lost the wheel, men got a cart onto four wheels. By
George Washington's time, human energy had created a
coach, carved and gilded, and suspended by leather straps
above four iron-shod wheels. It stands today in the carriage
house at Mount Vernon.

Another instance: In Ancient Greece, and perhaps earlier,
men knew the principle of the steam engine. The Greeks
spread over the known world after the Macedonians conquered it. Yet today on the Tigris and the Euphrates, men
are still paddling logs hollowed out by fire, as the American
Indians did, or drifting down these rivers in even more prim-
itive bowls of rawhide drawn over basket-work. After thus
traveling downstream, they walk back a thousand miles, as
the flatboatmen, a century ago, were walking back from New
Orleans to Pittsburgh.

In other places, during forty centuries, men built boats
with sails. In addition to sails, the Phoenicians used ranks of
oars. The Romans used two or three banks of oars, with a
slave chained to each oar. Through overseers using whips, the
captain thus had some control of the boat's direction and
speed. But this advance was lost. Columbus sailed in boats
wholly dependent upon the winds.

No one knows the future, and men who carry burdens on
their backs might not imagine a wagon. But surely, men have
always wanted enough to eat. Yet for six thousand years most
men have been hungry. Many of them have always been dying of hunger.

Hunger is normal to nearly all Asiatics and Africans, and
always has been. European working classes were hungry until
less than a century ago. Only three generations of Europeans
have enjoyed enough soup, bread and cheese, spaghetti. They
have never yet had enough meat, butter, milk, vegetables and
fruits. But no whole villages of western Europeans have
starved to death since 1848.

Famines have continued as before in Africa and Asia. Normally, over the greater part of this earth, a working man

14

The Living Authorities

gives sixteen hours of literally killing labor for one small bowl of rice. (His ancestors always have.) Every morning in peaceful Shanghai, made prosperous by its European settlements, policemen collected from the streets the bodies of men and women who had died of hunger during the night. It was a routine job.

When men try to make energy work, and it does not work, it fails to work because they are not using that energy in accordance with its own nature. A gasoline engine will never run on water, because it is not the nature of steam to explode when a spark touches it.

When for six thousand years, human energy does not work well enough to get from this earth enough food to keep human beings alive, it does not work because men are not using their energy in accordance with the nature of human energy.

Every human being, by his nature, is free; he controls himself. But in the Old World, men believe that some Authority controls them. They can not make their energy work by any such belief, because the belief is false.

But they do not question the belief, because when they submit to a living Authority's control, and can not get food, they can always blame that Authority. This is what they have always done. The history of every group of men who ever obeyed a living Authority is a history of revolts against all forms of that Government.

Look at any available records of any people, living anywhere at any time in the whole history of the Old World.

They revolt against their King, and replace him by another King; they revolt against him, and set up another King. In time they revolt against monarchy; they set up another *kind* of living Authority. For generations or centuries, they revolt and change these rulers; then they revolt against that kind of Authority, and set up another kind.

From Nebuchadnezzar to Hitler, history is one long record

15

of revolts against certain living rulers, and revolt against kinds of living Authority.

When these revolts succeed, they are called revolutions. But they are revolutions only in the sense that a wheel's turning is a revolution. An Old World revolution is only a movement around a motionless center; it never breaks out of the circle. Firm in the center is belief in Authority. No more than the Communist or the National Socialist (Nazi) today, has any Old World revolutionist ever questioned that belief; they all take it for granted that *some* Authority controls individuals.

They replace the priest by a king, the king by an oligarchy, the oligarchs by a despot, the despot by an aristocracy, the aristocrats by a majority, the majority by a tyrant, the tyrant by oligarchs, the oligarchs by aristocrats, the aristocrats by a king, the king by a parliament, the parliament by a dictator, the dictator by a king, the king by—there's six thousand years of it, in every language.

Every imaginable kind of living Authority has been tried, and is still being tried somewhere on earth now.

All these kinds have been tried, too, in every possible combination; the priest and the king, the king who is the priest, the king who is God, the king and a senate, the king and the senate and a majority, the senate and a tyrant, the tyrant and the aristocrats, a king and a parliament— Try to think of a combination; somewhere it has been tried.

In 1920 the Albanians tried four quarter-kings *and* aristocrats *and* a parliament. The Bedouin of Iraq today combine a tyrant and a majority. The Emir has absolute power of life and death; he owns all property, dictates all marriages, makes all treaties and raids and wars; if he makes one decision that the tribe does not approve, his subjects kill him and give another man his job. This works all right, too; except that the Bedouin do not get enough to eat.

Each of these kinds of living Authority, and every one of the combinations, has worked all right, except that its subjects did not get enough to eat.

The Living Authorities

Meanwhile, the thinkers from Plato to Spengler have profoundly considered the question, *What* Authority controls human beings? Every one of them has answered precisely that question.

Plato was a philosopher. He reasoned that the natural Authority is philosophers. He worked out in monstrous detail an ideal system, a totalitarian State (which he called a Republic) in which every human impulse is absolutely controlled by a few philosophers.

Spengler returns to the intangible Authority. He says the Authority is Civilization.

He explains that a Civilization springs (is born? or hatched?) from a changeless, formless, human protoplasm which clings to the surface of the earth, and plows and sows and reaps; this mass is The Eternal Peasant.

Each Civilization grows up, from infancy to youth to maturity. As an adult, it is Greece, or Rome, or England. Then it grows old and has cancer. The cancer appears as a small, unnoticed city; it grows, it becomes a large city, then a Metropolis. At this stage it is too far advanced for surgery; swiftly it swells into a Megapolis, and kills the Civilization.

The helpless human cells in the dying Civilization grow weak, and weaker, losing energy and courage and even desires. The Civilization dies, and they decay into the formless mass, The Eternal Peasant. From this mass another Civilization will spring, to grow up, to grow old, and to die of Megapolis.

This is brilliant and scholarly Old World thinking, now, at this moment. This view of human life is supported by an erudite analysis of all past history, and by a host of Spengler's intellectual followers.

Of course, any American who is not an intellectual knows that this world is not inhabited by gigantic, invisible creatures called Civilizations. He knows that ordinary men and women, using their energies, make a civilization and keep on making it, every day, every hour, and that nothing but their

17

constant, individual efforts can make a civilization and keep it existing.

I am a contributing creator of American civilization; it does not create me. I control the stem of this civilization that is within my reach; it does not control me. It can not even make me read Spengler, if I'd rather read a pulp magazine.

Yet on such reasoning as Spengler's, men have tried to act from the beginning of recorded time. On such reasoning, most of the inhabitants of this earth are trying to act now. They do not question their infantile belief that some Authority controls all human beings (except, perhaps, themselves).

Egyptians obeyed the Pharaohs, their living Gods; now the Japanese obey their Mikado. Alexander the Great was a military despot; so was Napoleon; so is Hitler. Twenty-seven hundred years ago, Lycurgus established a commune; twenty years ago Lenin was trying to establish a commune. Nebuchadnezzar was an absolute monarch; so was Louis XV when he governed this country from Labrador to the Gulf of Mexico. Genghis Khan was a tyrant; and what is General Franco?

From time immemorial, and still over most of this earth today, men have never ceased trying to find the Authority that controls human energy. Whether you look at Pharaoh's subjects, obeying a living God, or at Athenian Greeks obeying a majority, you see the same result: people did not get enough to eat.

Egyptians built the pyramids, and sold their children because they could not feed them. Athenians built the Parthenon, and went to their democratic elections through a thin sound of wailing from the pottery jars on their street corners, where babies were dying. Kind friends quickly put the new-born in a jar and set it in a public place, and came back again and again to listen, hoping that before the baby died someone might take her who could afford to feed a child.

If men and women do not want to live like that, then this is a fact: human energy does not work as human beings want it to work, under any kind of Authority that men are able to imagine or devise.

Here is a sketch of a grain-mill and bakery, in the grandeur that was Rome two thousand years ago:

"What a poor sort of slaves were there; some had their skin bruised all over black and blue; some had their backs striped with lashes and were covered rather than clothed with torn rags; some had their members only hidden by a narrow cloth; all were such ragged clouts that you might perceive through them all their naked bodies; some were marked and burned in the forehead with hot irons; some could scarcely see, their eyes and faces were so dim and black with smoke, their eyelids all cankered with the darkness of that reeking place, half blind and sprinkled black and white with dirty flour." [1]

Here are the English, just before Columbus sailed:

"The houses in what were called cities were built of stones put together without mortar; the roofs were often of turf. The cottages had no other floor than a dried and stiffened bull's hide. In Scotland the peasantry lived on the coarsest food, often on the bark of trees. Bread was accounted a rare delicacy. Over the border in England it was a little better. (Aeneas Sylvius) had bread and wine. The English women gratified their curiosity by breaking the bread into fragments and handing it to one another to smell and giggle at. The cottages were constructed of stakes driven into the ground, interwoven with wattles and covered with flakes of bark or the boughs of trees. The lot of the lower, the laboring, classes for many ages had undergone no amelioration; in a political sense, they were only animals valuable for what their work could produce. They were expected to manifest loyalty to the King and obedience to The Church. There was no career open to them, except to the grave." [2]

---

[1] *The Golden Ass of Apuleius*, Adlington's translation.
[2] Aeneas Sylvius' *Pon. Max. Asiae Europeaque Elegantissimo Descriptio*, 1534.

The Discovery of Freedom

Here are Americans, seven years after this Republic was established.

"Women and children in the month of December traveling a wilderness through ice and snow, passing over large rivers and creeks, without shoes or stocking and hardly as many rags as cover their nakedness, without money or any other provision except what the wilderness affords. Hundreds traveling hundreds of miles, they knew not why nor whither, except it's to Kentucky."[3] The snow was two feet deep, for naked legs to wade. Moses Austin, one of the richest men of Baltimore, had lost everything in the crash of the bull-market in western lands. He took refuge one night with twenty of these travelers in a cabin so small that they slept piled upon each other on the earth floor.

They were trying to reach a place where they could live. There were no jobs in the East. The poor had no work, no food; they hoped to get land in the West. But speculators owned every foot of western land; the Henderson Land Company owned Kentucky, and would sell land for $2.50 an acre, when, if there had been jobs, wages were 25 cents for a twelve-hour day.

So much for progress in two thousand years. And why consider such a short time? Two hundred and fifty thousand years ago, people lived in caves in France and Spain. People are still living in caves in France and in the Spanish Pyrenees. The cliffs of Chinchilla have always been inhabited. The pottery workers at Coria live in holes in the banks of the Guadalquivir, without windows or floors. In Italy, and in Greece, and in many places in France, human beings are still living underground.

When American Red Cross workers went into the Balkans after the first World War, they found families living in a clay bank in Montenegro's largest city. They were horrified. So was I. I wrote a piece about those homeless victims of war that should have wrung dollars from the stoniest American

---

[3] The Austin papers, quoted in *American Historical Review*, April, 1900.

pocketbook. Only, before I finished it, I went back with an interpreter to give some first aid to those miserable refugees. My sympathetic questions bewildered them. They were living as they always had lived, in their ancestral homes.

I should not have been surprised. Sixty-five years ago my own mother was living in a creek-bank in Minnesota, and it was not necessary then to say that her father was an upstanding, self-respecting, leading citizen of the community. Living underground was nothing unusual; less than sixty years ago, American families were living in dugouts all over the prairie States.

IV. The Planned Economies

SINCE history began, all the people of the Old World have always lived in what is now called "a planned economy."

When anyone says, "a planned economy," he means, a control of the human energy used in producing and distributing material goods, by an Authority consisting of a few men, and according to a plan made by those men—and enforced by the police.

Americans who have not lived in other countries can only imagine a planned economy, for they are used to living in an economy that individuals plan and control. Whenever an American decides how to earn or how to spend any money, or whether to drive his car or walk, or to get a job or go to college, or to plant corn or alfalfa, or to rent a house or build or buy one, he is planning and controlling the American economy.

One result of this individual planning and control is an enormous waste of things. No one can estimate its colossal sum, for normally a hundred million persons are adding to it every day, every hour.

An average American working man's garbage can would nourish bountifully any European lower-middle-class family. In every American city's slums, every morning before the garbage wagons come, immigrants stunned by this waste are picking over the contents of garbage cans, salvaging metal, paper, bones, fat, to sell to dealers. And Americans shudder to hear that human beings get their living from garbage cans.

In New York City's slums during the dreadful 1930's, when

The Planned Economies

most of the people in the tenements were living on relief, the little neighborhood bakers burned in the gutters every evening the loaves of that morning's bread which they had not sold that day. For in America everyone eats fresh bread.

Americans normally throw away every year an estimated hundred thousand tons of good white flour, in pies' lower crusts which they do not eat. Normally every month they throw away twenty thousand tons of white sugar, in the bottoms of coffee cups; they do not bother to stir sugar into coffee.

Every year they throw away 2,500,000 motor cars, not because the cars no longer run, but because new cars run better. Along the highways clean across this continent the old cars lie rotting away, fortunes in metal and leather and cloth. Europeans have been saying bitterly, "In America, the blind beggar rides in a Cadillac, guided by a faithful little Ford on a string."

I knew a mechanic who was out of work and broke in the worst of the depression, with a family to support. He picked up from the dumps in Wyoming enough sound structural iron and good steel cables to build a suspension bridge across Snake river, a bridge that the county could not afford to build at the estimated public cost of $50,000. He and his nine-year-old son built it, using a dragline-rig that he had made entirely from junk. It more than satisfied county inspection. The farmers who needed the bridge gladly paid $2,500 for it, and my friend, after paying for cement and gasoline, cleared about $2,000 for his labor. He plans American economy. Americans do.

During that depression, ten or twelve million Americans lost their jobs. Three or four million were on public relief. The others went on planning American economy and supported themselves and those on relief.

There is no waste of material things in other countries. In France, every cigarette stub in a gutter has always been carefully gathered up, and the tobacco from it is put into new

23

cigarettes. The Government has a monopoly of the processing and sale of tobacco in France.

In Italy, where the climate, the soil, and the people are the same as in California's Napa valley, during the recent Armistice a horde of fierce-eyed children pounced upon every cigarette stub, tin-foil package, orange peeling, or a horse's warm droppings. A quick snatcher might salvage enough in a day to exchange for a hunk of bread.

In the Balkans it is always a sin to let a crumb of cornbread fall. A peasant quickly picks it up from the earthen floor and asks God's pardon for such waste before he eats the crumb.

In the Middle East, the salt is salty earth; to leach out white salt would waste some saltiness. The Old World does not waste an atom of anything. It never has.

The billions of men and women who have lived and died young during all the centuries of Old World history, have always lived in a "planned economy." A planned economy does not waste any material thing. It wastes time, and human energy, and human life.

In communism, the men who establish the commune plan its economy. They can plan it only on the level of the living conditions that have already been created in that place at that time. (In 1900, no one could have planned a radio network.)

They always establish economic equality. To do this, they must plan an economy in which "every individual has his share of provisions and business set out." Therefore, no man can be permitted to live after his own fancy; that would not be communism, it would be individualism.

So no one living in communism can use his energy in a new way. Everyone in the commune must govern his acts in obedience to the Authority that decrees his share of business and provisions.

As long as he believes that this intangible Authority—the Public Good, the Will of the Masses, the Proletarian State,

The Planned Economies

the Law of Lek—does and should control him, he can not even assert his own will against it.

If he does assert his own desire to change living conditions —if, like King Agis IV, he tries to introduce money; or, like the woman of the Dukhagin, to have one whole hovel to himself, when the commune was not planned on any such high standard of living; or if in Amana, Iowa, in 1900 he had wanted to invent a motor car, or in 1940 to buy one—he cannot do this unless he shakes his comrades' faith in the controlling Authority. And this faith is all that keeps the commune in existence. If he succeeds in using his energy to change living conditions, he destroys the commune because he destroys that faith.

This is the history of scores of communes established in these States.

It is not true to say that communism maintains a low standard of living. Actually there is no standard of living. There cannot be one, because human energy creates all economic conditions in the human world, and creates them continuously in Time.

This planet gives nobody any food, clothing or shelter. A person is fed or not fed, housed or not housed, clothed or not clothed. But the quality of any food, clothing, or man-made shelter can not be known at any time in any absolute terms.

George Washington never heard of calories or vitamins; he lived on meats and starches through every winter; he never saw a glass of orange juice; his diet was so deficient that he lost his hair and teeth at an early age. His clothes were uncomfortable and unhygienic. He traveled on foot, on horseback, or in a springless carriage. His house had no toilet or bathtub, no furnace or heating stove, no light but candles. What was his standard of living?

It was so high that forty years ago not one American in ten thousand aspired to it.

Only an Old World mind can think in terms of a definite standard of living. Such ideas come from the ancient pagan

25

faith that this universe is static, changeless and limited. A realist now thinks in terms of dynamic, creative energy, and of human energies working to create an unknowable future.

So it can not be said that a communist economy is one of scarcity. If human energies are working effectively outside a commune, as they have been working outside the communes in these States, then in contrast, the communist standard of living seems to be low. This contrast causes discontent inside the commune.

But in any catastrophe, such as war or drought or economic shock, which temporarily disrupts a free economy, the communist economy will appear, in contrast, to be one of abundance. This contrast causes envy of the happy communists.

I well remember the incredible abundance of food in the Russian Dukhaber commune in Kansas—or was it southern Nebraska?—during the depression of the 1890's, when I and my parents were traveling among the hundreds of thousands of refugees, walking or riding in covered wagons along all America's dusty or muddy roads, looking for work and food. I can see yet those sleek, unmortgaged cows, those brimming pails of milk, those jars of butter in the spring-house, and the smiling Russian woman with her hair in golden braids, who spoke no known language, but opened the front of her blue blouse and took from next her skin a slab of cold biscuits. That was abundance to most Americans fifty years ago.

But all that can be said accurately about a communist economy is that it is static. At whatever level of living conditions a commune is established, at that level the living conditions remain as long as the commune lasts.

The reason for this historic fact is that nothing but a change in the ways of using human energy productively can change living conditions.

Since individuals actually control human energy, any change in its uses can come only from an individual's efforts, experiments, attempts to create things that do not yet exist. Most of these efforts inevitably fail, causing loss and waste.

The Planned Economies

Communism prevents such waste by preventing individual initiative in using human energy. This also prevents economic progress.[1]

Men have improved their living conditions in the Old World whenever they believed that living rulers were the controlling Authority.

Whenever they believed this, human energy worked spasmodically, in jerks, so to speak.

Take any few hundred years of Old World experience, outside the communes, and you see a succession of convulsive efforts and collapses, as if a living thing were roped down and struggling.

This is precisely what was happening. Human energy could not get to work at its natural job of providing for human needs, because whenever men began to develop farming and crafts and trade, the Government stopped them.

They believed that the Emperor was God, or the King was Divine, but he wasn't. Men in Government have no more power to control others than any man has. What they have is the use of force—command of the police and the army. Government, The State, is always a use of force, permitted by the general consent of the governed.

If this fact is not self-evident to you, talk to Americans who learned from experience what Government is. In nearly every American community there are men who lived in this country, somewhere between the Mississippi and the Pacific coast, with no Government whatever. They lived in anarchy, and every man carried a gun.

He had to carry a gun, because there was no Government. Government, as Jefferson said, is a necessary evil. It is evil

---

[1] The "progress" in Russia during the past twenty years has come from a dictator's efforts to industrialize Russia (that is, to bring living conditions up to the level already created in America). The imitation of America was Lenin's plan. The theory is that the dictatorship is temporary; that the communist commonwealth will be established when Russian production equals the present capitalist production.

The Discovery of Freedom

because it is a use of force, and force has no morality and no moral effect. It is necessary because—to date, and perhaps forever—a few men stupidly use force to injure others, and nothing but force will stop them.

When there was no Government, every man had to be able to defend himself, by force. He seldom shot anybody; the need for force is actually very little. But he had to carry a gun and be able to use it, on the off-chance that he might have to shoot it out with a Bad Man.

This state of affairs is a nuisance. Men do not want to lug guns around; they want to get on with their natural job, building towns, raising cattle, mining, drilling oil wells. To get rid of their guns, they had to get rid of the Bad Men. So they called themselves a vigilance committee, went after the Bad Man, and strung him up.

They did this clean across the country, from the Yadkin and the Mohawk to the Rio Grande and the Golden Gate. The invariable result was that the vigilance committee went bad.

This happened, because men recognize the brotherhood of man. Murder is everywhere abhorred.

So when a man had helped to kill another, disarmed and defenceless even though bad, he felt about his action, later, in one of two ways. He hated to remember it, he did not want to repeat it, he figured there was no need to do it again, and he dropped out of the vigilance committee. Or, having once broken the intangible bond of kinship that protects human life on this earth, he became at heart a killer.

The vigilance committee (it had scores of local names, the Bald Knobbers, the Sand-lotters) always began as a group of men who used force to stop robbers and murderers. It always became a group of men who robbed and murdered.

Only a still stronger force could stop them. So the peaceful men organized Government.

They chose one of their number and said to him, in effect, "We'll help you dispose of that gang, and after that, you attend to any Bad Man that shows up. One man can handle

The Planned Economies

that job, if he gives his whole time to it, and you're elected. You carry the gun from now on, Sheriff. And you, Judge, call on twelve of us to decide what the Sheriff ought to do with any Bad Man he catches. Now we've got a Government; we can get our work done without any more interference."

This is the essential element of all Government: force, used with general consent.

In any civilization, the use of force is the whole difference between Government and any other organized group of men. The need for Government is the need for force; where force is unnecessary, there is no need for Government.

Without the use of force, men direct the marvelous organized efficiency of the circus, loading, unloading, transporting and parading hundreds of people and animals, establishing and demolishing a tent-city on a schedule of minutes. One man directs all these intricate activities, by general consent. Anyone who doesn't consent can quit.

Without the use of force, men control the almost infinite complexities of radio, networks of human and other energies encircling the earth and working twenty-four hours a day on a schedule of seconds. Directors control it by the consent of thousands of men all over the earth. If a man in the Ural mountains, in the Sahara desert, in Australia, doesn't want to be at the mike when a man in New York wants him to be there, he can cut bait and go fishing. The only penalty is that if he quits, he has quit.

A traffic cop directs traffic by general consent, too. But he is Government; he has the use of force. When the traffic cop moves his thumb, a driver pulls to the curb. If he does not, he will eventually be stopped by force. He shows up in court when he is told to be there, too, (unless he has a pull at City Hall and uses it); if he does not, policemen will take him there, by force if necessary. He pays his fine, and with no back talk, or he will be put in jail by as much force as is needed to put him there.

A club member pays his dues because he wants to. If he does

not want to, he does not pay them, and he is no longer a member of the club.

A citizen (or, in the Old World, a subject) pays taxes because he wants to pay them. If he does not want to, he will pay them anyway, because Government is a group of men who have the use of force. They will take his property or his wages, by force, to pay the taxes they assess upon him. If he tries to lie out of paying, and they find it out, they will put him in jail, by force.

"And serve him right!" all the willing tax-payers will say, for Government is a group of men who have the use of force by general consent. Whenever, in all history, they have lost that consent, their subjects have thrown them out of Government and have given the use of force to another group of men. Government always derives its power (to use force) from the consent of the governed.

But a use of force is not *control*. No living ruler has ever actually controlled his subjects. There is no superhuman power in Government; men in Government have no natural nor Divine superiority to any other man. And no man can control another. No possible use of force can compel any individual to act. A use of force upon him can only hinder, restrict, or stop his acting.

In actual fact, *consent to Government is consent to a use of force to hinder, restrain, or stop individuals and minorities who act in ways that a majority does not approve or does not act to defend.* Stop, thief!

A "planned economy" is believed to be a Government's *control* of the productive uses of human energy. It is believed that the men in Government can control, for the general good, the men who produce and distribute material goods.

In thousands of years, they have never been able to do it.

The actual fact is that a "planned economy" is an absolute monopoly of agriculture, manufacturing, and commerce, held by men in Government and maintained—so far as possible— by police and military force.

The Planned Economies

Historically, this monopoly is always a use of force to hinder, restrict or stop the productive uses of human energy.

Its first effect is to prevent the use of human energy in new methods of production, or in producing new things. That is, it prevents economic progress.

The reason is that Government, by its nature, can not permit a competitor within the field of its activities. Everyone knows that Government is a monopoly of the use of force; it can not permit individuals to use force against each other, or against the Government, nor can it permit another Government to use force inside its frontiers; if it does, it ceases to be Government.

In the same way, a Government which is, for instance, a monopoly of the production, processing and sale of tobacco (as the French government was) can not permit a rival tobacco company to compete with it; if it does, it ceases to be Government.

When Government has a monopoly of all production and all distribution, as many Governments have, it can not permit any economic activity that competes with it. This means that it can not permit any *new* use of productive energy, for the new always competes with the old and destroys it. Men who build railroads destroy stage coach lines.[2]

Men in Government who imagine that they are controlling a planned economy *must* prevent economic progress—as, in the past, they have always done. For economic progress is a change in the use of men's productive energy. Only individuals who act against the majority opinion of their time will try to make such a change. And if they are not stopped, they destroy the existing (and majority-approved) Government monopoly.

To know the everlasting majority attitude toward new uses of productive energy, remember that your great-grandfather did not believe that railroads were possible. At the time, a

---

[2] Russians and Nazis are not developing *new* uses of productive energy. They are imitating uses previously developed in America, England, and France.

committee of learned men investigating the question for the British Government, reported that railroads were not possible, for the reason that the proposed speed of fifteen miles an hour would kill any human being; the human body could not endure such a pressure of air.

Remember what sensible men thought of Alexander Graham Bell's insisting that a wire could carry a human voice. Remember that ships could not be made of iron because iron does not float. Recall that the horseless carriage could never be more than a rich man's toy, not only because it cost at least five thousand dollars, but also because it ran only on macadam and therefore could never leave the cities. Or, what do you think of the experimenters in New Mexico who are working on rocket-ships to carry men from planet to planet? How much of your own money will you invest in a rocket-line from here to Mars? No majority will ever take up arms against their Government to defend such men as these.

Anyone who is running a going concern believes in it; he has also a selfish interest in it. The owners of river steamboats would never have encouraged the building of railroads. And when men in Government have a monopoly, they have the use of force (backed by majority opinion) to prevent anyone from attacking their monopoly.

A planned economy, therefore, is a use of force to prevent the natural use of human energy. This explains the historic fact, at first surprising, that in all history the earnest, sincere, hardworking ruler has done the most harm to his own people.

Old World Government has always been (supposed to be) an Authority controlling a planned economy. Actually it is a use of force to prevent material progress. The lazy, selfish, dissolute ruler neglects that job. Caligula, for instance, the worst of Roman Emperors, merely wasted goods in extravagant living and enjoyed torturing a few hundreds of his helpless subjects. People always get along comparatively well under a ruler like that.

It was sober, ascetic, conscientious Augustus Caesar who laid

The Planned Economies

the firm foundations of the misery in which all Europeans lived for generations. He began to establish a planned world-economy, the famous Roman Peace that the Roman legions gave the whole world's people by conquering them. (Just such a peace as Hitler, and some of his enemies, are planning now.)

That Roman Peace was designed to last forever. When Diocletian perfected it, its economy was so thoroughly planned and so well administered that farmers could no longer farm nor workers work, and Government took care of them on the relief that taxes provided, until the increasing taxes pushed so many farmers and workers onto tax-supported relief that there was not enough productive energy left to pay the taxes, and the Roman empire with its world peace collapsed into the Dark Ages.

Or consider the planned economies in this country two hundred years ago. Compare the Kings of France and Spain with the rulers of England.

That little half-an-island was blessed for centuries with some of the worst rulers that ever wore a crown. If King John, for instance, had been half the King that Henry the Second was, there never could have been a Magna Carta.

The only truly able Tudor was Elizabeth, and her father had left England in such an uncontrolled state that she had to use all her energy and wit merely to stay on her throne.

Never was a realm so little governed as Elizabeth's. She built up the British navy by doing nothing for it. She gave her sea-captains orders to do as they pleased, on their own responsibility and at their own cost; she would not even pay for the powder and lead with which they defended England against the Spanish armada. She never had a plan, except to wait and see what happened. With great firmness of character, she always decided to decide nothing today. By this highly intelligent means, she let her subjects found the British empire.

After her came the Stuarts. A charming, careless, self-indulgent breed of Divine Right Kings, the poodle dogs of their

33

species, with not a moral nor the slightest sense of responsibility under their curly wigs.

They governed so negligently that under their rule the very butchers and bakers and candlestick makers got up enough energy to chuck them off their throne, and enough independence of mind to behead one of them, Divine though he was supposed to be, and to make an ex-brewer the ruler of England.

Even after such a lesson, the Stuarts were so lazy that you find Charles the Second giving his Parliament this negligent order, "I pray you devise any good short bills that may improve the industry of the nation."[3] That was all.

This is no way to plan and control a national economy. While the King was uttering such useless words, his police were so out-numbered and terrified that it was no longer necessary to bribe them, and British commerce was thriving under their very noses. So many thousands of smugglers were exporting British wool from every port and cove that someone defined the island as a piece of land entirely surrounded by smugglers.[4]

Yet when the prospering British wool growers expanded production so rapidly that not even the innumerable smugglers could handle all their wool, Charles offered only one little remedy for overproduction: a decree that no corpse could be buried in England that was not wrapped in woolen cloth. This measure was enforced. But ghouls dug up the corpses to steal the cloth, which, through bootlegging, finally covered the nakedness of London's pantless workingmen.

The badly governed English at last revolted against the Stuarts, at the same time putting into English law a grant of

[3] *Parliamentary History,* Vol. 4, p. 291.

[4] English weavers made such poor cloth that they could not compete with continental weavers. To aid them by destroying the continental weavers, Parliament prohibited the export of British wool to the Continent. Of course this measure would have ruined the English wool producers, thus raising the cost of wool to English weavers and making their cloth worse. But, *as always in all past history,* grafters and smugglers rescued commerce.

The Planned Economies

some liberties that they had been lawlessly taking. Then they imported the best of rulers, the German line that is still on the throne. The Germans have always been the most thorough rulers and most submissive subjects in modern Europe. But English luck continued; the first two German Kings of England paid no attention to their job and did not even bother to learn English.

The third George was as austere as Augustus Caesar. So long as he was sane, he never for a moment forgot his duty. He toiled from candlelight to candlelight to prepare himself for governing, and as King he continued his ceaseless labor. He curbed English industry and commerce by more than two thousand new regulations.

But his subjects simply turned into grafters and smugglers and went right on expanding British commerce. In England itself, King George could not keep his subjects from getting bootlegged food, and (except the Canadians) his American subjects got away entirely. While they were doing it, the very London newspapers had the unprecedented audacity to print the discussions in Parliament.[5]

The rulers on the Continent were much more efficient. Production and commerce were so well controlled in the Germanies that they hardly existed. Obedience to Authority was the German way of life. The Landgrave of Hanou and Hesse had his agents round up 3,500,000 thalers' worth of his peasants and sold them like sheep to King George. And the Hessian peasants, broken hearted, obediently came to the unknown other side of the world and obediently killed Americans, without knowing or asking why, simply believing that they could do nothing else.

Meanwhile in France the planned economy was thoroughly

---

[5] Poor King George. In 1771 he wrote to Lord North, "It is highly necessary that this strange and lawless method of publishing debates should be put a stop to. But is not the House of Lords the best court to bring such miscreants before; as it can fine, as well as imprison, and has broader shoulders to support the odium of so salutary a measure?" Horace Walpole, *George III*, vol. 4, p. 280.

planned and enforced. "In every quarter, and at every moment, the hand of Government was felt. Duties on importation, and on exportation; bounties to raise up a losing trade, and taxes to pull down a remunerative one; this branch of industry forbidden, and that branch of industry encouraged; one article of commerce must not be grown because it was grown in the colonies, another article might be grown and bought, but not sold again, while a third article might be bought and sold, but not leave the country.

"Then, too, we find laws to regulate wages; laws to regulate prices; laws to regulate the interest of money; custom-house arrangements of the most vexatious kind, aided by a complicated scheme which was very well called the sliding scale—a scheme of such perverse ingenuity that duties varied on the same article, and no man could calculate beforehand what he would have to pay.

"To this uncertainty, itself the bane of all commerce, there was added a severity of exaction, felt by every class of producers and consumers. The tolls were so onerous, as often to double and quadruple the cost of production. A system was organized, and strictly enforced, of interference with markets, interference with manufactures, interference with machinery, interference even with shops.

"The ports swarmed with tide-waiters, whose sole business was to inspect nearly every process of domestic industry, to peer into every package, and tax every article; while, that absurdity might be carried to its extreme height, a large part of all this was by way of protection; that is to say, the money was avowedly raised, and the inconveniences suffered, not for the use of Government, but for the benefit of the people. In other words, the industrious were robbed, in order that industry might thrive.

"Indeed, the extent to which the governing classes have interfered, and the mischiefs which that interference has produced, are so remarkable as to make thoughtful minds wonder how civilization could advance in the face of such repeated

The Planned Economies

obstacles. In some of the European countries the obstacles have, in fact, proved insuperable, and the national progress is thereby stopped.

"Even in England, where [Government has] for some centuries been less powerful than elsewhere, there has been inflicted an amount of evil which, though much smaller than that incurred in other countries, is sufficiently serious to form a melancholy chapter in the history of the human mind.

". . . .Thus, to take only such conspicuous facts as do not admit of controversy, it is certain that all the most important interests have been grievously damaged by the attempts of legislatures to aid them. . . . Instead of leaving industry to take its own course, it has been troubled by an interminable series of regulations, all intended for its good, and all inflicting serious harm.

"Such are some of the benefits which European trade owes to the paternal care of European legislatures. . . . The first inevitable consequence was that in every part of Europe there arose numerous and powerful bands of smugglers, who lived by disobeying the laws. These men, desperate from fear of punishment, spread drunkenness, theft, and dissoluteness, coarse and swinish debaucheries, which were the natural habits of so vagrant and lawless a life." [6]

Indeed, nothing but smuggling kept the poor from starving to death under that Government monopoly, benevolently planned for their good.[7]

Weekly in the market places the captured smugglers were mercifully hanged for minor crimes of selling food, and for larger commercial activities they were burned alive or killed

---

[6] Henry Thomas Buckle, *History of Civilization in England*, Vol. 1, pp. 200, et seq.

[7] "C'est a la contrebande que le commerce doit *de n'avoir pas peri* sous l'influence du regime prohibitif; tandis que ce regime condamnait les peuples a s'approvissioner aux sources les plus eloignees, la contrebande rapprochait les distances, abbaissait les prix, et neutralissait l'action funests des monopoles." Blanqui, *Histoire de l'Economie Politique en Europe*, Vol. 2. Paris, 1845.

more slowly by the more agonizing torture of breaking on the wheel.[8]

Torture and death could not stop smuggling, because human beings must live. The use of force in an attempt to control the natural uses of human energy always hinders, restricts and hampers those natural uses, but it can not entirely stop them. Smuggling, graft, and piracy have always been part of history until this last century, because they are necessary protection of human life against the monopoly protected by force which is a "planned economy." Human life will survive on this earth in spite of hell and high water.

What the planned economies did, of course, was to prevent the development of civilization.

Whatever moral and spiritual values a man may develop during his lifetime, whatever heights of philosophy, ethics, art, he may achieve, depend first of all upon his remaining alive. The first necessities are food, clothing, and shelter from weather. The Old World remained brutal, bloody, inhumane and indecent for six thousand years, because never in all that time did men escape from planned economies long enough to establish a reliable food supply.

Every time they almost did it—as they did, during the upheavals and disorganization of Government in fights between groups for the governing power, which are called "the rise of" Egypt or Persia or Greece or Rome or France or Spain—they ended by establishing a firm, good Government, an Authority supposed to control them. This Government then enforced a planned economy with an increasing firmness,

---

[8] While Governments were thus "controlling" the natural uses of their subjects' energies in Europe, Americans were refusing to accept the Federal Constitution because it did not sufficiently restrict the American Government. They demanded, and got, a list of additional prohibitions, including one that forbids men in this Government to inflict "cruel and unusual punishments." Burning alive and breaking on the wheel were what they meant—only five generations ago. The Ogpu and the Gestapo are nothing new; they merely resume a Governmental use of torture that (only in the Americas and Europe) has been stopped, very recently, by the American and English recognition of human rights.

The Planned Economies

restricting the natural use of their energies until they could no longer get enough to eat nor support their Government. Then you see "the fall of" Egypt or Persia or Greece or Rome or Spain or France.

That is the history of planned economy for thousands of years.

The problem of human life on this earth is the problem of finding the method of applying combined human energies to this earth to get from it the necessities of human life.

This problem has never been solved by assuming that an Authority controls individuals. To the degree that men in Government have assumed this authority and responsibility, and have used their actual police force in attempting to control the productive uses of human energy, to that degree the energy has failed to work.

For instance: When the French weavers believed that Louis XIV controlled weaving, there was one whole season when they did not move a shuttle. They were waiting for the King to say how many threads of warp and of woof they might put into each inch of each kind of cloth. True, if they had not waited they would have lost their looms and perhaps their heads, for Government is a use of force. But it is a use of force that depends upon the consent of the governed. If the French people had not believed that the King should and did control weaving, they would not have been so ragged and cold that winter.

Another instance: More than two hundred years ago, the French in Missouri were producing wines that competed in France with the wines of Bordeaux. The Bordeaux vintners set up a howl to the King, for protection. He protected them, by prohibiting the exportation of wine from Missouri.

Notice that everyone, including the Missourians, believed that the King was controlling the production of wine. He was doing nothing of the kind; he couldn't. Human energy produces wine, and individuals control human energy. Louis XIV was using the force that is Government, and force can not

39

control human energy; it can only stop the use of human energy.

Missourians stopped producing more wine than they drank. If they had not stopped, they might have wrecked the vintners of Bordeaux. Certainly they would have planted more grapes, produced more wine, lowered the price of wine. They would have needed more casks, more boats, more settlers. America might be France today.

The King was encouraging settlements, to hold America for France. He was taking every care of the settlers. Still, there are two facts: They planted no more grapes. The settlements grew very slowly.

Here is another incident: In the spring of 1789, Moses Austin, the first American west of the Mississippi, applied to the Governor in New Orleans for permission to put millstones in a mill to be built at Mine à Breton in Missouri. He had the millstones there, and his request was mere routine, for Don Moses Austin was so important to New Spain that the King had given him one square league of rich mining land.

Six months later, he set his foreman to finishing the mill, while he rode to St. Louis to get the permit. It reached the authorities while he was there. He returned to his domain with it, and found that not a stroke of work had been done on the mill. In his absence, the foreman had gone fishing.

Moses Austin had made two large fortunes in the new States, and lost them in two nation-wide crashes, caused by collapses of land-speculating booms. There were no such calamities in orderly New Spain. But for some reason, amiable Moses Austin's temper became unreliable there. When the foreman returned from fishing, Don Moses fired him.

This could not be done. In New Spain, not even the most powerful Don could discharge the lowest workman without the Alcalde's permission. Don Moses Austin was summoned before the Alcalde in Ste. Genevieve, two days' journey from the unfinished mill.

The case was postponed from time to time, but finally all

The Planned Economies

witnesses were assembled. The Alcalde heard their testimony, reprimanded the foreman, and approved his discharge. Next year, Moses Austin got his mill to working, so that for the first time, Missourians were released from grinding grain by hand with pestle and mortar. A mill that could have been built in a month had taken a year.

The early history of nearly every State in this Union is crammed with such instances of "planned economy," for this country belonged to the Old World for as long as the history of the Republic.

The planned economy's invariable destruction of the Government that tries to enforce it, is an almost fatal result, because Government is necessary.

The human race is not yet so intelligent that all men can work together with no use of force to protect them from each other. So far, men have never been able to begin a civilization without first handing their guns to a policeman.

The policeman's—Government's—function is to stop the few robbers and killers who hinder the others' working. From what their work produces, the majority supplies the policeman with food, shelter and other necessities.

When the policeman turns his gun upon them all, in the delusion that force can *control* life-energy, he not only hinders and prevents their working for themselves; he also cuts off his own source of supply.

This is a very simple picture of what happens. The world seems infinitely more complex and complicated than that. Yet the most incomprehensibly complex mechanisms work upon very simple principles. A boiling tea-kettle explains the world's railroads and ships; a few marks on paper explain to a mathematician all of radio.

A "planned economy" destroys Government because when men use force in an attempt to control productive energies, *they have no means of knowing real costs,* and *these costs*

41

automatically increase at an increasing rate until the people can no longer pay them.

During the recent interim between wars in Europe, every American living there could observe this principle in operation.

The effects of the American Revolution have been disrupting the old planned economies of western Europe for a century. But remnants of these Government monopolies everywhere survive, and European belief in Authority has extended Government monopoly over many products of the industrial revolution.

Railroads, telegraph, telephone, radio, are Government monopolies everywhere outside this Republic. Salt and tobacco remain Government monopolies in many places. All Europeans and Asiatics take these monopolies for granted. It no more occurs to them that salt, tobacco, railroads, telegraph, telephones, radio, need not be owned by Government, than it occurs to Americans that the postal service need not be.

So an American abroad discovered at once that Government monopoly is absolute, and that therefore it operates under difficulties that make it destructive to the Government.

Being absolute, and maintained by police force, a Government monopoly need not please its customers.

A traveler in Europe obeys the railway officials and takes the service they provide, or he does not travel by train. He can not, so to speak, get mad at the New York Central and give his patronage to the B. and O., or vice versa, because Government monopoly has no competitor. The passenger who pays for his ticket has no effect upon that monopoly; it need not fear his displeasure, not lure him with club cars and Idaho baked potatoes. And it doesn't.

Government monopoly need not make a profit; it can run indefinitely on a deficit, as the American postal service does. Taxes make up the deficit; the Government collects them. French peasants who never set foot on a train in their lives,

The Planned Economies

lived on their famous soup to support the men who managed the French railroads.

The proper and necessary function of Government is the use of force. Old World Governments (for reasons I shall consider later) always use this force against each other, in war. Their principal function, therefore, is military force. In intervals between fighting, this force is potential and expressed in diplomacy, or power politics.

Since free men have created railroads, telegraph, telephone, radio, oil wells, modern factories, during this century, a Government that owns them must use them to serve its primary function. Every European government needs them for war, and it will build them and keep them running and make its subjects keep on paying for them, whether or not any subject ever uses them for their natural economic purposes.

Many Europeans regard the Baghdad railway as the final cause of the first World War. The Kaiser did not try to build the Baghdad railway because the Baghdadi Arabs raise dates that Berliners are eager to buy and eat. The German Government wanted that railroad to extend its political-military power, its use of force. The British Government does not object to a German's eating dates. The men in British Government prevented the Baghdad railroad because it would extend the Kaiser's use of force.

The Russian Czar's Government did not build the railroad across the empty Armenian plateau to make a profit by putting settlers on the land and hauling the food they would produce from it; Government need not make a profit, it takes what it wants. Government ran that railroad straight from the Czar's huge army-barracks to the Turkish frontier, missing Armenia's large capital city by four roadless miles. (As well my battered and indignant bones remember.) Nor are the great centers of Russian production in the Ural mountains now, for any natural economic reason.

No Government can manage an economic monopoly for economic purposes. The proper, necessary function of men in

43

The Discovery of Freedom

Government is the use of force. That is their job. They should regard their country from a political-military point of view. For example, when Texas entered this Union, men in Washington regarded that land as an area over which their use of military force extended; that was their duty. Just as it is a farmer's business to regard land as a source of crops.

When men in Government hold an economic monopoly, they must use it to serve Government's proper function, which is use of force.

The result is that the services of all the European remnants or extensions of "planned economy" are—to an American—notoriously bad. When I had been living for some years in Paris, I got an undeserved reputation for wit, in a small circle, by naïvely stating a fact. An American visitor, after trying for half an hour to get a Paris telephone number, asked me, "What on earth do you do here, when you want to telephone someone?" And I replied truthfully, "I take a taxi."

The Government monopoly, being maintained by force, does not depend upon its customers. Their desires have no direct effect upon it.

Therefore, the men in Government who manage the production and distribution of goods and services, have no means of knowing the real costs of these goods and services.

The real cost of any object or service that human beings need or want is the amount of human energy that they must use to get it.

Whether a man is earning money or spending it, or spading his garden, he measures the value of what he gets by the amount of energy that it costs him. If it costs too much, he will get something else; if both cost too much, he will get neither.

This natural measure of costs works directly upon an unprotected economy. The owners of sailing ships knew immediately when their service cost too much; their customers used steamboats. The river steamboat owners knew when their service cost too much; their customers went to the railroads.

44

The Planned Economies

The railroad and street-car monopolies knew when their costs were too high; their customers bought motor cars. The railroads took refuge with Government; the street cars are gone.

When an unprotected monopoly charges too much, the people destroy it by deserting it. The first faint pang of threatened desertion makes its owners sit up, right now. They know they are done for, as owners, unless they reduce costs—real costs, in terms of human energy.

But this threat of desertion does not exist for men in Government who have the monopoly of all goods and services that is a "planned economy." Their monopoly is absolute; it has no competitor; the people who pay its costs in human energy can not desert it. If its costs are too high, they pay them without ever getting the goods or using the service—as European peasants pay for railroads and in all their lives never travel farther from their birthplace than they can walk. Except when they are shipped to military training and to war.

So, to the men who manage European railroads, it always appears that the trains are giving all the service that anyone wants, at a reasonable cost—in the artificial terms of marks and francs and lira.

They have no means of knowing the real costs in human energy, because the people who pay those costs have no peaceful means of registering a protest that these costs are too high.[9]

And these real costs must constantly increase, because the attempt to exercise a control of human energy that can not be exercised, is a waste of human energy that must constantly increase.

I will illustrate what I mean:

Suppose that during the Armistice you bought a spool of thread in a French department store. Not that it is a spool; the thread is wound on a scrap of paper, for the thrifty French do not waste wood.

It takes a few seconds to say, "A reel of cotton thread,

---

[9] They may have a vote. Americans vote; how much does your vote affect the rulings of the Inter-State Commerce Commission?

please; white, size sixty." With leisurely grace, the clerk takes the thread in her hand, comes from behind the counter, and courteously asks you to accompany her.

She escorts you across the store, perhaps half a block, and indicates your place at the end of a waiting line. In twenty minutes or so, you reach the cashier's grating. He sits behind the bars on a high stool, a wide ledger open before him, ink bottle uncorked, and pen in hand.

He asks you, and he writes in the ledger, your name, your address, and—to your dictation—one reel of thread, cotton, white, size sixty. Will you take it, madame, or have it delivered? You will take it. He writes that. And the price? Forty centimes. You offer in payment, madame? One franc. He writes these amounts, and the date, hour, and minute.

You give the franc to the clerk, who gives it to the cashier, who gives you the change, looks at the thread, and asks if you are satisfied. You are. A stroke of his pen checks that fact.

The clerk then wraps the thread, beautifully, at a near-by wrapping counter, and gives you the package. You have spent thirty minutes; so has she; the cashier has spent perhaps five. An hour and five minutes, to buy a reel of thread.

French department stores were as good as the best in the world. The French are expert merchandisers. They knew pneumatic-tube systems; the Paris government owned one that carried special-delivery notes more quickly than anyone could get a telephone number. Department store owners admired the cash-systems in American stores. But if they had installed them, they would still have been obliged to keep the cashier, his ledger, and his pen and ink.

Why? Because in the markets of Napoleon's time, sellers cheated buyers. Napoleon protected the buyers. He decreed that the details of every sale must be written in a book, with pen and ink, in the presence of both seller and buyer, by a third person who must see the article and the transfer of money; the buyer must declare himself satisfied, and the rec-

The Planned Economies

ord must be kept, permanently, to verify the facts if there were any future complaint.

During this past century, French merchandising had grown enormously. It had completely changed; but not this method of protecting buyers.

I asked an owner of the largest French department store why Napoleon's decree was not repealed. He said, But, madame, it has been in operation for more than a hundred years! It cannot be repealed; think of the sales girls, the cashiers, the filing clerks, the watchmen who guard the warehouses of ledgers. They would lose their jobs.

He was shocked. He saw me as the materialist American, thinking only of profit, caring nothing for all those human beings.

I thought they were unemployed. They did not appear as unemployed on any record, but the actual unemployment in France and throughout Europe, was enormous. For every purchase in a French department store, something like an hour's time was unemployed; millions of hours a day. And the cashiers, the filing clerks, the watchers of those records, never did a stroke of productive work.

All this enforced unemployment made it impossible to do anything quickly. European life was leisurely; it had to be. This charmed the Americans gaily passing by, all the tedious waiting done for them, all the red tape untied, all the police stamps got onto their papers by Cook's or Amexco or their bankers or hotel porters. How serene, how cultured was European life, they said. No one hurrying, everyone with time for meditation and enjoyment, walking through the parks, sitting at café tables under the plane trees. How harassed, how hurried and rude and crude was American life in comparison, they said.

You recognized an American as far as you could see him, by the way he walked. Chin up, head high, briskly going somewhere, with an unconscious mastery of the earth he trod. No European moved like that. Europeans walked prudently,

47

The Discovery of Freedom

slowly. Their every gesture consumed time in merely letting time pass. That made their lives and their countries seem so restful, to Americans. And you can see precisely that same way of walking, that same sense of useless time, in the prisoners in any American prison-yard.

A friend and I bought a Ford in Paris. A French Ford, made—or perhaps assembled—by French mechanics, whose skill is unsurpassed in the world. I do not know what wages were paid to the men who made that Ford, nor how they lived, but I do know how skilled French workers, in general, lived, because I have friends of the French working class.

Their wages enabled them to live—where their class-status kept them, anyway—in the workers' quarters of the cities; that is, where the narrow streets are filthy with human excrement, because the tenements have no plumbing; where their food was bread and cheese and sometimes horse-meat; where their bedrooms have no windows because of the high tax on windows, and their teeth rot away in their jaws—for how can workers afford dentists?—and two of every three of their babies die less than a year old.

Taxes made the Ford cost in dollars twice what it would have cost in these United States; to a Frenchman, the price was a fortune. It was an ordinary Ford, then the butt of thousands of jokes in America. In Europe, our owning it announced (preposterously) that we were wealthy. A French worker, by careful planning and good luck and months or years of sou-pinching thrift, might own a bicycle.

Having bought this splendid Ford, my friend and I set out to get permission to drive it, and to drive it out of Paris and out of France. We worked separately, to make double use of time. For six weeks we worked, steadily, every day and every hour that Government offices were open. When they closed, we met to rest in the lovely leisure of a café and compared notes and considered ways of pulling wires. Exhausted, we rode home second-class in the subway. (Workers, of course, ride third-class in Europe.)

48

The Planned Economies

One requirement was twelve passport pictures of that car, taken full-face, without a hat. I exaggerate; regulations said nothing about a hat. But this was a Ford, naked from the factory; not a detail nor a mark distinguished it from the millions of its kind; yet I had to engage a photographer to take a full-radiator-front picture of it, where it still stood in the salesroom, and to make twelve prints, each certified to be a portrait of that identical car. The proper official pasted these, one by one, in my presence, to twelve identical documents, each of which was filled out in ink, signed and counter-signed, stamped, and tax-stamped; and, of course, I paid for them. One was given to me.

After six hard-working weeks, we had all the car's papers. Nearly an inch thick they were, laid flat. Each was correctly signed and stamped, each had in addition the little stamp stuck on, showing that the tax was paid that must be paid on every legal document; this is the Stamp tax that Americans refused to pay. I believe we had license plates besides; I know we had drivers' licenses.

Gaily at last we set out in our car, and in the first block two policemen stopped us. European policemen always go in pairs, so that one polices the other. I do not know whether this makes it impossible to bribe either, or necessary to bribe both. I never tried to buy a policeman.

Being stopped by the police was not unusual, of course. The car's papers were in its pocket, and confidently I handed them over, with our personal papers, as requested.

The policemen examined each one, found it in order, and noted it in their little black books. Then courteously they arrested us.

No one had told us about the brass plate. We had never heard of it. The car must have a brass plate, measuring precisely this by that (about $4 \times 6 \times \frac{1}{4}$ inches), hand-engraved with the owner's full name and address, and attached to the instrument board by four brass screws of certain dimensions, through four holes of certain dimensions, one hole in each corner of the brass plate.

My friend wilted on the wheel. "It's too much," she said. "Let's chuck it all and go by train."

"Gentlemen, we are completely desolated," I said. "Figure to yourselves, how we are Americans, strangers to beautiful France. Imagine, how we have planned, we have saved, we have dreamed and hoped that the day will arrive when we shall see Paris. At the end, here we are. We see with our eyes the beautiful Paris, the glory of French culture and French art. Altogether naturally, is it not? we seek to conduct ourselves with a propriety the most precise. In effect, gentlemen, what is it that it is that we have done? Of what fault it is that one accuses us? You see our passports, our cards of identity, our permission to enter France and to remain in France and to enter Paris and to live in Paris, and, unhappily, to leave France and to depart from Paris, for all joys must end, is it not? That is life. In fact, you have well examined all these, and you see that all are altogether completely in order, is it not? And the receipts for our rent, and for our window tax, and for our foreigners' tax, and for our income tax, and the quittance of our lease, all well made, is it not? all well viewed by the authorities. Good, that is that. But, it must be, the good logic always, is it not? It sees itself that we, we have committed no fault. It is not we who lack the brass plate; it is the car. Gentlemen, one must admit in good logic that which it is that is your plain duty; arrest the car. Good. Do your duty, gentlemen. As for us, we repudiate the car, we abandon it, we go—"

We were detained. The policemen accepted my logic, but courteously they said that the car could not stand where it was; parking there for even one instant was forbidden. My friend suggested that the salesman would take it back. Courteously the policemen said that, without the brass plate, the car could not move an inch from where it stood; that was forbidden.

The Planned Economies

"In all confidence, gentlemen," we said, "we leave this problem in your hands." We hailed a taxi and went home.

Mysteriously next day the car was in the salesroom. In two weeks the brass plate was beautifully hand-engraved. Exactly two months after we had paid for the car, we were able to drive it.

Of course we could not simply drive out of Paris. We were stopped at the city limit, "the barrier," while an official measured the gas in the tank and wrote the number of pints on our permit to re-enter Paris. This arrangement allowed us to choose the road by which we returned, for the permit was good on any road.

When we came back, the gas in the tank would be measured again, and we would pay the Paris tax on any pint we imported. That is just, isn't it? Should we, the wealthy who owned a Ford, be permitted to bring gasoline into Paris untaxed, while the middle classes paid the tax on the gasoline they used to clean their clothes?

These incidents illustrate the commonplace. Europeans, and other people everywhere, take such regulation for granted. If sometimes you fail to be as patient as they are, they say in surprise, "But naturally, it takes time to get permission."

Ask why you can't lift an innocent finger without permission, and your lack of the simplest reasoning power baffles them. One must always have a permit; how else could the authorities maintain the social order?

In every instance, that will stop you. There is no other way by which Authority can maintain a social order.

The tragedy of the Old World is that this *only way* by which Authority can maintain a social order must inevitably destroy the social order and any form of Authority that tries to maintain it.

The energy of a constantly increasing number of bureaucrats has always been subtracted from productive energy in the Old World.

In modern Europe, some years of every young man's life

51

The Discovery of Freedom

are consumed in training for war. But a far greater loss of productive energy is in the attempt to control productive energy. All their lives, all workers pour an enormous amount of energy into producing food, clothes, shelter, light, heat, transportation, all the necessities and comforts, and mountains of paper, pens, ink, stamps, filing cases, and acres of beautiful buildings, all to be used by men in Government who produce nothing whatever.

Men in public office do not use their energy productively; that is not their function. Their function is to use human energy as force to stop the uses of human energy that a majority does not approve, or at least does not defend. Men in Government must take the wealth they consume, from the wealth that productive men create.

The important question is, What amount can they take *safely?*

Because they use force, they have no means of knowing the answer to that question. They can always suppress by force any individual's, or minority's, objection to paying taxes; and of course they should suppress it; their function, as Government, is to stop by force any action that a majority does not approve or defend.

The inevitable disaster comes from the fact that, when men in Government try to control the natural uses of human energy in producing and distributing goods, the amount of produced wealth that they take must constantly increase, and the amount of energy that they subtract from productive energy must constantly increase.

The only way to make me stand in line for half an hour to buy a spool of thread, or to make me spend six weeks in getting stamps on paper when I want to drive a car, is to use the energy of persons who otherwise would be making more thread and more cars.

I submit to their so-called control because, under all the circumstances, I am willing to. But they must be right there on the job, or I wouldn't. No one would.

The Planned Economies

These men are a waste of energy in two ways. To live, they must consume the goods that productive men create; and, since they produce nothing, their own energy is subtracted from the amount of available productive energy.

Both these wastes *must* increase as time passes. They must increase because the fact is that all men are free; individuals control human energy. Therefore an attempt to control individuals is compelled, constantly, to come into closer contact with each one of them.

Nobody can plan the actions of even a thousand living persons, separately. Anyone attempting to control millions must divide them into classes, and make a plan applying to these classes.

But these classes do not exist. No two persons are alike. No two are in the same circumstances; no two have the same abilities; beyond getting the barest necessities of life, no two have the same desires.

Therefore the men who try to enforce, in real life, a planned economy that is their theory, come up against the infinite diversity of human beings. The most slavish multitude of men that was ever called "demos" or "labor" or "capital" or "agriculture" or "the masses," actually are men; they are not sheep.

Naturally, by their human nature, they escape in all directions from regulations applying to non-existent classes. It is necessary to increase the number of men who supervise their actions. Then (for officials are human, too) it is necessary that more men supervise the supervisors. Still, individuals will continue to act individually, in ways that *they* plan. These ways do not fit into Authority's plan. So still more men are needed, imperatively *needed,* to stop or to supervise these new ways of acting; and more men to supervise these supervisors; and more men to co-ordinate the constantly increasing complexity of all this supervision.

An attempt to exercise a control of individuals that in reality does not exist, must increase in volume.

The Discovery of Freedom

Bureaucrats are not to blame for increasing a bureaucracy; bureaucracy by its nature must increase. Consider those twelve photographs of our Ford. When cars were made by hand and no two looked alike, someone reasonably ordered that pictures be taken of a car, for identification. A million cars now look precisely alike; those pictures are worthless. The bureaucracy needs another bureau, to comb out of it all the orders which productive men, behaving in new ways, have made obsolete. Then how shall motor cars be identified? Another committee —which will become a bureau—is needed to decide such questions.

This tendency to waste energy is in all organizations of human beings. It develops in all business organizations; the larger the business, the greater the tendency to waste human energy. But an organization not maintained by police force, but dependent for its existence upon the multitudes of individuals whom it serves, encounters a natural check to this waste. If its costs in human energy are too high, its customers desert it. Business men call this check, "the law of diminishing returns."

There is a natural limit to the amount of human energy that Government can waste, too. Human energy on this earth must be used productively. Men cannot live, unless they use their energies to create their necessities from this earth which gives human beings nothing whatever.

But because men in Government are using police force, they have *no means of knowing what this natural limit is.*

Recently in Europe, it has been the limit of a majority's willingness to endure the increasing poverty that results from an increasing waste of human energy. No one could know that limit, because it depends upon the thoughts and feelings of a great number of individuals, no two of whom think or feel precisely alike, and all these thoughts and emotions are constantly changing in flowing time. The actual limit of their willingness could be discovered only by reaching it. Then the

The Planned Economies

discovery was too late. All was over for the men in that Government.

In the past history of the Old World, the limit of waste in Government's attempt to control productive energy has always been, not the willingness, but the ability of its subjects to endure starvation.

Sooner or later, the waste of human energy has become too great; the Government's willing subjects have not been able either to support their rulers or to defend them. In the constantly warring Old World, that ultimate failure of energy caused the bloody end of that Government and that civilization.

V. War

WAR has always been the primary function of Old World Government. Men living in the Old World use a large part of their energy in killing men and in destroying food, shelter, and all other necessities of human life.

Americans in general do not understand this. Neither do most continental Europeans understand the American attitude toward war.

When I was living in Albania I had a friend who was one of the finest persons I ever knew. He was an Italian of English ancestry. His mother and his maternal ancestors for many generations had been English. He was fourteen and his brother was nine, when their parents were drowned at sea. The boys had no other near relatives and from that time they were inseparable. They stayed together in schools and universities; they got from the King himself a special permission to do their military service together. They went together to Argentine, and in 1915 returned to join their regiment.

They were both wounded at Caporetto, and abandoned on the field. My friend reached his brother but was too weak to do anything for him. The brother died during the third night. My friend's wounds still required him to return to hospitals at intervals.

For weeks I tried to explain to him the American attitude toward war. He could not understand it.

I was confused, myself, for like most Americans I had taken it for granted that no one wants war. My friend had the best European schooling, Italian, German, and English. He was

War

widely and accurately informed; he was intelligent, open-minded, and eager to understand my puzzling country. The clue, he said, was in our attitude toward war. It baffled him.

He laughed at the superficial European belief that Americans are mere dollar-chasers. He knew several Americans intimately. He did not find them mercenary, nor cowardly, nor weak, nor—exactly—unpatriotic. American patriotism is peculiar, he said. Americans never say "my fatherland," "my motherland." What a peculiar attitude toward your country, to call it Uncle Sam. And notice, he said, the tone in which you say "Uncle Sam," or, "The States." It is affectionate; it has a sound of—what should he say? equality? tolerance?—as if a confident young man were speaking of a good old uncle. That is not the way in which a man speaks of his country, the fatherland, the motherland, the parent whose child he is.

And then, the curious American talk about war. He did not believe that it was entirely hypocritical. But would I explain the facts?

The United States are made by unprovoked military aggression. They attack the Indians and take half a continent; they attack Mexico and take Texas, Arizona, New Mexico and California; they attack Spain, and take Cuba; they attack the Filipinos and take their islands. Then why don't they hold and subdue Mexico, when American troops have taken Mexico City? Why don't they attack Canada while the mother country is embroiled in Europe? Why do the United States reverse all history, and fight for an older empire instead of helping to dismember it?

Now (in 1928) the United States are the strongest world power; why do they not have compulsory military training? They have used military power to dictate to all Europe; then why has the army no influence in our foreign policy? Why do the sons of our upper classes go into business or professions, why not into the army and navy? Why do Americans not honor their great Generals above such men as Edison and

57

The Discovery of Freedom

Hoover? Why, when General Pershing is an American, do Americans make a small-town editor the President of the United States?

One morning his servant brought a note, asking if he might see me at once, for only a moment. He came in, excited, apologizing for calling at that hour, "but I could not wait to tell you! It came to me in a flash, suddenly, just now. *It is materialism!* As you have said, Signora: Americans hate war because it kills men and destroys property. Suddenly, it comes to me. What are lives and property? Material things. All men die, time destroys all property. Lives and property have no value. The immortal value is the soul of a nation, and war regenerates the nation's soul. Americans can not see spiritual values. That is it, Signora; yes, yes, that is the truth. Deep down, at base, *au fond,* your countrymen are pure materialists. You see only the material world; you cannot see what war is, because it is spiritual."

He had seen his brother die at Caporetto, and he died in Ethiopia, a fine, brave, honorable man, who believed with his whole mind that an individual is a cell in the body of The State, that Authority controls all human beings, and that his own life had no value whatever but service to Immortal Italy.

That is the cause of war.

Men who have that pagan belief will always make war. They must make war, because of the nature of human energy. Not knowing that individuals control themselves, they do not recognize and accept that responsibility; they try to make their own energy work on a false basis. It will not work on a false basis, and one of the results of trying to make it do so, is war.

The people of the Old World have made almost uninterrupted war. For three thousand years, one year in fifteen has been an interval without war.

Let us have no more nonsense about capitalism causing war. Any schoolboy knows that Spartans made war. Men living in communism and under all forms of Government have always made war.

War

History is a spectacle of billions of human beings, naked and shelterless on this planet, with no food, no clothes, no shelter except such as their minds can imagine and their hands make. Not one of them could live if human energy did not ceaselessly attack this indifferent and dangerous earth; not one could live without the help of his kind. Yet they always use their energy to kill their kind and to destroy the food and shelter upon which human life depends.

This is suicidal. War does not only kill individuals; it attacks the very root of human survival.

War does not only destroy the material goods upon which human survival depends. War is an active, destructive denial of the facts of human life, the facts of individual liberty and human brotherhood.

No one who sees the plain fact that all moral and spiritual values of human life are in the individual, can possibly see any spiritual value in war. War comes from the individual's ignorance of his own nature, from his placing responsibility for the moral values of his own life in a fantasy, in a pagan god which he imagines exists outside himself and superior to him and controlling him—an Immortal Italy, a German Race, a Nation, a State.

Americans have fought many wars; they have even begun wars. They have never *made* a war. Every war that Americans have fought, they have fought to defend the individual against the aggressions of men who did not recognize the fact of individual freedom.

You hear it said that there will always be war, because men always want war. Is that true? Is human nature anti-human? Hardly. If it were, the human race would not have survived six thousand years.

Certainly, a majority always goes willingly to war. The pacifist is correct in saying that war would be impossible if they did not. Massacres would be possible, and slavery, but not war. War is a use of human energy, and individuals control human energy. Whenever a large number of men (called

The Discovery of Freedom

"a Nation," or anything else) go to war, that is proof that a majority of them is willing to go.

Certainly, too, human beings are fighters by nature. Living is a tough job; only good fighters can do it. Like it or lump it, this planet is no safe place for any living creature. Living is fighting for life, and when anyone does not know this fact, someone else is doing his fighting for him.

Anyone who says that economic security is a human right, has been too much babied. While he babbles, other men are risking and losing their lives to protect him. They are fighting the sea, fighting the land, fighting diseases and insects and weather and space and time, for him, while he chatters that all men have a right to security and that some pagan god—Society, The State, The Government, The Commune—must give it to them. Let the fighting men stop fighting this inhuman earth for one hour, and he will learn how much security there is.

Let him get out on the front lines. Let him bring one slow freight through a snowstorm in the Rockies; let him drive one rivet to hold his apartment roof over his head. Let him keep his own electric light burning through one quiet, cosy winter evening when mist is freezing to the wires. Let him make, from seed to table, just one slice of bread, and we will hear no more from him about the human right to security.

No man's security is any greater than his own self-reliance. If every man and woman worth living did not stand up to the job of living, did not take risk and danger and exhaustion beyond exhaustion and go on fighting for one thin hope of victory in the certainty of death, there would not be a human being alive today.

But fighting does not mean fighting one's own kind. If all men were not brothers, and if most men did not recognize the brotherhood of human kind, there would not be a human being alive.

Being natural fighters, boys find or invent reasons for fighting someone, usually another boy. They are still so nearly babies that they have not learned how to control themselves, and, like babies, they are still protected from their real enemies. Thirteen-year-old Auguste Chouteau, who took command of twenty-six boatmen and responsibility for bringing a fortune in trade-goods on flatboats from Fort de Chartres up the dangerous Mississippi against the spring flood of breaking ice, and landed the goods safely and began building the trading post of St. Louis in a wilderness, did not waste his time and energy in fighting another boy.

Men whose minds and circumstances are childish will fight each other, too. Brawls flare up from the natural fighting spirit of child-minded men when they are protected from their natural enemies. In fire, flood, earthquake, pestilence, these same men will fight as allies against their common enemy.

And a few men, fighting each other, do not make a war. A hundred, five hundred, ten thousand men, fighting each other, make at most a riot. Only a Government can make war.

The cause of war is the delusion that Government is an Authority, controlling individuals. Of course, whoever controls an act is responsible for its results. If Government did control individuals, then the men in Government would be responsible for their subjects' food, shelter, clothing, health, education, religious beliefs, marriages, in short for their whole lives.

Old World rulers, as well as their subjects, have always had this pagan belief. Hitler's delusion is nothing new. All the Kings, Emperors, Czars, aristocrats, upper classes, have always believed that they control, and are responsible for, the majority whom they regard as their inferiors.

But human energy, like any energy, works only under its natural control. Like any energy, it can be prevented from working in any given instance, but nothing but its natural individual control can control it.

So long as human beings live, human energy can not be stopped. When the pressure exerted to stop it is too great, it explodes destructively, in war.

61

The Discovery of Freedom

Examine any war in history; you will find that its cause is an attempt by men in Government to use the proper function of Government, force, as the *control* of human energy.

Not long ago, Europeans believed that Government's proper function was to control its subjects' religious beliefs. If the King did, or could, control any other man's faith, certainly he was responsible to God and to his subjects for every soul in his realm. And he would serve God, and do good to the conquered, by extending his realm.

Partly from this cause, came the wars called religious wars. Why are there no wars for religion today? Because today most men know that force can not control anyone's beliefs.

Today it is said that a conflict of economic ideologies causes war. In Russia, Italy, Germany and Japan, men in Government have tortured and slaughtered multitudes whose ideas differed from theirs. These countries now make war. And what is the one element that modern Communism, Fascism, National Socialism and Bushido have in common? *A fanatic belief that Government is Authority that controls individuals.*

Most wars in history come from Government's attempt to enforce an imaginary control of the productive uses of human energy. The "planned economy" hinders, restricts, and reduces production. But human energy must be productive, to keep people alive. When force obstructs it, people suffer privation and hunger. In rebellion against this misery, they rebel against the ruler whom they hold responsible for it.

So history is full of wars of rebellion. Behind the rebel leaders, are men who are hungry. Their rebellion breaks up the mechanism of attempted control; for a little while they are able to improve their living conditions, and for this they thank the new ruler, or the new form of Government. But in the Old World, they always believe that Authority controls them. So all the rebellions have never greatly improved the wretched living conditions that come from trying to make human energy work on the false assumption that individuals do not control it.

War

In the brief history of these United States there is an instance of the connection between this false belief and war. The most atrocious, bloodiest and most costly war of the last century was the war between these States. Its cause was the Federal Government's so-called "Protective" tariff.

This tariff is a restriction of trade. Its original purpose was to protect this country's infant industries. Ordinary Americans fought it until 1896. Ten years ago, American farmers began taking money from all American tax-payers in payment for reducing this country's food supplies, on the ground that this payment is "the farmers' protective tariff."

From the first, this Protective tariff worked as all attempts to control productive human energy have always worked. It made everyone poorer. But the owners of the infant industries, still pagan-minded, still regarding wealth as a static quantity, and Government as Authority, imagined that this restriction of trade was making them prosperous.

How could they prosper, they reasoned, except by taking prosperity from someone else? If this universe is static, wealth does not increase; a man can get a dollar only by taking it from another man. The idea that prices can go down while wages and profits increase, naturally never entered their heads, because in all history this had never occurred.

The Government's kind protection was taking money from most Americans and giving it to the factory-owners, thus making their customers poorer and reducing the market for factory products. Believe it or not, this is what the factory-owners wanted, and they got it and kept it, by buying Daniel Webster and assorted lots of cheaper Congressmen, both northern and southern.

Ordinary dumb Americans fought that tariff for a hundred years, because it was counter-revolutionary and because it was a use of force to take money from most citizens and give it to a few. Southern Americans fought it politically until 1860, for the same reasons and also because they were selling cotton on the world market and wanted to buy manufactured goods at

63

world prices. They claimed a right to nullify the tariff in their own ports; they did open their ports, and the Federal Government threatened war and made them close them.

The election of 1860 decided that this tariff would be raised still higher. So Southerners claimed the right to leave the Union, which all States had until then maintained, and they did leave it. They formed a Government, and when Federal troops would not withdraw from their States, they attacked the Federal troops.

That was the most brutal war that civilized men had ever fought. In that war, Americans revived a barbarity that had not been practiced since Genghis Khan, but is Hitler's method today: cold-blooded atrocities committed on unarmed civilians and women and children, by regular troops acting under orders.

Northerners fought to save the American Revolution by saving the Union. Southerners fought to save the Revolution by defending the rights of the States.

During the war, European troops moved into Mexico, thus proving that the Northerners were right. A shift in the Constitutional balance of power in this Government, ever since that war ended, may yet prove that the Southerners were right.

That war cost the lives of half a million Americans. It cost a generation's loss of energy in the north, and half a century's loss of it in the south. The war and its effects were caused by a little intrusion of the ancient planned economy here, a little use of force as an attempted control and an actual restriction of the productive uses of human energy.

The form of the Government makes no difference. Whether the ruler is a majority, as in Greek democracy, or a King or a dictator or elected members of Parliament, if men in Government use the force that *is* Government in an attempt to control human energy, one result is war.

Since the ruler is believed to control his subjects, it is believed that he makes the war. What actually happens—as in

War

the case of the religious wars—is that he can *not* control his
subjects. His imaginary control fails to work.

So the ruler (and his subjects) recognize that something is
hampering his control. This is true; the opposition is in the
nature of human energy. But neither the ruler nor his subjects
reject their delusion that he controls them. They reason that
his control does not work well because it is not strong enough,
or because it does not cover a large enough area of the earth.

The ruler, whoever he may be, therefore increases his use
of force in more determined efforts, and as the results are always more disastrous, his subjects make a war of rebellion
against him, or they make a war to enlarge the frontiers of
his imaginary Authority.

An Old World frontier is a bayonet-line that marks the geographical limit of a ruler's attempt to control individuals. The
Government's actual use of force is stopped there, where the
guns and garrisons of another Government face his.

Since Government's planned economy has always kept people poor, the almost static living conditions through all Old
World history seem to verify the pagan belief in a static universe. All Old World thinking about economics assumes that
wealth cannot be increased, but must be divided.

So the Old World ruler (and his subjects) assume that to
get prosperity, they must take it away from someone else.
They see no means of raising their standard of living, except
by using force to move the frontiers beyond the farms and
mines and factories that are already created.

No doubt many Germans believe sincerely that in order to
live, they must enlarge the German frontiers. And so long as
frontiers are limits of a Government's use of force in an attempt to control human energy, this will appear to be true.

For twenty years, all European Governments have been
starving Europeans. Imagine every State line in this Republic
fortified, garrisoned, guarded by two lines of soldiers and police and two lines of bureaucrats, all taken from this coun-

65

The Discovery of Freedom

try's productive population and supported by the remainder of that population.

Imagine that no train nor car nor person nor package can cross any State line here, without twice being stopped and twice being examined, nor without police permission to leave one State and police permission to enter the other. Imagine that from one State you can take or send only fifty dollars, from another ten, and from some States no money at all, so that no one outside the State of Michigan can buy a car; and imagine that the currency changes at every State line, and that merchants use one kind of money, and travelers another, and that at any moment a Government decree may change the value of either kind. Imagine that some States do not admit cigarettes and some exclude ready-made dresses and others require a deposit of the total value of a car or truck to insure that it will not be sold within the State, a deposit that will be returned when the car leaves the State at the point where it entered. And try to do business, try only to live, when only Florida will admit Kansas wheat, and Maine can export potatoes only in exchange for Texas carrots, and Syracuse china can be exported only to Vermont and only to the extent that New York State's politicians permit an importation of Vermont maple sugar, which New York's bee-keepers oppose as an invasion of their market for honey. Go on imagining; you can not equal the European reality.

This is what a belief in Authority made of the American insistence, during and after the first world war, upon "self-determination of peoples."

The inevitable reaction to such a state of affairs is war. Too much energy is subtracted from productive energy. Too much force is opposed to the natural uses of men's energies. The people are hungry. And will they curb their Governments? Will they abolish such a use of force? Does that kind of action occur to them?

Not at all; they blame their rulers. They rebel, and change their rulers. That is what they have done, in Italy, in Greece,

66

in Austria and Roumania and Poland and Germany and Spain.

The pattern is as old as human life. The new rulers use more and more force, more police, more soldiers, trying to enforce more efficient control, trying to make the planned economy work by piling regulations on regulations, decree on decree. The people are hungry, and hungrier. And how does a man on this earth get butter? Doesn't Government give butter?

But Government does not produce food from this earth; Government is guns. It is one common distinction of all civilized peoples, that they give their guns to Government. Men in Government monopolize the necessary use of force; they are not using their energies productively; they are not milking cows. To get butter, they *must* use guns; they have nothing else to use.

So you hear that the causes of war are economic. You hear of wars of hate and revenge. You hear that nationalism causes wars, and that only a World State and a "planned" world economy (which is what Hitler is fighting for) can bring world peace. (Another Roman Peace, and another Dark Ages.)

Well, there is a frontier between Missouri and Kansas. Men of different cultures, antagonistic ideologies and ancient enemy-races met at that frontier, eighty years ago.

Missourians were aristocrats, tolerant, self-indulgent, slave-owning descendants of the Catholic Cavaliers; their political faith was rooted in Magna Carta, feudalism and the feudal class-rights of man.

Into Kansas came the hard, narrow, fanatic Protestants from New England, iconoclasts, hating aristocracy, hating feudalism and class-distinctions, standing for individualism and human rights and the abolition of slavery.

Behind the Missourian was French Missouri, that had been French for almost two hundred years. With the New Englander was the German, the "lop-eared Dutch," so newly come from the crushed revolutionary efforts in Germany that he spoke only his native language. They met, on this frontier, the German and the French, whose ancestors had fought each other on the Rhine since before Caesar went into Gaul.

If you speak of a conflict of cultures, there was one. A conflict of political ideologies? There it was. Hate? Revenge? when the feudal slave-owner met the wild-eyed fanatic who was stealing his slaves and betraying them to starvation and gangs of murderers? when Germans met French, with memories of a thousand years of war between them?

Missourians and Kansans killed each other for six years before the guns spoke at Fort Sumter and two Governments made war. Kansans and Missourians are not precisely fond of each other yet. Listen to the crowds' roars at the annual "Turkey" football game between Kansas U. and Missouri U. You do not hear that sound at football games anywhere else. Kansans have not forgotten the border raids and the Lawrence massacre; Missourians remember the burning of Independence and Order Number Eleven; now, after eighty years.

But the Missouri-Kansas line is not an Old World frontier. No one guards it. No one wants to move it, because it is not the boundary of an imaginary control of individuals and an actual use of force.

Recently there has been a faint general belief that American Government is Authority. It stops your car on a State line, as if that line were an Old World frontier.

ALL CARS STOP, the sign says. Someone questions you a little, not quite knowing why. You see another sign: OIL TRUCKS STOP HERE. Americans are almost believing that Government controls the energy that produces oil from the earth. That is an old story to Missourians who remember that Louis XIV imagined that he controlled the production of wine.

Some fifteen hundred such assertions of a non-existent Authority have actually been put on the statute books of these States. And, when the Old World attacked this Republic, and

War

Americans had to fight for their lives and for the recognition of human liberty on this earth, fifteen hundred of these Hitler laws were tangled around their feet in their own country.

Americans are so carelessly rich that they let those laws stand so long as they were hindering American production and trade. But when they hindered this fight for life and liberty, in eight days every State abolished them.

That is what Americans do, when they see their enemy. This Republic is not the Old World. Not a State line in it, nor the national boundary, is an Old World frontier.

If Missourians believed that Missouri's Government controlled them and therefore must provide for them, the politicians in Jefferson City would have to guard the Missouri-Kansas line with police and troops, and staff it with bureaucrats examining permits and cars and purses and shipments of goods. There is no other way by which men in Government can attempt to control individuals.

Then Missourians would need Kansas wheat and oil and salt and revolving doors from the world-monopoly of their manufacture in Independence, Kansas, just as they need these things now. Kansans would need Missouri's apples and lead and zinc and bauxite, just as they need them now. To men in each Government it would seem necessary to get these things into their own State, to relieve the people's increasing poverty. And Government has only one means: war.

Both Missourians and Kansans are good fighters. They would fight that war to a standstill, and resume it again and again, until it might seem that the only way to end it would be to crush Missourians utterly, or to smash every Kansan beyond possibility of recovery.

This solution might seem necessary, if you did not know that utterly crushing the enemy has always been the method used to end war. For six thousand years that method has been ending war. It does not end war, because war is not caused by the enemy.

War is caused by the ancient pagan belief that Authority

controls individuals, and must and should control them. This belief is in individual minds, and no force whatever can change any man's mind. War will end when a majority of men on this earth know that every man is free. Each person must see for himself that everyone is self-controlling and responsible.

So long as any large group of persons, anywhere on this earth, believe the ancient superstition that some Authority is responsible for their welfare, they will set up some image of that Authority and try to obey it. And the result will be poverty and war.

Part Two

THE REVOLUTION

I. The First Attempt

THE beginnings are unknown. All over this earth are ruins of civilizations about which we know nothing whatever. These sixty centuries may have been a Dark Age. Perhaps all men once knew that men are free.

Our record of this knowledge begins with one man. There is no historical proof that he ever existed. The story holds its self-evident truth.

It begins about four thousand years ago. The wars of Kish and Shipurla were then as far past as the wars between Greece and Persia are now. Ur was the center of world-empire, about as old as England now is. Elamites and Arabs were attacking Ur, and Babylon was young in the west.

This man traveled from Ur toward the far west, with his father, his wife, and an orphaned nephew. They were shepherds. Their flocks kept them moving always to fresh pastures. When Abraham died very old, his grandsons buried him in what is now Turkey.

He had taught his increasing family that men are free.

Many gods were then believed to control all things. Gods of water made water flow, gods of air moved the winds, gods whispered in trees, roared in thunder, or with gentle rain watered the crops. These gods required services from men at certain times. The god of fertility must be served in the spring or he would not make seeds sprout. (So we still celebrate May Day.) Gods always controlled every human being. As water could not run nor rain fall nor plants grow, so a

73

man could not think nor feel nor move except as a god controlled him.

Fifteen hundred years after Abraham died, a Greek loved a woman only because a god had shot a poisoned arrow into his heart. This little god on our Valentines was real to a Greek. Greeks were as sure that these gods existed, as Americans are sure that electricity exists.

The logical Greeks could explain men's acts only by supposing that crazy gods controlled them. In senseless rages, the father of gods roared thunder and flung bolts of lightning. Gods and goddesses foolishly quarreled and, using men as weapons, they made wars. They hung invisible over the battles, snatching the javelin aside or driving it into the enemy's body.

Abraham said that none of these gods exist. He said that God is One Creator-and-Judge.

God is The Right, he said; Rightness creates the universe and judges men's acts. (As water judges a swimmer's rightness in swimming, God judges rightness in living.) But God does not control any man, Abraham said; a man controls himself, he is free to do good or evil in the sight of God.

This observation of reality made little impression on the world at the time.

After many adventures, Abraham's numerous descendants went to Egypt for food, during one of the usual famines. It seems that they became a rich and highly privileged class, having a pull at court with a clever kinsman who was reducing the Egyptians to slavery. Generations grew richer and richer, more and more secure, of course making no objection to slavery. (It wasn't *their* slavery.)

Then the old, old, endless repetition occurred once more. A new man came to power, saying (and I quote,) "The children of Israel are more and mightier than we; come on, let us deal justly with them."

The oppressed Egyptians leaped to it. They grabbed the Israelites' economic security and began liquidating them. They made their lives bitter with hard bondage, in mortar, and brick, and all manner of service in the field; all their service, wherein they made them serve, was with rigor. They killed them, and killed their babies; they increased their hardships until the remnant was wretchedly dying.

Then Moses rescued them. He got them out of Egypt, and across the Red Sea, alive. Six weeks later they turned on him bitterly, wailing, "Ye have brought us forth into this wilderness to kill us with hunger."

They would do nothing for themselves. Slaves are fed; they had been fed in Egypt. Whenever Moses did not feed them, they howled that he was killing them. You wonder how Moses could have stuck it out for forty long years.

Over and over he told them that they were responsible for themselves, that each one of them was free; that they could not have a god nor a King to control them and be responsible for them. He was always trying to pound it into their heads. "Ye are not murmuring against me, but against the God of Abraham." For the children of Israel were always murmuring.

Whenever they could sneak a chance, they made a pagan god.

At last Moses yielded so far as to give them ten commandments. Not one of these tells a person what to do. They are negatives, addressed to the motives of an individual's acts. When slaves want a master to give them orders, what are they to make of such an order as, "Thou shalt not covet thy neighbor's goods"?

Three of the ten prohibit any image, picture, or description of God. Each individual must act according to his own idea of Rightness.

When you think of the pagan world as it was in the historical time when only the Israelites held this truth, you see their preserving it as the great achievement of all history.

The struggle went on for centuries. Leader after leader, poet, philosopher, warrior, kept insisting upon the fact of individual self-control, individual freedom.

The Discovery of Freedom

Gideon was a warrior. He "rose up, with those around him," and fought magnificently against overwhelming odds, 135,000 Midianites against him in one battle. He subdued them so that they lifted up their heads no more, and the country was in quietness forty years.

Then the men of Israel said unto Gideon, "Rule thou over us, both thou, and thy son, and thy son's son, for thou hast delivered us from the hand of Midian."

Here is an appeal not only to the conqueror, but to the father; an offer of hereditary monarchy. Anyone who believes that a ruler has real power will take such an offer. A selfish man wants it selfishly; an unselfish man wants to use it to do good to others.

Gideon said unto them, "I will not rule over you, neither shall my son rule over you. The Lord shall rule over you."

But these kingless people wanted to escape from the relentless responsibility of freedom. A hundred years later they were begging the wise man, Samuel, "Now make us a king to judge us, like all the other nations."

The thing displeased Samuel, and he told them in plain terms what they were asking for:

"This shall be the manner of the king that shall reign over you: he will take your sons and appoint them for himself, for his chariots, and to be his horsemen, and some shall run before his chariots. And he will appoint him captains over thousands and captains over fifties, and will set them to ear his ground and to reap his harvest, and to make his instruments of war.

"And he will take your fields, and your olive yards, even the best of them, and he will take the tenth of your seed and of your vineyards, and he will take the tenth of your men servants and your maid servants, and your goodliest young men, and put them to his work.

"And ye shall cry out in that day, because of this King which *ye shall have chosen*."

Here is a precise statement of the source of any Government's power, and of the effects of any Government's attempt

The First Attempt

to control human energy—the taking-away of energy from production, the waste of energy in bureaucracy and war.

Nevertheless, the people of Israel refused to listen to Samuel and they said, "Nay, but we will have a king over us, that we may be like all the nations, and that our king may go before us and *fight our battles.*"

It is impossible to exaggerate the importance of this disclosure of the fact that men are free. Its ultimate effect upon the world was bound to be terrific.

This view of the nature of man is scientific; it is observed fact, tested by experience. All pagan belief to the contrary notwithstanding, human beings do not behave like seeds or tent-caterpillars. It is self-evident that a man is not a cell in a commune or a mass or a class or a race, or in Immortal Italy or The German Race or Society or The State, or in any other mystic bee-swarm that can be imagined. Everyone knows that he is himself, and that he controls his own acts—even though he may believe that this is not true of anyone else.

But Abraham's discovery went no further. He stated the nature of human energy. This knowledge is essential; no one can live well, in any way, unless he knows the nature of his own energy. But this knowledge alone is not enough. Men always knew that steam lifts the lid of a pot; the knowledge is not useful until someone devises a method of using it, a steam engine.

Knowing the nature of human energy is not enough, because one person's energy is not enough either to preserve his life or to make it the kind of life he wants. His energy must be combined with the energies of others; he must know a second fact, that all men are brothers. There still remains a problem of method, the method by which men can act according to their real nature and their brotherhood.

The great leaders of the Israelites could not even tell them that all men are brothers.

They were a very small group, surrounded by powerful

pagan empires; Egypt in the south, Armenia, Persia, Chaldea, Babylonia, Assyria, in the north and east, and in the west, Rome.

The most promising young Israelites were always falling in love with pagan girls. The pagan achievements awed them all. When you see the incredible walls of Baalbek or Tadmor, in ruins as they are now, and even with the memory of New York's towers behind your eyelids, you are struck dumb. The simple Israelites who saw those gigantic cities in their magnificence, dwarfing their thronging populations, must have been stunned.

They would have melted humbly into those pagan multitudes, if their strong men had not stood in the way and driven them back with threats, telling them that they were like no other people, that they were set apart, chosen to know the truth and hold to it.

They wanted to be "like all the other nations." But to be like any other people, they must forget that men are free.

That is the truth that they held. Therefore, of course, they were anarchists. They lived and prospered for centuries, with no government whatever.

Everyone knows that anarchy is the natural relationship of human beings, and that it works perfectly well. Father and mother and their grown children got along all right with uncles and aunts and cousins, and no policemen. If they quarreled, they settled the quarrel themselves. Even executions were not formal; a majority acted directly and killed the criminal with stones. Having no Government, the Israelites used their energy in production, cultivating and harvesting crops, caring for flocks, and making clothes and shelters.

But pure anarchy can not build cities, nor conduct an extensive commerce, nor develop production beyond the handcrafts. Some kind of organization is necessary for these activities. This is a problem of method, which the Israelites did not even attack.

They went back to the pagan submission to an (imagined)

The First Attempt

Authority. They made a King. And Solomon built a city and a great temple, and extended their industry and commerce, and lavishly wasted their wealth in riotous living. They were like other nations. Like other nations, they were defeated in war; their city and temple destroyed. Their conquerors used the then-ancient custom of mass-deportation (revived in Europe by the Allies in 1924, and now used by Hitler) and left less than a fifth of the Israelites in Palestine. Vassal-subjects of Rome, the remnant in Judea slavishly obeyed their priests.

Yet the sound of that word, Judea, has always alarmed the Old World.

Today the people called Jews are literally a race of all mankind. Like Americans, they have no common ancestry, no common religion or political philosophy, no common appearance, habits, manners or customs. They have no nationality nor common language. They have in common only one thing, a tradition. It is the tradition that Americans have—an inheritance from men who once asserted, against the whole world, that men are free.

With reason, the Old World hates the Jews. Four thousand years ago, a Jew said that men are free. Two thousand years ago, a Jew preached that men are free. In medieval Europe, the Jews came from Spain, knowing that men are free. That knowledge will destroy the whole Old World concept of the universe and of man, it will break up the foundations of Old World nations and States, and shatter the very basis of their subjects' lives.

So they are afraid of the Jew. They ward him off; they shut him out; they build walls around him; they kill him. Their actions show that they are afraid.

Every attack upon Jews, from exclusion from this country's public universities to the ghettos and the massacres in Poland today, are the acts of men who are afraid.

And who leads these attacks? A tyrant. Wherever tyranny is strongest—in 15th-century Spain, in Czarist Russia, in Nazi

The Discovery of Freedom

Germany—attacks upon the Jew are most mercilessly atrocious.

All over the Old World, again and again, for two thousand years, hatred of the Jews has flared up. It is always the hatred that comes from fear, and always—every time, in every instance—it is begun and fostered by men who are afraid of the knowledge that men are free.

Christ came not to bring peace, but a sword that would destroy kingdoms.

Again and again, in sermons and parables and acts. Christ said that all men are free. He attacked the priests and drove them from the temple. He flouted their pretended control and openly, ostentatiously, broke their laws. He said that the whole law depended upon the truth taught by the prophets.

He added the truth that all men are brothers.

Multitudes followed Christ, but they did not understand. They thought they followed a King of the Jews, who would lead them in revolt against Rome and establish again the kingdom that Gideon had refused and Solomon had accepted.

Historically, the times were ripe for a revolt in the Near East. From a high mountain, the record says, Christ saw the kingdoms of the world, and refused them.

And if it were a historical fact that a man had come from Palestine then, to be the Emperor of Rome, what actual power would he have had? All the armies and the police can not make a better world. The Emperor had nothing but the use of force, that can hinder and restrict the individual energy that makes the human world, but can not control and use it.

The maker of human destiny is the individual. Here, within each living man and woman, is the self-controlling energy that makes this human world. Each person has the responsibility for what this world is.

So Christ spoke to the individual. He spoke of the God of Abraham, the God that is Rightness, and does not control any man but judges every man's acts. (Does not every mechanic know that this is true, to the smallest detail? Does anything

The First Attempt

work, does any act succeed, that does not conform to the real nature of things?)

Christ spoke of the real nature of human beings, of the freedom, the responsibility, the dignity and the power of the individual. *Whosoever* shall say unto this mountain, Be thou removed, (and shall not doubt in his heart) he shall have whatsoever he saith. The meek shall inherit the earth. Our father in heaven, thy kingdom come, for thine *is* the kingdom. How hard it is for them that trust in riches to enter into the kingdom of God. (How difficult, for men who trust illusions, to see a fact.)

He spoke of the brotherhood of man. Love thy neighbor *as thyself*. Do unto others as ye would be done by. A new commandment I give unto you, that ye love one another.

Three centuries after Christ was executed, the Roman World Peace was dissolved in the human misery its "planned" economy created, and the Christian Church was an increasing power whose leaders believed that it controlled even the thoughts of men.

II. The Second Attempt

ABOUT thirteen hundred years ago a self-made business man began the second attempt to establish the fact of individual freedom in practical affairs. This man is a historical figure, as solid as George Washington.

He was an orphan, of good family, but cheated out of his property inheritance. As a child, barefooted, ragged, hungry, he worked sixteen or eighteen hours a day and slept on bare ground under the sky. He had no schooling whatever, but he had ability and he got ahead. In early middle age he was a highly paid executive, widely known and respected.

He traveled, buying and selling goods throughout the greater part of the civilized world. Babylon was long forgotten, and the Roman empire had ceased to exist. For three hundred years, Constantinople had been the world's center. The thriving modern cities were Baghdad, Damascus, Antioch, Alexandria.

To understand this man, think of a seasoned business executive today, practical, shrewd, humorous, friendly, nobody's fool. A man who earns, say $25,000 a year; a sufficient but not spectacular success. Comfortably well off, though not extremely rich, he marries his employer, a business woman of ability, and they retire, to live in Coral Gables, Florida.

He and his wife often served coffee to their friends. The entertainment was conversation. The host's opinions were so radical that for some three years he used prudence in expressing them. But little by little, he expressed them more publicly, and arguments begun in his livingroom spread all over town.

The Second Attempt

He agreed with Abraham. There is only one God, who does not control men. Each individual is self-controlling and responsible. The pagan gods do not exist.

This idea created terrific excitement, for Mohammed was expressing it in Mecca, the shrine of the most renowned pagan gods. The greatest of these was the strange, heavy, black stone, known to have descended from the sky. Pilgrims came from all over the world to worship it, and the most famous poets displayed their poems in the Ka'ba that sheltered it. Mecca lived on pilgrims, as Miami lives on tourists. The Meccans were not merely enraged by Mohammed's blasphemy; it hit them where they lived.

He went right on saying what he thought. There is no superior *kind* of man; men are humanly equal. The Emperor has no actual power over anyone. In Mohammed's observation and belief, a priest is no holier or more powerful than any other man, either.

The priests called down their most blasting curses upon him. These had no effect.

Mohammed said that some men are prophets. The greatest, he said, are Abraham, Moses, and Christ. "It is not meet for God that he should have any son; God forbid!" God is the Creator, constantly creative. "When he decreeth a thing, he only saith unto it, Be; and it is." [1]

His view was that the priests corrupted Abraham's teaching when they assumed authority to rule the Jews. Christ attacked the priests, and reasserted the truth. But the Catholic and Greek priests now corrupted Christ's teaching, by claiming authority to control Christians.

This showed, he said, that organization is evil. There should be no priests. Each individual must recognize his direct relation to God, his self-controlling, personal responsibility.

Increasing numbers did. The priests themselves had made Mecca a sanctuary; no blood could be shed there. They could

---

[1] *The Koran*: 19th Sura, Sale's Translation.

The Discovery of Freedom

only make life so miserable for these heretics that they left Mecca. Mohammed's ideas spread far and wide. Men came to Mecca only to hear him. Medina, two hundred miles away, asked him to come and be its emir.

Mohammed prudently kept this offer in reserve. He went on talking in Mecca. "They say, Become Jews or Christians, that ye may be directed. Nay, we follow the religion of Abraham the orthodox, *who was no idolator."* [2]

Surely, the gods themselves could not bear this. Mecca's most respectable citizens, one man from each family incurring an equal guilt, drew their knives to shed Mohammed's blood in holy sanctuary. They stormed Mohammed's house. He had just left, in no confusion.

He made tracks for the south. Hot on the trail came the Meccans. Leaving no tracks, Mohammed was traveling northward to Medina.

A small town in palm groves, Medina lived mostly on the date-harvest and a few flocks of sheep and goats. The pilgrim road passed by it. Mohammed's arrival made a great difference. He and his Meccan companions waylaid a rich caravan belonging to his would-be murderers, and brought in immense spoils. Increasing numbers of pilgrims stopped in Medina, and Mohammed converted them to the belief that there is one God, and no gods in the Ka'ba at Mecca.

Mecca's income was cut at its root; the town crashed into the worst depression in its history. The Meccans saw that they could not live in the same world with Mohammed's ideology. Industriously they prepared for war, and set out to destroy Medina.

A terrifying rumor of their approach sped before them. Mounted, and well armed, spearsmen, swordsmen, and archers, they far outnumbered the total population of the little town.

Quietly, before dawn, they approached it. Medina slept

[2] *The Koran:* 2nd Sura.

84

The Second Attempt

peacefully in the palm groves. Screeching a war-cry, the Meccans charged furiously into volleys of arrows that disrupted the charge. The survivors pulled out of the welter of fallen horses and men. There was not a sound nor stir in Medina; not a defender to be seen. Nothing like this had ever been known before.

Mohammed had invented trench warfare. He had placed the men of Medina in trenches, curved around the town. To charge into a trench was suicide. To leap it was to be surrounded. Volleys of arrows were futile, they sped only to earth.

The Meccans drew off and consulted. They kept on consulting. They galloped furiously back and forth before the trenches, yelling insults, daring the men of Medina to come out and fight like men. No one did.

This went on for days. Medina had ample provisions. The Meccans ate all theirs. Finally, unable to think of anything else to do, they turned back toward Mecca, two hundred miles away. News of their unfought war doubtless reached there before them.

Certainly it traveled as fast as camels, to all the bazaars of India, Persia, Arabia, Byzantium, Palestine, all northern Africa and every oasis in the Sahara. It is the kind of news that no one forgets to tell.

Historians have never been able to explain the terrific force of Mohammed's simple statement. Hilaire Belloc says with loathing that it "arose out of nothing, out of the hot sands to the East, and spread like a fire." Carlyle marvels, "As if a spark had fallen, one spark on what seemed a world of black unnoticeable sand; but lo! the sand proves explosive powder, blazes high from Delhi to Granada!"

The knowledge that men are free swept across the known world as swiftly as Americans swept across this continent.

Mohammed remained six more years in Medina. Then he traveled to Mecca as a peaceful pilgrim—leading thirty thousand good fighting men, well armed. A deputation met him

85

outside Mecca and welcomed him to the holy city, a sanctuary. The Meccans accepted his religious views and made no objection when he removed the idols from the Ka'ba.

"Use no violence in religion," he said. "Fight for the religion of God against those who fight against you, but transgress not by attacking them first."[3]

Two years later, he died. He had fought, and won, two battles. All the tribes of Arabia from the Red Sea to the Euphrates declared that men are free, that there is but one God, and that Mohammed was one of the prophets.

In eighty years, the world was Moslem from the Indian Ocean to the Atlantic. The Mediterranean was a Moslem lake and the western gate of the known world had a new Arabic name: Gibraltar.

Then came the first great creative effort of human energy. It created the first scientific civilization.

American schools teach American children the European past. Pagan Greece and pagan Rome; the transformation of the Empire to The Church during the Dark Ages; the Renaissance, the Middle Ages, the Kings and the barons; the Reformation, modern Europe, the rise of the capitalist class, the revolt of the masses: that is Europe.

During the stagnation of Europe that is called the Dark Ages, the world was actually bright with an energetic, brilliant civilization, more akin to American civilization and more fruitful today for everyone alive, than any other in the past.

Millions upon millions of human beings, thirty generations, believing that all men are equal and free, created that civilization and kept on creating it for eight hundred years.

To them the world owes modern science—mathematics, astronomy, navigation, modern medicine and surgery, scientific agriculture.

To them the world directly owes the discovery and the exploration of America.

---

[3] *The Koran*: 19th Sura.

The Second Attempt

These men were of all races and colors and classes and all former cultures and many religions; by no means all of them were Moslems. They were former subjects or descendants of subjects of all former empires. There is no one name that applies to them all. Europeans called them Saracens.

Their own records of the eight hundred years of their civilization, its institutions, and the causes of its collapse, are largely locked in the Arabic language. Since American scholars and intellectuals in general are European-minded, an American can get only glimpses of the Saracens' world, seen through European indifference or hatred.

What makes the difference between living now, and living fifty years ago? You think of electricity, telephones, cars, radio, plastics, and you answer, "Science."

Yet twenty-two hundred years ago, there were scientists. Before Rome was an outlaw's camp in the far west, Aristotle was saying, "If a man grasps truths that *can not be other than they are,* in the way in which he grasps the definitions through which *demonstrations take place,* he will not have opinion, but knowledge."

A great scientific civilization flourished in Greece before historical time. You can see its ruins now on Crete and on the mainland. No one knows even the name of the people who created it. Their houses had central heating and modern plumbing; the women wore modern clothes. There is an interesting legend of the man who made wings, flew from Crete toward Sicily, and fell in the sea. These people had no weapons of war. The ruins show that armed men suddenly attacked and burned their cities, and, as the saying goes, wiped out their civilization.

When, for any reason, men stop creating a civilization, many of them go on living and bringing up their children. The Cretans today are not Greeks. (Just try to call a Cretan, a Greek!) The Albanians are not Greeks. The Macedonians were never Greeks. No European scholar knows Aristotle's

The Discovery of Freedom

ancestry, but certainly his point of view is not Greek. (The illiterate Albanian mountaineers say that he was Albanian, and give you his ancestry for a dozen generations; whatever that is worth.)

His father was court physician to Amyntas the Second, King of Macedon. Aristotle went to the best university, Plato's Academy in Athens. He had no use for Plato. He tutored young Alexander the Great and tried to teach him some sense. When Alexander set out to conquer the world, Aristotle left him and founded a school of science. It flourished until Alexander's successor suppressed it. Aristotle quietly went on with scientific research.

No known century has ever lacked scientists. Whenever Authority was weak, men opened schools of science. Then a more efficient ruler suppressed them. The Emperor did this again in the 6th century, and textbooks tell you that "Science expired in Greece." Later you learn that Science, nine hundred years dead, "revived" or "was awakened" in Italy.

All such phrases, of course, are nonsense far inferior to such good nonsense as "Twas brillig, and the slithy toves did gyre and gimble in the wabe."

What happened was that, a little while before Mohammed retired from business, the police closed all schools of science in the Byzantine Empire. A scientist could shut up, or he could sit in a dungeon, or he could get out of the Empire (if he could).

Naturally, a great many got out. In the west, Rome was a ghost town and gangsters roamed over Europe. The north was barbarian. In the east, Persia at the moment was comparatively liberal. The scientists went to Persia.

In its turn, the Byzantine Empire's energy was failing under good strong Government. The Persians swept across Asia Minor again, and this time they heard Mohammed's declaration that individuals are free. The men who believed this could not be suppressed.

Within a century, the Moslem world included India, Persia,

The Second Attempt

Arabia, Syria, Palestine, Egypt and all northern Africa to the Atlantic, Gibraltar, Spain, the Balearic islands, southern France and southern Italy and the Italian islands. It encircled the Persian Gulf, the Caspian Sea, and the Mediterranean. Not a frontier separated all the people in that enormous area.

These people were children of men who had lived in all the former empires; they had the same racial heritages, the same cultures, languages, customs. But now they no longer believed in pagan gods. They knew they were free.

The first thing that men naturally want to do is to attack the material world. To live, they must attack it. The natural aim of human energy is to make this earth habitable for human beings. When no false belief obstructs human energy at its source in the individual, men attack this earth to adapt it to human needs and desires. Then they need scientific knowledge, which is knowledge of the material world.

The refugee scientists in Persia were popular now—respected, admired, listened to. No Authority suppressed them; no police kicked them around. They opened their schools; from Baghdad to Granada, their schools were crowded with students. In two centuries, they were great universities, the world's first universities.

For hundreds of years, these universities grew. The University in Cairo was more than a thousand years old and still had forty thousand students, when I was there.

These universities had no organization whatever. (Mohammed said that organization corrupts knowledge.) A Saracen university had no program, no curriculum, no departments, no rules, no examinations; it gave no degrees nor diplomas. It was simply an institution of learning. Not of teaching, but of learning. A man, young or old, went to a university to learn what he wanted to know, just as an American goes to a grocery to get the food he wants.

Men who knew (or thought they knew) something, and wanted to teach it, opened a school to sell their knowledge. Success depended upon the demand for the knowledge they had. If they prospered, other teachers joined them. So the schools became universities, and century after century public-spirited men added buildings, just as individuals and groups of alumnae add to American universities.

The teachers lectured in open classrooms. Anyone was welcome to listen. An incoming student wandered about, listening. When he decided upon the teacher he wanted, they discussed privately whatever he wanted to learn and needed to study, and agreed upon fees. Then he joined the class regularly. If he was not satisfied, he could quit at any time and find another teacher. When he had learned what he wanted to know, he left the university to use his knowledge. (No doubt his teachers would give him letters of introduction, if he wanted them.)

A thousand years after the Saracens built these universities, far away in time and on a continent that they never knew existed, a revolutionary leader, Thomas Jefferson—who knew little or nothing about the Saracens—realized the dream of his life when he created the University of Virginia. His dream was a new kind of education.

Proudly, almost bragging a little, he wrote to a friend in the medieval-university system of Harvard, "We shall allow them [the students] uncontrolled choice in the lectures they shall choose to attend. Our institution will proceed on the principle . . . of letting everyone come and listen to whatever he thinks may improve the condition of his mind."

For more than nine hundred years the University of Cairo proceeded on precisely that principle. Until the end of the 19th century, Europeans were not able to impose upon that university any tinge of the European belief that minds acquire knowledge, not by actively seeking to know, but by passively being taught whatever Authority decides that they should know.

In these universities, teachers offered all the learning of the past, translated into Arabic. The students in general did not want metaphysics; they wanted science. They wanted Aristotle

The Second Attempt

and Galen and Euclid and every scrap of knowledge that had been added to theirs.

The Greeks and the Romans had seen in India the Hindu symbols of numbers. But Europeans were still using the clumsy Roman numerals that do not permit arithmetic, and they were still adding, subtracting and multiplying by clicking little balls along wires, as the Chinese still do. So were the Saracens. Now, they seized upon the Hindu numbers, that did not hinder their minds or their acts.

Americans call these figures Arabic; they number these pages. A row of them is on every typewriter, and at its end there is a circle: zero.

The Saracens' free minds first grasped that concept: zero. Nothing: an absence of any number, that *is* a number. They added zero to the nine numbers that had been known.

Any mathematician will tell you that, without zero, there could not be mathematics. Without zero, Americans would have no engineering, no chemistry, no astronomy, no measurement of substance or space. Without zero, there could not be a skyscraper, a subway, a modern bridge or highway, a car, an airplane, a radio, a city water supply, or rayon or cellophane or aluminum or stainless steel or a permanent wave. There could not be modern science, the modern world, without zero.

Having zero, the Saracens developed arithmetic and added algebra and quadratics. To Euclid's geometry they added plane and spherical geometry.

Applying this mathematics to sun, moon, and stars, they produced astronomy. Across three continents they built observatories. They invented the sextant and the magnetic compass, and accurately calculated latitude, and, not quite so accurately, longitude. They deduced the shape and movement of the spinning earth, around its axis and around the sun, and they measured its size.

If a Saracen navigator who died eight hundred years ago, could stand today in the chart-room of the Queen Mary, he would profoundly admire the detail, the printing, and the changes in the charts, but he would have no more difficulty in understanding them than a man who knew ox-carts had in understanding the first carriage he saw. A Saracen captain could take the Queen Mary's charts and instruments and navigate that steamer across the ocean today. The one instrument that baffled him would be the Sperry gyro-compass; he could use it, but he would not understand the electric energy that keeps it spinning.

The Saracens gave Europeans the information that the earth is round, its measurements, the sextant and the magnetic compass, and the portolani, the maps and charts that Columbus took with him on his voyages.

They also did more than anyone else to make Americans healthy.

First they translated Galen's works into Arabic. (Europeans got these later from the Arabic.) Then they did a lot of original research in medicine and surgery. Nine hundred years ago they were using the entire American medical pharmacopoeia of today, excepting only the recently discovered chemical compounds. There was not another great advance in medicine, from the Saracens' time to the American century.

From the Ganges to the Atlantic, the Saracens built medical schools and hospitals. One of these was in Salerno.

I find no authority for saying that Europeans first learned medicine and surgery from this school. But, while this school was flourishing in Italy, Italians built the first hospitals in Europe. Within a week's journey of the Saracens' great school of medicine and surgery, Italians were performing the first surgical operations ever performed in Europe.

I doubt that even in the Dark Ages any doctor cut open an important, paying patient without having some idea of what he would find. (He could not learn that in Europe, where at that very time The Church was forbidding dissection.) And when I learn that these patients recovered from operations removing gall-stones, I do not think that a "revival of Science"

The Second Attempt

saved their lives. I think the Italian doctors had studied surgery in the Saracens' hospital-school of surgery.

They used local anesthetics for these operations. The Saracens had discovered local anesthesia. The next great attack upon pain was the discovery of general anesthesia, in Massachusetts General Hospital in the United States of America, late in the 19th century.

In 13th-century Milan, Italian doctors and surgeons were making cures that all other Europeans thought were miracles. At the same time, the Doges of Venice decreed (and are supposed to have invented) quarantine, of *both contagious and infectious* diseases. That's an odd inspiration, to come to men who had always believed that pestilence was God's anger vented upon mankind.

Both Milan and Venice were thriving commercial cities, thriving entirely from trade with the Saracens.

In fact the whole Renaissance, the "revival of learning in Europe," inexplicably "arose" in Italy, that long, narrow peninsula with Saracen civilization brilliant at its tip, and its every port opening to the Saracens' sea.

Precisely one hundred years after Mohammed died, the Saracens moved into central France. Near Tours a frantically assembled army of Europeans met them. Defeated in the one battle, they retired to Provence and Spain. They did not attack Europe again.

The fanatic Catholic Europeans regarded the Saracens as anti-Christ, the devil on earth. Saracens regarded Europeans as barbarians. A few bands of Catholics remained in the bleak and barren Pyrenees and sometimes harried the Spanish frontier. For five hundred years, the border guards kept them out of Spain.

In Spain the Saracens built great centers of science and art and production and commerce, Cordova, Granada, Seville. From India and Africa and Cathay, students came to the universities in Spain, and from Spain students went to the

93

universities in Baghdad and Delhi. Farmers in rich southern Spain poured into the cities an increasing abundance of foods and raw materials, and out of the cities poured an increasing wealth of goods, woolens and linens and cottons and silks, mosaics, enamels, porcelain, glass, gloves. Ships thronged in the ports, unloading spices, ivory, camphor from the Isles of Spice, tempered steel and finely-wrought brass from Damascus, horses from Arabia and saddles of leather softer than velvet, from Morocco across the straits.

Five hundred years; Saracen Spain was three times as old as these United States are now, when from darkest Europe Pope Urban the Second sent half a million fanatics to attack the Saracens in Palestine.

This unprovoked aggression began a world war that lasted until the United States subdued the "Barbary pirates" in the Mediterranean. Pirates they were, no doubt; but they did not know it; they thought they were fighting the Europeans, who had attacked them first.

From the European chroniclers of this war we get almost our only glimpses of the Saracens' world.

The cause of this war was a struggle for Authority in Europe. The Church was divided; there were two Popes, and Pope Urban was the weaker.

No one knows, positively, what his motives were in starting the Crusades. Apparently he wanted the three results he got. The Crusades enabled him to oust the other Pope; they diminished the killing in Europe; and during the absence of the fighting men, The Church became The Authority.

There was good reason for the Crusades; it is truly doubtful whether Europeans would have survived if the Pope had not got rid of the barons. Their ceaseless wars were killing too many people by starvation.

For more than a century, The Church had been decreeing peace in Europe. First, the Popes declared the Peace of God; no one paid any attention. Then they decreed the Truce of

94

The Second Attempt

God, a long week-end from Wednesday night to Monday morning. If the ruling classes would only take that vacation every week, then common men could farm and trade on Thursdays, Fridays, and Saturdays. Sunday was of course God's day. And on Mondays, Tuesdays, and Wednesdays the ruling classes could go on trying to move their frontiers, and killing each other's farmers and traders. But The Church was not yet strong enough to enforce this Truce of God.

The Saracen world was peaceful at the time, except for a family quarrel among the Turks, newly converted pagans who had recently seized Baghdad. The Christian Emperor of Constantinople was fighting barbarians in what is now Hungary.

In Europe, Pope Urban the Second summoned all the barons to a great council, and made a speech that roused them to frenzy. He called upon them to save the tomb of Christ from the children of the Devil, and he gave complete forgiveness of all sins to every man who would go, and instant entrance to Paradise to any man who died on the way to kill infidels.

The fighting Europeans at once began what historians call the remarkable phenomenon of the Crusades, an outburst of greed and highly practical politics, and of a natural desire to get out of that Europe to Heaven, which lasted for two centuries.

"Free the Holy Land!" was its slogan.

Moslems had held the Holy Land for five hundred years and Christians had been worshiping at its Christian shrines, which Moslems reverently guarded. Christian shrines are Moslem shrines and Jerusalem has always been a Holy City to Moslems, who revere Abraham, Moses, Gideon, Samuel, and Christ as prophets of God.

Saracens had set the guard that still stands—or did, when I was in Jerusalem—at the Church of the Holy Sepulchre. Night and day for more than a thousand years an armed Moslem has stood there, to keep Christians from killing Christians of rival sects at the tomb of Christ.

95

The Discovery of Freedom

On the most holy day of the Christian year, the guard retires. For the twenty-four hours of Easter Day, no infidel presence profanes the tomb from which Christ rose. Then occurs the miracle; fire from the tomb lights candles in the darkness, and Christians kill Christians.

At sunset of Easter Day every year, the Moslem guard returns to his post and the police of Jerusalem carry the Christian corpses out of the Church of the Holy Sepulchre, sometimes hundreds of bodies, sometimes only dozens.

There are some two hundred sects of Moslems. They have never quarreled at the mosque of Omar, which is Mohammed's shrine in Jerusalem. No Christian stands guard there.

Nearly half a million Crusaders crossed the Bosporus in the first Crusade. The sympathy of the Christian Emperor in Constantinople was with the Saracens; he did all he could to hinder, harass and divide the Crusaders, while at the same time getting rid of them himself. They defeated the Saracens in one battle, and besieged Nicea. The Emperor made an alliance with its Saracen defenders, and moved his own troops into the city.

The Crusaders went on to Antioch, and besieged it. They devastated the surrounding country so thoroughly that they almost starved to death. Under the eyes of the guards on Antioch's walls, they cooked and ate the Saracens they killed.

They could not take Antioch. A *Christian commander of Moslem troops* in the besieged Moslem city, betrayed it to them. He let them in secretly at night; they massacred the whole population. The bodies rotting in the streets and the wells caused a mysterious sickness that killed thousands of them.

They went on toward Jerusalem, finding only deserted villages and towns on the way. From impregnable walled cities, the emirs sent embassies offering to pay the Crusaders not to disturb them. An envoy from the Sultan of Egypt, who held Jerusalem, met them, bringing the Sultan's suggestion that

The Second Attempt

they fulfill their vow to their Pope by entering Jerusalem peacefully, as pilgrims.

The Crusaders moved warily, in this country of magic. Certainly they were surrounded by the sons or close allies of Satan himself, for long before the news could reach these infidels by any earthly means, they knew that the Crusaders were coming.

With Christian guides who joined them along the way, the Crusaders went on toward Jerusalem. South of Beirut, a miracle occurred. Over their heads in the air, a hawk wounded a pigeon. It fell to the ground. Attached to its leg was a silver cylinder containing a strange thing, unknown to the Crusaders —a piece of paper with marks upon it. The Christian Syrians explained that this was Arabic writing, and read it.

"The emir of Akka to the lord of Caesaria, greeting. A race of dogs, stupid and quarrelsome, hath passed by me, moving without order. As thou lovest the Faith, do what thou mayest, and have others do, all that may hurt them. Send this word to other citadels and fortresses." [4]

In two years, the Crusaders had fought two open battles and a few skirmishes; they had unsuccessfully besieged two cities and taken Antioch by treachery. Of the 426,000 Crusaders who had invaded the country, 30,000 reached Palestine.

They found the palm groves, the vineyards, the orchards of figs, the villages and towns and the white-walled city of Ramlah deserted.

A hundred Crusaders rode into Bethlehem and found it a Christian town built around the Cathedral of the Virgin Mary. The people, priests and monks entertained them royally. They rode back toward Jerusalem, and came to the peaceful church of the Blessed Mother of Christ, in the garden of Gethsemane on the Mount of Olives.

[4] From "The Chronicle of the Anonymous," quoted by Harold Lamb in *The Crusades: Iron Men and Saints*, p. 214.

The Discovery of Freedom

For five weeks they attacked gray-walled Jerusalem on its heights. They battered its walls with every known engine of war; from thirty miles away they hauled timbers and built thirty-foot towers, and under a rain of boulders and pitch and Greek fire they advanced the towers and rushed across blazing drawbridges into hand-to-hand fighting on the tops of the walls. They took Jerusalem, and for two days and nights they slaughtered men, women, children, babies, in the houses, down the alleys, over the roofs. Around the mosque of Omar where the pavement is flat, their horses charged fetlock-deep in blood. Only one little group of the many Christians in Jerusalem, huddled together in the last extremity of terror before these bloody killers and unable to make them understand any known language, suddenly sang in Greek a part of a Christian mass; and the Crusaders, recognizing it, swerved by and left them alive.

Jerusalem, then, was one of the feudal kingdoms that the Crusaders established during successive Crusades, in Palestine and Syria and, unhappily for the Christian Armenians, in Armenia Minor. These kingdoms lasted for about eighty years. The Saracens did not attack them. The Christian Kings held Jerusalem for years with less than a hundred soldiers.

Before the Crusaders had reached Jerusalem, they had begun to adopt the Moslem dress. In a few years, they were living, eating, behaving like Moslems. Their sons, born in these Crusaders' kingdoms, *grew up so tolerant that they let Moslems worship in the Christian churches.*

How does it happen that the Crusaders found so many Christians living among the infidels? Why, Christians lived there all the time. They were part of the Saracens' world. Moslems did not exterminate people whose religious belief was different; here they still are, in lands that the Moslems held for a thousand years—the Armenians, Albanians, Greeks, Copts, Maronites, Druses, Jews, Parsees, Yezedees, Hindus, to mention a few.

It was Europeans who massacred heretics, to the last infant

whose parents had the slightest knowledge that men's minds are free.

Europeans slaughtered the Albigenses, the Waldensians, the Socinians, the Huguenots, the Covenanters, and scores of other groups. Five hundred years after the Crusades, Protestants and Catholics were fleeing to the American wilderness to save their lives from European fanaticism.

Before they took Jerusalem, the Crusaders had met the Saracens only once in open battle. From that day they respected them. In contrast to the bludgeoning Europeans, the Saracen fighters were swift as wind. They wore light helmets of Damascene steel, and a body-armor of gilded steel mesh that stopped an arrow but was so sheer that a whole suit of it crumpled into a handful. They were lean, agile, quick, and they rode small horses as swift as their thin, flexible swords. They attacked the flank of their enemy's army, and wheeled and formed and attacked again with incredible speed.

The iron-armed and iron-armored ranks of Christendom charged straight forward with a full-throated roar, "God wills it!" But the Saracens, under their flying green silk banners, swept like a wave and struck at the flank, calling out an ululating cry that sounded to the Crusaders like the howl of wolves. La ilaha illa-llaha!—there is only one God.

When the Crusaders went out of Jerusalem to attack Ascalon, they were already adopting the Saracens' battle tactics.

They were still unable to guess the uses of a great deal of their loot. At Antioch their bewilderment was pitiable. They sat down on beds and leapt up terrified by a movement beneath them; they had never seen a mattress. They did not know how to deal with the draperies, carpets, cushions, the silks, linens, leathers, the unknown metals, strange utensils, and clothes. The fabrics seemed magical; chiffons, that clung like cobwebs to fingers, and, their chronicles say, a silk that changed its color.

They sniffed at strange liquids in curious containers; they did not know what an oil-lamp was. Gingerly they tasted unknown substances; a white powder, delicious but perhaps poisonous; they had never heard of sugar. In small gold boxes and in tiny tubes with jeweled stoppers were other substances with strange tastes; they had not seen cosmetics. (Saracen women used all the cosmetics that American women use, and a few more. No other women in history were ever so well-groomed, until this generation of American women.)

In Antioch, and again in Jerusalem, the Crusaders whose castles were rude stone walls and floors of earth or damp stone covered thick with rotting reeds, came into rooms like jewels, the floors tiled, the walls and ceilings of mosaic. By a low couch covered with taut, snow-white linen stood an ebony taboret; a finger-tip could not feel the lace-work of mother-of-pearl set into its top. A delicate lattice-work of an unknown wood mysteriously let one look out through the window, though no one could look in, and a faint scent came from this lattice-work. It was sandal-wood.

Wondering and rummaging, peering into hiding-places, dragging out and killing some quivering thing, a child or a slave, the Crusaders came upon objects that seemed to be made of some kind of jewel. Could there be in this country so many jewels, so large? These vessels were transparent. But not jewels; seize one, it crushed to pieces that cut the hand. It was glass.

It was a country of magicians; all Europeans heard that it was.

But the most amazing thing to the Crusaders must have been its cleanliness. (Americans are the cleanest people on earth now.)

The Crusaders got wet in the rain or when they crossed rivers. And a bath was a solemn rite that every page performed, after his all-night vigil before the altar, on the morning before he was made a knight. But Moslems bathed five times a day.

This was Mohammed's idea. After he died, the friends whom he called his "companions" gathered up every saying of his that anyone had written down or remembered, and made a book of them, the Koran. His point of view was always tolerant, and practical. They pestered him about the pagan rite of turning toward Mecca in prayer; several times he said it didn't matter which way anyone faced; finally he said, Let it go; face toward Mecca. They wanted his decision about gambling and drinking; he said, "In both there is great sin, and also some things of use unto man, but their sinfulness is greater than their use." Asked how many wives a man should have, he replied that too many wives distract a man's mind from his business affairs, and mentioned Solomon's well-known troubles with wives. Urged to say precisely how many wives are too many, he said that four are plenty. But on the subject of cleanliness he was a fanatic.

Probably in reaction from the filthy Christian ascetics, he said emphatically that a clean body is essential to a clear mind and a pure spirit. Everyone should bathe often, and always in running water; one can not bathe clean in standing water because the water becomes dirty.

He tied cleanliness to his plan for keeping the truth in men's minds without a church organization. Let everyone repeat to himself, morning, noon, and night, and in mid-morning and mid-afternoon, the fact that there are no pagan gods. And before saying this, bathe in running water. (Remembering trade, he added that men crossing deserts could use sand.) Mohammed himself always washed his hands before and after eating, and rinsed his mouth.

So the Crusaders came into a country where it seemed that everyone was always bathing. Fountains were everywhere, for Moslems saw no reason to go to church to say that there is only one God; they bathed and repeated that fact wherever they were, interrupting work and business only a moment or so. These innumerable, flowing fountains made a profound first impression upon the invading Europeans.

Anyone, or any group, that wanted to, built a fountain, just as anyone built a mosque. There was no more organization about a mosque than in a university. A mosque's courtyard is quiet, and pleasant with its splashing fountain; beggars and philosophers sat there. Some had made money enough, some had inherited money, some lived on alms in order to give their whole time to thinking about the nature of the universe and of man. Five times a day, one of them climbed the mosque's minaret and called out that there is no God but God. Those to whom it was convenient repeated the fact in the mosque, after bathing at its fountain, and someone might read aloud from the Koran, or not. Men in the neighborhood kept the mosque repaired if they wanted to; if they didn't, it fell to ruin.

Imagine the Crusader who had grabbed a small kingdom in Syria, dining for the first time with a neighboring emir. A King wearing harsh leather, coarse wool and eighty pounds of iron-chain armor, and used to gnawing meat heartily from the bone, tossing the bone to the dogs, and pouring down his throat a quart of ale.

The stone walls and stone-paved courtyard of his host's castle would be home-like, and rooms like those he had looted would not surprise him. He would see, now, how silk garments should be worn. But what did he do, when a servant offered him a silver bowl with an open-filagree cover, and poised a slim pitcher above it? If he lifted the cover and looked into the bowl, it was empty. The pitcher was full of warm, rose-scented water.

Before the Saracen ate, he washed his hands in scented water poured over them; the water vanished through the bowl's filagree cover. He wiped his hands on a linen damask or a terry-cloth towel (our bath towel). A servant set between the host and his guest an inlaid metal tray, and placed upon it a porcelain bowl of food. The Saracen ate with his fingers, as Europeans did, but he did not wipe them on his clothes; he washed them again.

The meal was served in courses; platter after platter, bowl after bowl. After each course, the Saracen washed his hands, and dried them on a fresh towel.

The Second Attempt

Not one dog sat yearning for bones and scratching fleas. The floor of tiles or polished stone was shining clean. On a dias, the host and guest sat on thick-piled, silken rugs, richly colored, and clean. Before a Saracen entered a house, he left his shoes outside.

The meal itself was amazing and strange. The meats were prepared in ways unknown, with seasonings and sauces. There were salads, and frozen sherbets. There was a strange drink, in tiny cups—coffee, with sugar in it. No European had ever seen many cereals, vegetables, and fruits that the Saracens ate: rice, and spinach, and asparagus, lemons, melons, peaches.

The world's first scientific farmers were producing them.

In Europe, the serfs and oxen hauled wooden plows that scratched the earth, and the crop was whatever God willed. The land was twice plowed every year, and half of it always lay fallow, for the earth grows tired and needs rest. When Richard of England crossed Europe, he must have been proud of the strong English land; in England, only one-third of the fields lay fallow.

But not an acre of arable land ever rested in the Saracens' world. From the Atlantic to Cathay, across three continents, the Saracen farmers were fertilizing the land, deep-plowing and contour-plowing, and irrigating, and *rotating their crops*. They were pouring into the markets an abundance of nearly every food that the earth produces, and taking in return such a wealth of goods as the world had never seen before.

These goods are still renowned: damask linens, mohair fabrics, muslin, Morocco leather, Syrian silks, oriental rugs, mosaics, inlaid woods, glassware and porcelains, enamels, filagree and inlaid work in metals. Damascus steel was never equaled until very recently in these United States, and it is not yet surpassed in quality. In 1919 at the Peace Conference, the French demanded and got Syria, and stopped the manufacture of Syrian silks, a Saracen manufacture fifteen hundred years old and still producing silks with which the famous weavers of Lyons could not compete.

103

The Discovery of Freedom

Americans owe directly to the Saracens our southwestern and Californian architecture, our cotton industry, our asphalt paving, and a long list of such things as beds, table and bed linens, small occasional tables, strawberries, ice-cream. Americans speak Arabic when they say, mattress, sofa, cotton, talcum, sugar, coffee, sherbert, naphtha, gypsum, benzine. Our cars run, our streets are paved, our houses are furnished and our bodies clothed with things that the Saracens created.

The Christian kingdoms in the Saracens' world lasted less than a century. The heirs of their Crusading founders became indistinguishable from the Moslems in their customs, manners and dress, as the other Christians were in that civilization.

Then the Moslem emir (who was a Kurd) proposed an alliance with England. He offered his sister in marriage to Richard the Lion-Hearted, who was crusading at the time. But Richard intended to return to England, and sensibly he refused to take home a Moslem Queen.

Since the Christian King would not make peace, the Moslems attacked and took Jerusalem. They did not sack it, and as soon as its defenders surrendered, they released their prisoners. The terms that the victorious emir imposed upon the invaders were, that they must go home. He gave them forty days in which to dispose of their property or pack it before leaving.

During the forty days, the people in Jerusalem bitterly complained to the emir that the departing Christians were seizing everything they could lay hands on. They demanded that the emir stop this plundering. The emir replied, "If I stop them, they will say that I have broken my word. Let us give them an opportunity to praise the goodness of our religion."

He let the people in Jerusalem protect their own property as best they could, and the Europeans got away with quite a lot of loot.

But the returning Crusaders brought back to Europe the first idea of a gentleman that Europeans had ever had. Until they invaded the Saracens' civilization, they had never known that a strong man need not be brutal. The Saracens were splendid fighters when they fought, but they were not cruel; they did not torture their prisoners, they did not kill the wounded. In their own country, they did not persecute the Christians. They were brave men, but they were gentle. They were honorable; they told the truth, they kept their word.

This ideal of a gentleman especially impressed the English. It is still producing perhaps the finest class of human beings on earth today, the men and women of the British ruling class. It is an ideal that permeates all of American life. This is what surprises so many people in many parts of the world, when they see and meet the common American soldiers and sailors.

From such dim indications an American can get some idea of the people with whom the Italians were dealing, before and while they were "awakening" Europe.

At that same time, the Jews were in Europe, from Spain. Subversive ideas spread also from them; for instance, the rumor that the earth is round. Roger Bacon (when he could get out of jail) was corresponding with Saracen scholars in the universities of Spain. The feudal system's equilibrium, that had been so perfect through the 12th century, was threatened by questions in men's minds. The Church was more and more strictly suppressing new heresies.

All Italians were prospering from trade with the Saracens. Italian merchants, traders, sea-captains, sailors, were constantly meeting men of greater knowledge and wider experience than theirs, richer men, better dressed, better fed, cleaner and better groomed; men who thought and acted quickly, and independently. They had better methods of navigating ships, quicker ways of computing costs and adding bills. With incredible swiftness, they dispatched their business affairs over great distances.

To the Italians, this speed must have been the most startling thing in the Saracens' world. A European who traveled eighteen miles in one day had done something to brag about for years. A Saracen thought nothing of sending a parcel two hundred miles and getting a receipt for it tomorrow.

A thousand years ago, the Saracens' pony express habitually covered two hundred miles a day, anywhere on land from Morocco to Bokhara or the Ganges. At a pinch, it could do two thousand miles in eight days. Such speed over such a distance was not equalled until the pony express ran from St. Joseph, Missouri, to San Francisco.

The Saracens' postal service was swift, secret, free, and universal. You can see a remnant of it today in Ragusa (Dubrovnik) on the Dalmatian coast.

Ragusa was one of the Free Cities that "rose" in Italy during the dawn of the Renascence. Italian traders created them. The Free Cities were the only places in Europe at that time, where men could manage their own affairs. And Ragusa, at least, was a place where a man might believe whatever he believed, with no interference.

While Authority in Europe was still whipping up fanaticism to crusading fervor, Europeans in Free Ragusa were building churches of equal beauty and dignity for men of all faiths; a Roman Catholic church, a Greek Catholic church, a mosque and a fountain for Moslems. This is religious freedom.

Under the arcade of the market place, above the door that led to the offices of the city government, you see today a painting of Mother Ragusa, the Free City. The colors are still clear and fresh. Grouped around Mother Ragusa's knees, and equally enclosed by her arms, are children of all peoples; the Norman, the Mongol, the African, the Slav and the Levantine. Here is human equality and human brotherhood.

Below the portrait stands a marble bench on which three judges sat every day, to hear and judge in public any case brought before them. They represented the Free City. They were bound to judge all men with an equal justice.

Ragusa prospered enormously. Its merchants rivaled and

The Second Attempt

often outstripped the Venetians. An earthquake completely destroyed the city in the 16th century; they rebuilt it immediately with all its churches, in such speed that they could not pause to determine property lines, and therefore agreed to build the correct number of shops, all of equal size, leaving adjustments to be made afterward. Prosperity was hardly interrupted. Ragusa was so important that Catholic Spain sought the Free City as an ally, and Ragusa's ships sailed with the Spanish armada against England.

In rebuilding Ragusa, the merchants improved their postal service. They built dove-cotes all along the tops of the city's double walls, under the battlements, and thousands of descendants of the Saracens' pigeon post still flutter about them.

The Saracen cities, and Ragusa, required every foreigner to pay as entrance fee at the city gates, two carrier pigeons from his town. You can still see the barred cages, open now, where the foreign pigeons were filed under the name of their home.

When ships set out on the Adriatic, or caravans on the road that ended in Cathay, the traveling salesman took with him as many Ragusan pigeons as he might require to pay his entrance fee to other cities and to carry his correspondence to the home office. By pigeon he sent back sales reports and market news and his next address. In Ragusa a clerk took the replies, in their sealed cylinders, to the pigeon master, who selected the proper pigeon and attached and dispatched the letters.

This postal service covered land and sea from the Atlantic to the Indian Ocean. For speed and privacy it was not equalled again until Alexander Graham Bell invented the telephone.

Roman post roads are famous, and indeed they were excellent for their purpose, which was military. They were useful to The State, to the privileged class in the Roman Republic, and later to families that had a pull with the Emperor or Empress. But look for swift transportation and communication available to all ordinary men, and you find that the Saracens created them.

Look for the people whose lives are adjusted to a fast tempo, the people who travel swiftly and far, who communicate with each other quickly over long distances, people who attack space and time and create a civilization rapid, vibrant, depending on speed. Two peoples have done this: the Saracens and the Americans.

Here are two groups of people, as unlike as can possibly be. On the deserts and mountains and in the steamy fertile river-valleys from the Ganges to the Atlantic, there were Hindus, Mongols, Chaldeans, Assyrians, Armenians, Persians, Medes, Arabs, Greeks, Egyptians, Phoenicians, Hittites, as many African peoples and a thousand others whose ancestors had worn that soil to dust under their feet before history began.

Ten centuries later, on a virgin continent of primeval forests and great rivers and fresh-water inland seas, there were Spanish, Norwegians, Africans, Dutch, Germans, French and English and Scots and Irish and Swedes, whose ancestors had been here for less than two centuries.

In both cases, suddenly, "As if a spark had fallen, one spark . . . on explosive powder," there is a terrific outburst of human energy.

In both cases, these people create a civilization having these features:

It is scientific, constantly increasing and using scientific knowledge. Its essential function is not war, but production and distribution of goods. It is tolerant of all races and creeds; it is humane. Its standard of living, including standards of cleanliness and health, is the highest in the world. Its tempo is increasingly rapid, and great speed in communication and transportation is necessary to its existence.

Saracens created that kind of civilization. Americans are creating that kind of civilization.

What have they in common, a Saracen who lived eight hundred years ago, and the American flying overhead today?

They share a common human situation on this earth, and

The Second Attempt

a common human *nature,* and both live in conditions that do not prevent them from using their natural freedom.

The Saracens' civilization ceased to exist. Why?

I lived for some years in the remnants of the Turkish empire, and in Syria and Iraq I looked for such traces as I could find of an answer to that question.

It seems to me that this second attempt to establish conditions in which human energy can work under its natural individual control succeeded, as it did succeed for almost a thousand years, because anarchy was not quite as pure among the Saracens as it was among the Israelites.

All these peoples were already living in many kinds of groups when most of them became Moslems. They created a civilization embracing all the social customs, tribal traditions, and ways of human association that remained from all the cities and empires that had ever existed between the Ganges and the Atlantic.

So their anarchy was more an anarchy of groups than of individuals. Many individuals were completely free in it. But apparently most of them preferred to remain in tribal or family groups, and to accept many forms of authority that could not be enforced.

For example, families made contracts of marriage, subject to the consent of bride and groom. Moslem marriages are still precisely this. They are not religious sacraments. Neither are they civil contracts; and here, I think, is the weakness that eventually ended the Saracens' civilization. There was no civil law.

Marriages were an agreement between families; if it were necessary to enforce the terms of the agreement (which included property settlements from both families) the aggrieved family enforced them.

The only safeguards of property seem to have been possession of the property, individual honesty, and public opinion.

Well, cabins were never locked on the American frontier

where there was no law. The real protection of life and property, always and everywhere, is the general recognition of the brotherhood of man. How much of the time is any American within sight of a policeman? Our lives and property are protected by the way nearly everyone feels about another person's life and property.

But the Saracens seem to have had no civil law whatever. There were Mohammed's recorded opinions, and those of other wise men; Moslems accept these as rules of conduct. There were the emirs, leaders of groups; like leaders of political parties in this country. There were the Caliphs; the word means, Successor (to Mohammed). The Arabian Nights tell how the Caliphs used their influence.

There were men everywhere, whom their neighbors depended upon to give judgments, like the judgment of Solomon in the case of the two women who claimed the same child. I knew such a Cadi very well; he was an expert cabinet-maker and earned a good living at his trade.

A westerner who has seen a quarrel flare dangerously in an Arab bazaar will never forget it. One voice, one word, pierces that din of bargaining; the sound shocks the turmoil to utter silence. Out of it comes a mob-roar. "Brothers! you are brothers! Moslems, remember you are brothers!" With that roar goes a mob-rush. Get out of it, quick.

It is over in a moment. Scores of hands tear the quarreling men apart, snatch the knives from their fists or sashes. An unperturbed din of bargaining rises again, while small crowds of men who can leave their own affairs surround the angry men and go with them to the nearest Cadi, who, if he wants to keep his reputation for wisdom, must then and there settle the quarrel in a way that satisfies everyone's sense of justice.

You admire the method, because it works. But it is not law.

Actually it is the way in which men always, everywhere, keep the peace, when no one of them has a recognized right to use force. Then each one feels his responsibility. This is the

The Second Attempt

way Americans kept the peace on the frontier, and keep it now on fishing and hunting trips and in clubrooms.

The Saracens evidently got along very well for nearly a thousand years with no law. They modified, in many ways, the pure anarchy of freedom. From the past, they kept tribal customs. They increased the natural authority of parents over children, and the natural influence of wise, able, successful men and women. Workers formed fraternal groups; these still exist, more than a thousand years old. The fraternity of boatmen clusters around every ship that anchors in the Bosporus, and takes no passengers or freight ashore until the boatmen's chief and the ship's captain have agreed upon terms suited to that day's and that ship's circumstances.

All these are methods of using free energy flexibly, in mutual action. They are ways of controlling combined human energies without restricting individual freedom. How many of such methods there were in the great days of that lost civilization, precisely what they were, how they worked or failed to work—who knows? The subject does not interest Europeans, and I can not read Arabic.

There must have been many methods of controlling by mutual consent, all the activities of that busy civilization spanning three continents with trade, discovering and increasing and applying scientific knowledge, creating and distributing an unprecedented wealth of goods and of knowledge, literature, art, architecture—constantly improving all living conditions.

There was no Authority. There was no State. There was no Church.

Men were spending enormous sums of money in building roads and observatories and universities and hospitals and mosques and fountains and public gardens. Scholars were collecting and exchanging manuscripts and books; architects were creating the world's most beautiful buildings. Traders were managing businesses extending thousands of miles. How did they do it? What methods did they develop, from eight hundred years of experience?

All those complexes of free energies, operating across three continents and three seas, involving millions of persons in inter-dependent relationships, were geared to speed, the speed of the pony express and the pigeon's flight.

When the Turk's blitzkrieg struck, it tore that world apart. The pony express ceased to run; the pigeons fluttered over their sacked towns.

Nothing remained to hold together the millions of living persons who had been creating that vast, delicate and intricate civilization. By no means all of them were Moslems. All races, colors and nations were Moslems, mingling, with no distinction between them but their individual qualities as men; the one thing that Moslems have ever had in common is their belief, and their daily saying, that there is only one God.

No single organization, religious, political or social, extended over that whole tri-continental civilization. And there was nothing to take their place; there was no Law.

I think there is a natural necessity for a civil law, a code, explicitly stated, written and known; an impersonal thing, existing outside all men, as a point of reference to which any man can refer and appeal. Not any form of control, for each individual controls himself; but a law, acting as a not-human third party in relationships between living persons; an impersonal witness to contracts, a registrar of promises and deeds, of ownership and transfers of ownership of property; a not-living standard existing in visible form, by which man's acts can be judged and to which men's minds can cling.

In the 15th century, the savage Ottoman Turks first realized that men are free, and became a cyclone of energy striking the Saracens' world. In that world, fifteen generations had lived and died since freedom was an electrifying discovery. You may be sure that practical men took their free action for granted and never thought about it. Suddenly the average man was helpless, broke, unable to deal with a world that no longer

The Second Attempt

worked. A business man, he was no philosopher. He knew he was not responsible for this collapse, yet a practical man knows that effects come from causes; something must be responsible.

Between the 15th century and the 17th century, the Moslems forgot the God of Abraham, Christ, and Mohammed. They came to think of God as Authority, controlling men. I believe they could find no other explanation for the ruin of their world. They said it was an act of God; it was completely unreasonable, so they said that God is Unknowable. And this belief, prevailing among the millions, affected the newly-converted Turks, so that they, too, reverted to paganism. The Saracen world and the Turks who had conquered it, sank into stagnation.

Turkey was the Sick Man of Europe. From 1820 to 1924, the men who governed the Five Powers of Europe gathered solicitously around that sick bed, to hack off hunks of the patient. Human energy in Turkey was so weak that the people would not act, either for or against the Sultan. In the white-lace marble palaces along the Bosporus, there could be nothing but palace-intrigues.

I remember a Young Turk in 1923. He was young, and passionately admired everything western. He was rapturous because Turkish women were now working in factories, like western women. Hats were fundamentally important to him, and he demanded an edict forbidding Turkish women to wear veils. Mustapha Kemal issued that edict later; Turkish women felt as American women would feel if a nudist dictator ordered the police to permit no woman to wear any clothes in public. That edict was called, "freeing Turkish women." It shut a generation of them into their houses for the rest of their lives.

This Young Turk assured me that Turkey was awake at last; that Mustapha Kemal was a great liberator, who would keep European invaders out of Turkey, and compel Turks to act like Europeans; or else.

He said, "Praise be to God, at last we Turks are rebelling against God, like you Americans!"

The Discovery of Freedom

I was shocked. He was amazed that I did not know my own country. He explained, as to a baby moron, "Surely you know that God made the world. God made the mountains and rivers. You Americans refuse to accept God's will. You cut down the mountains; you make the rivers run as *you* will, Ah, but that is magnificent! Man's will against God's! And you do it, you succeed! All praise to God! we Turks, too, we are rebelling against Him!"

Moslems had gone back to the static, changeless universe and the controlling Authority. They had escaped from the responsibility of freedom. Moslem life was stagnant for six centuries because Moslems no longer knew that individuals control themselves and are responsible for their own acts and their own lives and for the human world they make.

From Sultan to slave, every good Moslem lived in submission to the Unknowable, as Spartans submitted to the Law of Lycurgus, as savages submit to tabu, as communists and fascists and nazis submit to The Party, and as some Americans believe that individuals should and must submit to an enforced Social Good, to the Will of the Majority, to a Planned Economy, to many other pagan gods that do not exist.

Through Italy, the Saracens gave Europeans "the awakening of Europe." Through Spain, the last flare of their energy gave the world the discovery of America.

Of course Columbus did not discover America. Irish, Danes, Norwegians, Basques, and at least one Spaniard saw America before Columbus did. The Breton fishermen apparently refilled their water-casks every season from New England's rivers. A map now in Venice, drawn three hundred years before Columbus was born, shows Newfoundland correctly, where it is.

Generations of sailors had known there was land in the west. For two centuries at least, Europeans had heard that the earth is round. Many had the Saracens' measurements of it. In longitude, these measurements were inaccurate by some eight thousand miles.

The Second Attempt

Columbus had to quell a mutiny on his ships, because he used these inaccurate measurements. The Spice Islands did not appear where they should. When he did see land, it was approximately where his charts showed India. He had no doubt that it was India, and assumed that he had somehow missed the islands.

The Saracens had no use for these measurements, no reason to sail around the earth to India. They were in India. Cathay and the Spice Islands were on their doorstep.

But Europeans needed a route to India, and the Crusades taught them that they did. The riches of the world were in the East, and the Saracens had them. Europeans were the Have Not nations, and they knew it.

For two hundred years their sailors coasted along the shores of this continent, and all that time the Kings and the Popes heard that the earth was round, and European scholars had its measurements and charts showing that the land in the West was fabulous Cathay and Ind and the Isles of Spice, overflowing with ivory and silk and gold.

Then why did not European energy leap to follow the Irish, the Norwegians, the Danes, the Bretons and Basques, as Spanish energy leaped to follow Columbus?

The nature of any energy explains its behavior. The explanation of men's acts, or failures to act, is found in the nature of human energy. Individuals control human energy, and they control it in accordance with their view (true or false) of the universe.

In the 13th century Europe, you find Roger Bacon—called "the father of modern science"—spending much of his life in jail, because Europeans believed that men did not control their own thoughts.

Roger Bacon was actually free, of course. Whenever he got out of jail, he went on corresponding with the universities in Spain, and sooner or later he said something, and was put back into jail. He controlled his thoughts, his speech, his acts; no one else could. But he was one man among multitudes who

The Discovery of Freedom

believed that the Church and the State controlled them. The Kings and the Popes believed this, too; they believed that they were responsible for the inferior multitudes, and did their best to control them.

So whenever a man like Roger Bacon said what he thought, these Authorities used their real power, force, to put him into a dungeon, where only a jailor could hear him speak, and stone walls and chains kept him from acting as he wanted to act.

But the Kings and the Popes, you may think, were free. Access to India would have made them enormously rich, and they had heard that India was within their reach. You may wonder why they did not send expeditions to the land whose coasts their sailors had seen.

They could not, because the pagan belief that Authority controls individuals does not only prevent individuals from acting freely. It also prevents the men who act as Authority from using their subjects' energies in new ways.

Here you have the very root of Old World thinking. Belief in a controlling Authority rests upon the belief that nothing *is being created,* that all things *have been created.*

In six days God created the earth and all that is therein; then (the ancients believed) Creativeness ceased forever; there is no more *creative* energy; on the seventh day the Creator became Authority controlling what *had been created.*

The whole idea of Authority controlling the universe and man, depends upon seeing the universe as completed, finished, motionless, changeless.

For if the universe is not completed and static; if, instead, dynamic Energy is creatively operating; then a thing that is impossible at this instant will exist in the coming instant; then all things are changing into new, unprecedented things; to-morrow cannot be known today, and nothing that exists today can control tomorrow.

No Old World mind dares to admit the terrific thought that

116

The Second Attempt

Reality is Creative Energy, that Change is in the very nature of things.

True, everyone sees changes in the visible world; seed changes to plant and flower, and flower to seed. But to Old World thinkers the acorn and the tree are one thing, *oak;* its visible form changes (or seems to change) but *oak* does not. Visible forms are illusions, they say; Reality is static, no Creative Energy is operating. (Yet this energy creates new things all the time—apricots, seedless oranges, scentless marigolds. Not long ago in Texas, for no reason that anyone can discover or guess, one single bough on a grapefruit tree created a thing that never existed before: red grapefruit.)

The discovery of Progress is very new; Massachusetts was more than a hundred years old when (in 1735) a European suggested the possibility that Progress might exist. Wild young radicals in the Boston taverns argued that Progress is possible; young Benjamin Franklin was one of them, and all respectable Boston frowned upon such dangerous radicalism. That's why Benjamin left home and went to Philadelphia, to begin a career where no one knew that he held such subversive ideas.

So in Europe the Kings and Popes, whose authority was derived from belief that Authority controls a motionless universe, could not admit that this earth spins in space. If this earth does not rest upon something immovable, then there is energy.

The truly great intelligence of medieval Europeans saw at once that Energy operating in the universe may be *creative.* If there is Creative Energy, if God is creating, then this universe is not finished, changeless, static; and if it is not, then Authority is not its control.

The Europeans' whole world rested upon the pagan belief that Authority controls all things including men. When they heard that this earth spins in space, their whole minds and souls recoiled in horror. That is why they implacably hated the Saracens, whom they saw as anti-Christ, the Devil on earth, rebelling against the Authority of God.

117

The Discovery of Freedom

The Kings and the Popes could not look for the East in the West; that would admit that the round earth spins in space; that would admit that the principle of the universe is Energy, and possibly Creativeness, Change, Progress. This is why they forced Galileo to recant his statement that the earth moves. ("But it does move," he muttered, uncontrolled, after he saved himself from burning at the stake by loudly declaring that it does not.)

So no one could come out of Europe to discover America.

It was Columbus, a Genoan sailor who knew Saracens in every port, who sailed west to India so confidently that the King of Portugal could not beat down his terms. All expenses, paid in advance; an Admiral's commission, in advance; vice-regal power over all lands he reached, forever hereditary in his family; *and* ten percent of all valuable metals ever discovered in those lands, to the end of time; that was what Columbus demanded, and he would not take a penny less.

In Spain, that had been a great center of Saracen civilization for nearly eight hundred years, he found the Christian princes who agreed to those terms. He made the deal with Isabella and Ferdinand in the army camp outside Granada, where their troops were besieging the Saracens.

That summer he sailed, and that summer Granada fell. Granada the beautiful, the great fountain of learning and science and art and commerce that the Saracens had been creating for hundreds of years, was their last stronghold in Spain.

Seven hundred and seventy-five years before, their ancestors had come into Spain. In three years, they held all Spain to the Pyrenees. Only a few Spanish Catholics remained in the mountains, not worth conquering. They harried the border a little, as the wild tribes beyond Khyber Pass annoy British India; border guards attended to them, while in Spain the Catholics, Jews, Greeks, Berbers, Negroes, all the peoples called Saracens, were building Madrid, Seville, Cordova, Granada, Valencia, all the cities, with their libraries, universities, observatories, their schools of architecture and literature, their expanding markets, prospering traders and craftsmen and artists, and all over the fertile south the farmers were developing newer methods of scientific farming that gave the land no rest.

Little by little, as Churchmen grew more powerful in Europe, they gave more help to the Catholics in the Pyrenees. They fought their way into Spain, as the Crusaders had gone into Palestine. They took Aragon, and Castile. But though they advanced, they could not establish their authority. They were able to take cities and provinces, only on condition that they left them free.

Spanish Catholics who were living in the Saracens' civilization were willing, or more than willing, to welcome Catholic Kings, but they would not give up their Free Cities. From the weak invaders they demanded, and got, Magna Cartas; signed documents guaranteeing their freedoms.

When Granada fell, the Saracen troops retreated to Africa, and on their heels came Isabella's and Ferdinand's troops, driving out hundreds of thousands of Jews. (800,000, some records say.) There would be no more religious freedom in Spain.

But no Authority controlled the people in Spain, yet. The cities were Free Cities, like those in Italy. And the people had been born and brought up in Saracen civilization; for centuries their ancestors had lived in that civilization.

The barrier of hatred between Europe and Spain was gone; Spain was now part of Catholic Europe. But the living men and women in Spain were no more European than the French are German today. The Catholic conquest of Spain merely broke down a barrier and let the living human energy of the Saracens' world into European history. Its effects were terrific.

From Spain, energy leaped the Atlantic, in the hundreds and thousands of men and women who sailed with Cortes, Pizarro, Ponce de Leon, Balboa, Magellan, all the explorers and conquistadors who put this hemisphere on the map and

The Discovery of Freedom

led the way around the round earth; and in the thousands who marched with De Soto and Coronado from the Gulf to the Ohio and from the Rio Grande to the peaks of Colorado, and came so near to meeting in Kansas in 1545, only half a century after Columbus saw an island that he thought was India.

Youngsters like Hernando de Soto in his teens, riding away from home alone, on a lean horse, with a sword and a spear and nothing else whatever but his fearless self-reliance; hundreds and thousands of young men like that—they discovered America.

And they came from Spain, only from Spain. Other Europeans did not stir for a hundred years. Three generations of them did not move from where they sat. Not though they knew that the earth is round, and that the fabulously rich half of it waited to be explored. One man comes sailing under an English flag; later, here comes his son, under that flag; and who are they? The Cabots; Italians; two more men like Columbus, from the center of the Saracens' Mediterranean.

Columbus might have come and gone and made no more difference than Eric the Red or Alonso Sanchez, if human energy had not leaped from Saracenic Spain, if thousands of men had not taken their lives in their own hands and risked them, on their own responsibility, in the unknown.

(Americans are writing history for American children as if writers still lived on gifts from flattered Royal Highnesses. King Henry the Navigator, who never reefed a sail, discovers a route to India around the tip of Africa. By a clever trick, he gets the Pope to give him the whole unknown half of the earth. But Spaniards are exploring it. The King of Portugal quarrels with the King of Spain about that, so the Pope divides the New World between them. And that piece of parchment causes Spaniards to explore it. Little children of America, learn your history lesson well: How powerful are the Authorities that make this human world. And the carts that pull horses.)

The Second Attempt

Here are three historic facts, which no one can dispute: Two thousand generations of Spaniards had been living in a civilization where every man could act freely. For one century after the fall of Granada, Spaniards were less submissive to Government than any other Europeans. During that century, Spaniards explored and conquered the New World and conquered Europe.

In that century, Spaniards crossed the unknown ocean and discovered and seized sixty degrees of latitude and one-sixth of the earth's circumference. They explored and conquered Cuba, the Caribbean islands, Central America, Mexico, Peru, Chili, New Granada, Venezuela, and North America to the Missouri river and the Golden Gate. They took the Philippines. They created the first world-empire, that all but encircled the earth.

In Europe, Spaniards took Portugal and the Low countries and almost the whole of France; the King of France was a prisoner in Madrid. They continued the Crusades against the infidels and took the Balearic islands, Sicily, Sardinia, Naples and Milan. They took northern Africa. They took the Germanies. In the center of Europe, the King of Spain was Emperor of all these lands. In the west he dominated England, whose Queen was his daughter-in-law; in the east his troops met the Turks at Vienna and flung them back into the Balkans, defeated.

That is the whole record of Catholic Spanish energy.

It lasted one century, three generations. One century later, Spanish energy was not able to get food enough to keep Spaniards alive.

The change in Spain when Granada fell was only a change in meaning. You could not have seen it on the surface of things. The Saracen emirs had known that men are free; the Catholic rulers believed that Authority controls men. But expediency made Isabella and Ferdinand *grant* certain liberties to their subjects.

A Spanish merchant who had been prospering in Seville,

The Discovery of Freedom

for instance, went right on prospering. All the energy of Saracen civilization that had been creating that civilization was turned, by the lure of unknown lands and the Authority of the new Kings, into conquest and war, but there was all the outfitting of ships and armies; business boomed.

Business men and workers saw nothing changed. The emir had known that every man is self-controlling and responsible for his own affairs. The King granted him permission to manage his affairs. A busy man saw no difference. If anyone pointed out this difference to him, no doubt he replied, "Oh, that's theories. I'm a practical man, I've no time to waste on theories. Everything's all right; the cloth market has never been better than it is right now."

Some two million Moslems remained in Spain. The King's troops made them Catholics. Why should a Catholic object to that? All men should be Catholics; all right-thinking men are Catholics; if any man can't see the truth, he should be made to. The killing and torturing is bad, but it's the only way, and the end justifies the means. The end is good; it is saving their souls. Anyone who protests must want them to be damned.

Tortured, slaughtered, burned alive in their blazing houses or rounded up when they fled, the surviving Moslems did become Catholics. So that was all right.

But, converted, they continued to act like infidels—reading their Arabic books, playing their athletic games, wearing their silk robes, and bathing, always bathing.

Church and State prohibited these heathen customs. Police burned the Arabic libraries, and searched the converts' houses for Arabic books to burn. Reading, writing, or speaking Arabic was strictly forbidden. Police stopped the Moslem games. In every city, town and village the public baths (our "Turkish" baths) were converted to other uses, or razed to the ground. The converts were forbidden to bathe secretly in their homes.

Well, that does not affect the liberty of a Spaniard who does not know Arabic, nor want to play games nor to bathe. Does it?

The Second Attempt

Still it seemed that the converts—now called Moriscos—did not wholeheartedly accept the Authority that acted only for their own good. They were suspected of bathing in secret. There was a doubt as to what they really thought.

To find out what they thought, the Spanish priests began the Inquisition. The name is accurate; it was an investigation. The Church was responsible for the individual's salvation, and responsibility must be control; no one can be responsible for any thought or word or act that he does not control. To control the beliefs of these Moriscos, it was necessary to know what their beliefs were.

Torture was the only means of finding out. No lie-detector, nor psychological test, existed then. Torture was the only known way of reducing a man's mind to a state in which, presumably, he could not lie. Recently the Russians and the Germans have used torture for this same purpose.

The investigation revealed a heathen taint in the minds of Spaniards who had never been Moslems. The freedom of thought in Spain was more appalling than anyone had suspected. All the force of The State was barely able to suppress it.

A sincere desire to do good was the whole motive of the Inquisition. A kinder man never lived than Charles the Fifth of Spain, Emperor of the Holy Roman Empire that Hitler now wants to resurrect, who ordered his subjects killed by scores of thousands. He was not cruel, and I mean it; he did not want to cause pain, he wanted to prevent it. Obstinate heretics who insisted upon being responsible for their own opinions must be burned alive, but Charles the Fifth ordered that every one of them who repented and submitted to Authority must be killed mercifully. He did not doubt that he was responsible for his subjects' salvation; he had to wipe out those whose minds were corrupted, just as a farmer must kill a tubercular cow, for the health of the others.

At the end of Spain's first century, the chiefs of the Inquisition despaired of rescuing the Moriscos. God only knew what these children and grandchildren of anti-Christ truly believed. And more than a million of them were still in Spain.

Some Churchmen advised the King to deport them. Others urged a massacre; they begged the King to act not only for the good of Spain, but for the whole world's good. To an objection that there might be one truly Christian Morisco, they replied that killing him could do no harm, since God knows His own and would take him to Heaven. Deporting these children of the Devil would scatter the infection, not end it.

But they lost the argument. The Moriscos were merely driven from their homes and herded to the seacoast. Starving, dying of thirst, and robbed, beaten, murdered along the way, few of them lived to reach the African deserts. Not one was left alive in Spain.

All Spanish intellectuals burst into one great song of joy and hope. Now Spain was clean. Now every Spaniard was wholly obedient to Church and King. Alone of all European countries, Spain was now one united mass of loyal men, believing and acting as one being. Every thinker and poet in Spain celebrated in book and song this glorious event, this blessed time, the dawn of Spain's Golden Age.

It was the end of Spain.

The loss of a million Moriscos was not so important. Billions had died in Spain during those nine centuries of vigorous human energy. Millions were still living in Spain. But it was true; hardly one was left who knew that men are free.

From three generations of Spaniards, the most self-reliant had gone to the New World and the wars. Now the Moriscos, with their secret thoughts, were gone. Spaniards really were united in one common belief, the belief that Authority controlled them and was responsible for them. And human energy in Spain simply ceased to work.

Losing a million workers caused an economic shock. But the wars caused economic shocks; so did the fall of Granada; driving out hundreds of thousands of Jews had been an eco-

The Second Attempt

nomic shock at the very beginning of this vigorous century.

There was still plenty of energy in Spain to till the fields and man the looms and keep trade thriving. But human energy is individual energy, controlled according to individuals' beliefs. Great stretches of the Morisco's fertile land, depopulated then, have never again been plowed. When Spaniards were hungry, they flocked to the cities, to The Church, to the King, who should feed them. As if fishermen should come to the cities, for fish.

Again and again in history, this happens. Always, when people look to Authority for the things that only their own energy can create, they flock to the cities where their energy can produce nothing. During Rome's declining centuries, Romans did this. During the past ten years, a few million Americans have been doing this. During the past twenty years, starving Russian peasants have crowded into the cities—for food.

Thirty years after the last knowledge of freedom was gone from Spain, the Government could not get even a dribble of taxes from provinces that once had filled the Royal treasury to overflowing, and outfitted in addition all the ships and thousands of men who sailed to the New World. In Seville, where two thousand looms had been working, barely three hundred moved. The whole civilized world had been buying Spanish gloves; now Spain produced no gloves.

Travelers report that monasteries were enlarging and multiplying everywhere; property was flowing to The Church; hordes of priests thronged the streets; villages were dwindling, fields poorly cultivated, the people were hungry. Protestant writers say that The Church was devouring Spain.

But The Church seizes no property. The Church does not entice a single person to leave the fields or the market place. No one is ever compelled to enter a monastery or the priesthood.

There is security in The Church, for mind and soul and

body. Spaniards wanted security, the security that children have a right to expect from an Authority they obey.

Madrid's population declined from half a million to 200,000. In the middle of Spain's second century, the 200,000 were starving, and the Governor of Castille with armed troops and executioners was scouring the countryside and seizing food from the peasants, to feed Madrid. Why did he not buy it? He could collect no more taxes.

Tax collectors were tearing down houses and selling the materials for anything they could get, to apply on the owner's taxes. In some towns they demolished more than two-thirds of the houses. And where would they get taxes next year?

Villages were completely deserted. Villagers wandered in bands, looking for food. They died along the roadsides, all over Spain. The King slashed official salaries, even of the highest nobles, even of the Royal household; and slashed them again, two-thirds; and could not pay them. Unpaid soldiers left the frontiers unguarded and ravaged the country, for food.

For almost eight hundred years, human energy in Spain had produced such an abundance of food, comforts and luxuries as the world had never before imagined. After Granada fell, human energy continued to operate in Spain and through Spain upon the New World and Europe, for two more generations. The third generation no longer knew that men are free, and energy weakened in Spain. The fifth generation could no longer support the Government, and their children died of starvation.

In 1699, the British Minister to the Spanish Court could not buy bread in Madrid. Like everyone else, he had to ask the Government for bread. The Corregidor gave him an order for bread, and he was obliged to send men conspicuously armed with "long guns" two leagues from the city to get the bread and bring it back, for only armed men could protect bread in the streets of the capital of Spain.

Twenty thousand starving peasants came into Madrid that

day, from the country where the plows were rotting in the weedy fields.

From that time, foreigners ruled the Spanish people. Spain's Prime Ministers were French, Italian, Austrian; Irish soldiers propped up the Spanish monarchy. The ambassadors of Spain were not Spaniards.

When the French were losing the war that Americans know as the French and Indian wars, France slipped Louisiana to Spain—in order not to lose it at the peace conference. And the Lord High Admiral of Spain, who sailed into Lake Pontchartrain to take possession of this continent west of the Mississippi for the Spanish Crown—and who quelled rebellious New Orleans by hanging nineteen leading men from his yardarm—was Admiral O'Reilly from Ireland.

Spain had practically ceased to exist.

III. The Feudal System

DURING their Dark Ages, Europeans were creating the feudal system. This system is unique in the Old World, because the men who created it attempted to hold a double-view of Reality. They tried to combine the ancient pagan superstition that Authority controls a static universe, with a knowledge that men are free.

A strange thing happened when an Emperor accepted the Christian faith.

Christ proclaimed individual liberty and declared that this truth would destroy kingdoms. And an Emperor, to strengthen his autocracy, urged and compelled his subjects to be Christians!

This astounding action was possible only because Europeans had modified their idea of Christianity.

The God of Abraham, Moses, Christ and Mohammed is One God. The first Christians, as well as the Jews and Moslems, saw the universe as, precisely, a universe; a unit; one thing, indivisible. They saw a human being as a unit, indivisible. By your fruits, your acts, shall ye be judged; because your acts *are* you. Faith without works is dead; a man acts in accordance with his belief, a faith that does not shape his acts does not exist in him. Energy operates under control and can not be separated from its control; how, then, can there be a separation between a man's self and his acts, between his soul and his living body?

These first Christians were few, and, like the Israelites, they held a truth that isolated them from the vast pagan world.

The Feudal System

Like Americans in a foreign country, they naturally drew together in small groups. For centuries these tiny groups were scattered, each one surrounded by multitudes of pagans.

Hilaire Belloc, an English Catholic scholar, says that by the third century, a man who had studied Christ's teachings and believed them and sincerely lived a Christ-like life, did not even think of calling himself a Christian. A Christian must be admitted to a small, exclusive group; he must submit absolutely to its discipline, and he was subject to expulsion if he had any opinion that differed from The Church's decrees.

Lenin copied this structure and discipline from the Early Church, in his organization of the present Communist Party. Hitler copied it from the communists. It is an effective method for a small minority to use against an overwhelming majority.

By this method, The Church preserved Christian doctrine; by this method, The Church survived through the centuries while the Roman world was collapsing under its planned economy. The Church emerged from that chaos as the only coherent group in the ruins of the Empire.

Meanwhile, the leaders of The Church had shaped its doctrines. Four of the greatest of these thinkers are called the Fathers of the Church. The strongest, most intelligent and most effective of these was St. Augustine, who for nine years had been a Manichaean priest.

Through all these early Christian centuries, the majority of European pagans were Manichaeans. Mani was a reformer, who attacked the older Sun-worship, brought its doctrines more up-to-date, so to speak, and swept Europe with a wave of religious enthusiasm.

He saw the universe as just about what the Roman world was at the time. There had been, he said, a catastrophe. The Sun-god had once kept Darkness subdued, but now everything was mixed together in confusion, in a battle. In all things, Light and Dark (Good and Evil) were fighting each other. The battle would end when all light was again in the Sun.

There were sparks of light in all things, including men.

The Discovery of Freedom

The peculiar function of the Manichaean priests was not to increase light in men, but to be transmitters through which God, the Sun, drew all good (light) back to himself. Thus they served both the Sun and mankind, by hastening the end of the battle and of the universe.

So the Manichaeans saw the nature of things, not as unity, but as war between opposites; war between Sun and Dark, between soul and body, heat and cold, wet and dry, up and down, right and left, north and south; war everywhere, in every thing.

St. Augustine served this faith as a priest of the Sun for nine years before his Christian mother's prayers aided him to see the greater truth in The Church. He became a Christian, a Bishop, and the most influential of the Four Fathers of The Church.

When the Emperor Constantine began to defend the Faith, The Church was a bulwark in a crumbling Empire. The Bishops saw the universe as a struggle between good and evil. They believed that the whole material world is evil, and that The Church is the Authority created by God to redeem mankind from Original Sin and to lead and win the war of the spiritual world against the material world.

Every European Christian believed in this war between two worlds, and he believed that his body was in the material world and his soul in the spiritual world. He also kept his pagan belief that the universe *has been created,* and is now static and controlled by Authority.

Since everyone believed that Authority controlled him, and that he was divided into two parts, everyone believed with no surprise that his soul belonged to God (or the Devil) and his body belonged to his master. Where he himself came into this picture isn't clear, but apparently that question never occurred to him.

Pope Innocent the Third, who after the Crusades, made The Church the strongest power in Europe and actually came very near to establishing a lasting European peace, stated what

The Feudal System

all Christians believed: "As God placed two great lights in the starry heavens, a greater light to preside by day and a lesser by night, so He established in the realm of the Universal Church two great powers, one to rule the souls of man and one to rule their bodies."

For more than a thousand years, Europeans lived in a constant struggle between priests and barons, as commonplace to them as the struggle between politicians at election time is to Americans.

All the values in human life which (because of that long conflict in Europe) many Americans still mistakenly regard as opposed to material values—all ideals, morality, humane feeling, and recognition of such facts as the brotherhood of man and the spirit's control of the body—The Church preserved, fostered, and fought for, during those ages of misery and human degradation in Europe.

But, as the phrase goes, The State controlled The Church during those ages. The phrase means that the barons commanded more fighting men than the Bishops.

A Bishop had a genuine power over men's minds, because they believed that he had, but in battle he didn't have a fighting chance against larger numbers of armed barons and their vassals.

Now if God controls men, logically a Bishop who is God's personal agent can not be bossed by a baron. So for centuries the Popes with logic on their side and the Emperors with the fighting men on their side, struggled to decide the issue: Does The Church control The State, or The State control The Church?

No third solution occurred to anybody.

Indeed, that controversy still continues in Europe. It was one cause of the recent civil war in Spain. Mussolini must make terms with the Vatican. Hitler dares only cautiously to attack The Church. The Church of England is still precisely that; an Englishman is granted religious freedom, of course, he may be a dissenter if he likes, but the Government collects taxes from him to support the Church of England, and aristocrats appoint the clergymen. Not so long ago Americans heard on their radios the abdication of a King of England, and knew that it ended a struggle between the King-Emperor and the Archbishop of Canterbury.

Even in these United States, a shadowy claim of all churches to be Government is still recognized, in the fact that American churches, like all Government, pay no taxes.

During the century after Pope Urban the Second began sending the fighting men out of Europe, The Church became the strongest power. A majority of Europeans then believed so surely that the Pope was Authority on earth, that no Emperor could successfully defy him. And under the Authority of The Church, Europeans developed the feudal system to its perfection.

Men of great learning and intelligence believe today that the feudal centuries were the highest point of civilization that men have ever reached. Hilaire Belloc says of the feudal system, "A civilization which was undoubtedly the highest and the best our race has known, conformable to the instinct of the European, fulfilling his nature, giving him that happiness which is the end of man." [1]

It is hard for an American to imagine that feudal world. For it seems to be an actual fact that in the feudal system an individual hardly existed, even in his own mind.

In a way incomprehensible to Americans, everyone felt that he lived in two worlds. In the invisible world, all souls were equal. God's mercy and justice were alike for all; to God the Emperor's soul was no more precious than the slave's. And this spiritual world was the *real* world.

Men truly felt that this material world was temporary. A man thought of this earth and his own body rather as an American thinks of his clothes. He would discard them soon, and step into the real world.

---

[1] *Europe and The Faith*, p. 243.

The Feudal System

Temporarily in this temporal world, everyone had his place and was neatly kept in it. Born a peasant, a man *was* a peasant. He could make no effort to be anything else. He could take no risks, suffer no failure; he had no responsibility whatever for his own fortunes.

This absence of responsibility, of ambition, of any belief in Change, is also an absence of many causes of discontent.

In the feudal system, everyone was as secure as can possibly be. The serf was fastened to the land that he worked; he could not leave it, nor lose it. He worked it as he was told; his share of whatever crop God sent was fixed. He could not risk, nor gain nor lose, anything. If another baron seized the land, still the serf was right there on it, secure.

Everyone was as secure as that, in his class. He owed a certain duty to his class, and received a certain protection. His class owed a duty to each other class, and received from each a certain return.

To the knight, the class of serfs owed obedience and labor; the class of peasants owed obedience and labor and certain quantities of certain foods delivered at certain times from the produce of the peasants' communal land. The class of craftsmen, in their various guilds, owed the knight and the baron a loyal deference and certain quantities of goods of all kinds, everything needed for their households and their wars.

To these working classes, the knights and the barons owed justice and military protection. The knights owed the baron their military service; the baron owed to knights and pages, justice and military training and leadership. To the King, the baron owed his military service and that of his knights and vassals.

The king was also a baron; his own serfs, peasants, and craftsmen supplied his needs. To them, to his own knights and pages, and to the lesser barons in his realm, the king owed justice and military leadership.

Individuals act in accordance with their faith. They create the human world in the image of their God. Medieval Europeans believed that the universe is static and changeless, that God is no longer the Creator, but a controlling Authority, and that in God's invisible world, all souls are equal.

Therefore, they introduced into the ancient pagan world of despots and slaves, this Christian knowledge of human equality; they created the feudal system.

This system was not so simple in practice as in theory. It was infinitely complicated by the real nature of human beings, who are not cells of a class. They created all kinds of exceptions, but at the same time, patiently they fitted these exceptions into the system. By the 12th century, they had crystallized the smallest details of behavior.

For instance: A craftsman owed his apprentice food, shelter and training in the craft; the apprentice owed his master obedience and faithful labor. But the apprentice could not demand a bed; his master might let him sleep on bare ground. On the other hand, the master's wife might send him on errands, but no one could require him to wash the dishes or mind the baby. Every human relationship was worked out as minutely as that. No one need ever decide what to do.

That was a social system. Please notice the word. When, in speaking of the ways in which human beings live and manage their affairs, you say "system," that is the kind of thing you mean. At least, I hope you do; for to talk of "a system" when discussing ways of living that are not systems, is idle nonsense.

The feudal system was the most perfect social system in history. It even had a safety valve, to release any pressure of energy in it. An exceptional, ambitious, and gifted boy might get his master's permission to learn to read and write, and enter The Church. Church discipline was strict, but The Church represented the spiritual world, and in it, all men were equal. Any priest might become the Pope. A serf's son did become a Pope.

Outside The Church, the class-structure was one that living men could not create nor endure unless they were convinced that the universe is static and divided into two parts. They could not have borne its stagnation, if they had suspected that progress is possible. They would have rebelled against the inequalities of wealth and of power, if they had not felt that this world is only a waiting-room, from which they were going to Heaven.

The practical value of the feudal system was that it segregated fighting. War is the essential function of every kind of Government whose subjects believe that it is Authority controlling them; so war was the essential function of the feudal system. But the Authority of The Church opposed war, and exempted the working classes from fighting.

War was the sole and exclusive business of knights and barons, and they attended strictly to it, taking only Saturday afternoons off for a few rounds of highway robbery. War raged across the feudal countryside as normally as cyclones and grasshopper plagues in pioneer Kansas, and much more destructively. As every child in London now knows the sound of bombs, so every child in feudal Europe knew the sound that Chesterton celebrates—"the intolerant trumpets of honor, that usher with iron laughter the coming of Christian arms."

Frequently, too, God's wrath descended in epidemics of cholera, typhus, bubonic plague, and common folks died by thousands so swiftly that survivors could not bury the corpses, while lords and ladies fled to house-parties in the country, for the duration.

But the system allowed enough human energy to work well enough to feed and shelter almost everyone. Famines were not so frequent as before. Burghers and their wives, and even some peasants, wore shoes on holidays. Craftsmen and artists built the beautiful Gothic cathedrals, and no one minded living huddled around them with no more sanitation than cattle have in pens.

This system truly was the greatest height of European civilization. But in its perfection it lasted little more than one century. An enormous amount of energy was lost when the Black Death swept across Europe, killing in some places a

The Discovery of Freedom

third of the people, and in other places more than half the people, who of course had not the faintest notion of cleanliness or of medicine. Then from the Saracens, the Italians were getting a more accurate idea of the universe and of human beings.

Pico della Mirandola was preaching the dignity of the individual, and saying, "To thee alone is given a growth and a development depending on thy own free will." In England, Roger Bacon was writing, "One individual is worth more than all the Universals," and, "God has not created the world for the sake of Universal Man, but for the sake of individual persons."

Italian traders were making their Free Cities. And their business boomed. In the Free Cities, everyone was making money, and the standard of living was sky-rocketing.

Yet these Italians still imagined the static universe. Though their own energies were creating a changing world, their pagan minds believed that wealth *had been created* and that there could never be any more of it than existed in their 13th century.

So when other Italians made another Free City near by, and also began to prosper by creating more goods and more trade, the older Free City's traders roused up their townsmen and attacked and stormed the rival city and destroyed it utterly. That was the way they handled competition.

(As if Chicagoans today would destroy Milwaukee, Detroit, Cincinnati, St. Louis and the Twin Cities, in order to take their prosperity. Or as if General Motors would destroy the Ford plants, to get more of the market for cars that never expands; or as if Kresge's would burn all the Woolworth stores, to get all the dimes that can ever be spent; or as if workers would do less work, in order to get more of the changeless amount of work in this world; or, logically, as if one man killed all other human beings on earth, in order to get all the wealth that they produce.)

Then the energy of Spain, which Authority poured into war,

The Feudal System

swept through Europe's shaken feudal system, and German reformers attacked it.

This German attack upon The Church was not an attack on the pagan belief in Authority; the Reformation was a struggle to get Authority. Germans began it, and German thinkers have always been pagan-minded. The Roman Empire never conquered the Germans; they never learned the Roman concept of law. The Roman Catholic Church never quite conquered them and taught them the feudal sense of human rights.

There is, of course, no human difference between a German and anyone else. But the people who live on that part of the earth called Germany have always lived just outside the borders of Europe. Their way of thinking has never been quite European. So, when The Church was Europe, rebellion against The Church came naturally from the German thinkers, and naturally spread among the German people and their tribal kindred, the Dutch.

But it was not a true revolutionary movement. The Reformation was at first an effort to reform The Church, and then the leaders of the protesting groups, the Protestants, denied the Authority of the Pope and declared that they were the Authority. As everyone knows, the Puritans and the Pilgrims brought to America, not "freedom to worship God," but a theocracy that claimed to be the Authority dictating to everyone's conscience.

Only three or four generations of Europeans lived in the perfected feudal system. After that, they were born in a time of confusion. New ideas were all over the place. Everyone argued about everything. The earth was said to be round. Protestants said that the Pope was not infallible. Kings were trying to run their realms as if they owned them. The barons, who obeyed feudal customs but had never obeyed another baron, refused to be bossed by a fellow-baron who was a King. All over Europe the barons and Kings were fighting. Columbus saw India in the west— What's that? In the west? Yes, the

137

earth is round. Armies erupted from Spain; war in the Low Countries, war in France, war in the Germanies—and the heathen are attacking Vienna. The Devil has all the Dutch; forty thousand and more are slaughtered and burned at the stake, and still there are heretics. Heaven help a man who tries to make a living in times like these.

This is called "the rise of Monarchy" and "the rise of Nationalism," because during some centuries the Kings defeated the barons everywhere on the continent of Europe.

If you hold the pagan belief that some Authority controls individuals, and the feudal belief that God places each person in his proper place in the temporal world, you naturally conclude that a King who rules the barons has a God-given right to rule them. And, of course, to rule all lower classes.

So continental Europeans easily believed in the King's divine Right. It followed that the King's children, inheriting his Divinely-endowed nature, must be a kind of human being superior to all other kinds.

The balance of rights and duties between the classes was gone, when Europeans believed that Kings and Princes partook of the Divine nature of God.

But all the other feudal beliefs remained, and do to this day: the belief that the universe is changeless; the belief in Authority; the belief in classes; the belief that there must be a social system, that social system and Government are the same thing, and the belief that whatever, or whoever, controls individuals must make everyone secure in social order.

These are all feudal beliefs, and modern Europeans began to advocate them passionately after the Kings assumed Authority over the feudal class-system. For the more earnestly the King tried to enforce the social order, and a control of production which his ministers planned, the less his subjects were able to produce. And the Government's attempted control of men's energies constantly consumed more and more of the wealth that they produced, and constantly subtracted more and more energy from the productive energy in the nation.

138

The Feudal System

A Nation is merely an area in modern Europe, enclosed by frontiers that are geographical limits of a Government's use of force. When power-avaricious Kings broke the feudal system, they claimed for themselves all controlling Authority and responsibility, and said, "I am the Nation."

This idea of The Nation was a new idea, but Kings who wrecked the feudal system had to have some new idea, because everyone knew they were governing everyone they could subdue by force, regardless of races, languages, cultures, religions, or any other common ground between the governed people. A King, like any other man, must have some ground to stand on; some religious basis. If none already exists, one must be invented. Just as Hitler today invents The New Order, so Kings and their supporters invented The Nation.

There is no more natural or sensible reason for any Nation in Europe, than there is a reason why any State in this Union should be a nation. Germany is no more a German Nation than Wisconsin is, and Louisiana is a French Nation if France can claim to be. Normans and Gascons and Bretons and Provencals never mean France when they say, "my country"; they mean Normandy and Gascony and Brittany and Provence. Bavarians have not as much in common with Prussians as they have with Czechs, and Sicilians and Tuscans and Venetians and Neopolitans never have been Italians to each other.

The Nation is nothing at all but simple force. Not in a single Nation are the people of one race, one history, one culture, nor the same political opinion or religious faith. They are simply human beings of all kinds, penned inside frontiers which mean nothing whatever but military force.

The only thing that permits any of these Nations to exist, is the belief in the minds of almost all the persons penned inside these frontiers, that Government naturally controls their business, their work, their communications, their travels, their salt and tobacco and windows, and (to a greater or less extent) their newspapers, their public meetings, their theatres, their religion, and their personal habits. Workers have always been obliged to have permits to work, traders to trade, manufacturers to produce goods; communication and transportation have always belonged to Government; a new bathtub or a window in anyone's house has always been Government's affair; every contract between individuals must always be registered in a Government office (and taxed): a police agent always sits inside every apartment house or hotel entrance (and locks the doors at the evening hour set by the police chief) for Government must know everyone's comings and goings and callers.

This ancient belief in Authority is the whole basis of such shadowy "nationalism" as actually exists. If there is no other Authority to obey, Europeans can only obey an Authority that calls itself National. As a lost child will obey any adult, so a Breton who has lost his own King will obey the Government of France, and a Bavarian will obey the Government of Germany.

On the continent of Europe (excepting only France) all Europeans obeyed their Kings until the first World War. They have never questioned Authority. Their only outcry has been, and still is, that Authority does not control them *properly*.

Inside these modern National frontiers, the workers have been working harder and getting little more than their ancestors did in the feudal system. So the so-called revolutionists attack their Governments and ruling classes, accusing them of not controlling the social system *as it should be controlled*.

Socialist, Social-Democrat, Communist, Fascist, National Socialist (Nazi) all demand that Government make a better social system; that Government control the men who produce and distribute goods; that Government create security for men on this earth.

The basis of all this thinking is ignorance of creative energy; it is ignorance of the real nature of human beings; it is the ancient, pagan superstition that Authority controls a static, limited universe.

This belief is at least six thousand years old. Acting upon

The Feudal System

this belief, human beings have tried every one of these ideas now advanced as revolutionary, and many more; they have tried every conceivable way of making a human world in which human energy can work at its natural job of making this earth habitable for human beings, and never in one of those centuries have they succeeded (with that pagan belief) in using their energies well enough to get them all enough to eat.

Yet they keep on trying, because individuals control human energy in accordance with their religious faith, whatever it may be. And belief in Authority controlling a fixed, limited, changeless universe is the pagan religion.

If this belief were true, then a human world controlled by some kind of human Authority would work. Then such a world would have worked, at least once, at least fairly well, during six thousand years of efforts to make it work.

It does not work, for the same reason that a perpetual-motion machine will not work, because the attempt to make it work is based on a false belief, and not on fact.

IV. The English Liberties

ONLY the English kept the values of the feudal system. On their sea-guarded island, apart from Europe, the English barons successfully resisted the Kings.

King Henry the Second first attacked the feudal system in England, so sensibly that he almost destroyed it. He attacked its justice.

Justice is a moral problem that men have hardly begun to solve. It comes from the necessity to act in accordance with facts. Men have always known that there are facts in the nature of things, to which human beings must conform. (There is gravitation; better not walk off a cliff. There is human brotherhood; better love thy neighbor *as thyself*). So in all times they have doubted that one man is able to judge another. Justice is always felt to be a standard not made by men.

Pagans obey the whims of gods, as explained by their priests. Democratic Athenians believed that justice is the will of a majority, on the theory that ninety men are right and ten are wrong. Using this theory, they killed off their intelligent and honest men. Pontius Pilate also obeyed a majority, though more skeptically.

Roman law protected Roman citizens (not Roman subjects). So when a chief of police carelessly told his men to torture St. Paul, the prisoner had only to say, "I am a Roman citizen," to bring the chief himself abjectly apologizing. "I am a citizen, too," the chief said, as a fraternity brother, but he had to brag that he was rich: "With a great price, obtained I this freedom." His prisoner was still coldly superior; St. Paul replied, "I was born free."

The English Liberties

By "freedom" they meant that no man in Roman government could torture and kill them just because he took a notion. The Gestapo was only for Roman subjects. A citizen, St. Paul could appeal to Roman law; and it executed him because he did not worship pagan gods.

The feudal Europeans left justice to the elements, to fire and water. Bind an accused man and throw him into deep water; if he drowns, he is innocent; if he does not drown, he is guilty. ("Born to be hanged, you'll never be drowned.") That was the ordeal by water; the ordeal by fire worked on the same principle. For knights, there was the ordeal by combat; God gives success to the right. That is true, as every scientist knows, and every man who ever adjusted a carburetor. But feudal Europeans, like pagan Greeks, imagined that God personally controlled the spears and swords (as today they might imagine that God's invisible hand adjusts the carburetor) and those trials by combat caused sceptics to say, "Might makes Right."

King Henry the Second took advantage of this scepticism. His grandfather had invented Circuit Courts: King Henry established them, and invented juries. He published through his realm the news that any man who demanded the King's Justice would be tried before a judge, and his case would be decided by twelve men of his own social class (his peers).

Innocent or guilty, would you rather face a feudal ordeal, or judge and jury? Exactly. King Henry's justice was so popular that gradually he built up an authority stronger than any baron's. The feudal system was well on its way out, when he died.

Richard the Lion-hearted was his heir, but Richard went away crusading. His brother John, though somewhat insane, was next of Royal blood. He taxed the barons brutally; he seized their lands and castles; *he married their daughters to commoners.* Of course the King dictated marriages, but this atrocity would destroy classes. The outraged barons protested. The King's officers seized their wives and children and starved them to death in dungeons.

The Discovery of Freedom

The barons rose in armed revolt. At Runnymead their stout vassals defeated King John's; the barons caught King John and scared him into signing an agreement to return their estates and to obey feudal customs.

This document is Magna Carta. It abolished judges and juries, restored trial by ordeal,[1] and bound the King to respect and preserve the feudal rights of all classes.

Magna Carta is the charter of English liberties. It is a King's admission that even Royalty is bound by feudal obligations. Therefore, by implication, it grants to every Englishman his class-rights.

In France and Hungary and Catholic Spain, the Kings signed Magna Cartas, but later repudiated them. No English King was ever quite able to down the British barons and abolish the English Magna Carta.

The political principle of England today is the feudal principle of a social order of classes, in which every individual has the rights and duties of his class-status.

The English lower classes maintain this class-system with a dogged tenacity. A Duke might try to meet a butler, a taxi-driver, or a farmer (in the American language, share-cropper) on a basis of human equality, but none of them would let him.

The ruling classes, who derive their ideal of the gentleman directly from the Saracens, and their social responsibility from the feudal system, always maintain the feudal recognition of human equality in the spiritual sense. They recognize their duty to the lower classes, and the right of every individual to certain privileges, or freedoms.

In England, so to speak, no one can compel an apprentice to mind the baby. Britons never will be slaves.

There is no British Constitution, in any American sense. This is another of the confusions between the English and the American languages. After American revolutionists had in-

---

[1] Trial by ordeal was legal in England until 1819, though gradually it had become obsolete.

The English Liberties

vented Constitutions and French revolutionists had copied the idea, the English began to speak of "the English Constitution." They mean, by the word, what an American means when he says of another man, "He has a strong constitution." They mean a general state of British Government.

Their Government has gradually been made through centuries by accumulated customs and points of view and laws and civil wars.

The only written Constitution of England was Cromwell's. An ex-brewer, he led the Puritan rebellion against the Stuarts, and made himself dictator of England. His officers wrote the Instrument of Government. It gave supreme authority for life to the Lord Protector (naturally Cromwell). It recognized the age-old feudal assembly of barons, to "talk deeply" and "to watch the King wear his crown." Cromwell lived only six years as Lord Protector. His Instrument died with him, and the English brought back the Divine Right Stuarts.

The civil wars went on for centuries. Many refugees fled from them to America. Eighty-eight years before the American Declaration of Independence, the English abolished Divine Right in England, and transferred much of the King's authority to the assembly of barons, the House of Lords.

Land poor, the Lords could not pay the costs of the Royal Court, and rich commoners refused to, because they had no control of the King's spending. Naturally they did not expect any equality with the nobly born, but they stubbornly would not pay taxes unless they were given some way of holding the taxes down. So they were let into Parliament as a lower class, a House of Commoners, or Commons, and allowed to control the Royal treasury.

This concession was more important than the Lords contemptuously realized at the time. Their sons, more realistic, flocked into the House of Commons. That House has slowly gained importance, until now it can ask questions of the Ministers, and, by "going to the country" in a special election and

The Discovery of Freedom

getting popular support, the House of Commons can overcome a decision of the Cabinet.

Unfortunately, many Americans do not understand the English people nor the British empire. Neither do continental Europeans.

Americans, whose ancestors discarded feudalism in 1776, today look at the British empire in Africa and Asia, and ask how the English can hold millions of men in unwilling subjection, and still say that they stand for freedom.

Continental Europeans, whose ancestors abandoned the human values of feudalism and went back to an ancient tyranny, sneer at the English as a nation of shopkeepers, hypocrites, and double-crossers.

Neither of these points of view is valid.

The English stand for the true values of feudalism. British Government always grants that every individual, in his class, has human rights, dependent upon and subject to the whole social order. This social order, and this grant of rights, the English give to every Englishman and every British subject. A naked savage has his human rights, in his class, under British justice. The solitary British administrator, full of fever and quinine, who doggedly does his duty in a topee and mosquito-boots, and rules and takes care of the savage, claims no more for himself than his own human rights in his own class. He does not regard the savage as his social equal, and he does not consider himself the social equal of an Earl. In the sight of God and British justice, all men are equal; in this world, each man has his place.

As the first ex-President of the United States said courteously to an English guest in his house, Mount Vernon, "Yes, yes, Mr. Bernard, but I consider your country the cradle of free principles, not their armchair. [The English] walk about freely, but then it is between high walls; and the error of their Government was in supposing that after a portion of its subjects had crossed the sea to live upon a common, they would

The English Liberties

permit their friends at home to build up those walls about them." [2]

This element of freedom, of individual action within class limits, which the English kept from feudalism and developed and fought for through centuries of bloody civil war while all continental Europeans abandoned it, is the element in English life that created the British Empire.

The natural human desire to use human energy to improve the conditions of human life, had a leeway in which to act, in England. Therefore the English became, as continental Europeans truly say, "a nation of shopkeepers." The essential function of the continental Nations is the ancient function: war. The essential function of England is trade.

In the 17th and 18th centuries, Englishmen (with the King's permission) went out to make profits. It was not British Government that established colonies; it was the Virginia Company of Gentlemen Adventurers, the Massachusetts Bay Company, the Hudson's Bay Company—trading companies. The East India Company went into India; Cecil Rhodes went into South Africa.

The continental Kings *planned* Empires; they sent nobles and soldiers to seize land, and peasants to colonize it; their Ministers planned and "controlled" its settlement and cultivation. In America the King of Spain gave free land and a six-months-old pig to every settler's family, a barrel of grain to every adult, a hoe to every child over six years old.

The Kings and Queens of England chartered traders and let them trade. Raleigh's whole colony vanished; Captain John Smith had some troubles in Virginia; two-thirds of the colonists in Massachusetts died during the first winter.

British Government planned no Empire, and took no care of settlers. It intervened only when the trading companies had to use force to protect their trade. Then the British navy took Manhattan island and the Hudson valley away from the

[2] Allan Nevins' *American Social History as Recorded by English Travelers*, p. 33.

147

The Discovery of Freedom

Dutch, and the British army took Canada and India away from the French, to stop competition with British trade.

This feudal element of granted liberties makes the British Empire unique. It is the only Empire ever created by individuals using their energies to increase the available supply of useful goods. Governments created the other Empires, using military force in war to enlarge the area of their use of force. In a world of war-made Empires and war-making Nations, the British use war only as a necessary protection of Britain's primary function, which is trade.

The same element of liberties causes the unplanned flexibility to circumstances, that made Elizabeth's little half-an-island into an earth-encircling Empire. This lack of planning, which obliges England's rulers to change their minds with changing situations, is what the continental Europeans call "English perfidy" and the English call "muddling through."

Make no mistake about it; the English saved the only knowledge of human rights on earth, when it was lost everywhere else. And England for centuries has been the land of liberties.

But a grant of liberties, no matter how extensive, is not full recognition of the fact of individual liberty.

Ever since Italians "awakened Europe," all Europeans have talked about liberties and freedoms. Words in different languages do not mean the same thing; Americans delude themselves by assuming they do. When St. Paul's jailer said, "freedom," he meant safety from the Gestapo.

Very few Europeans have ever known what liberty is. All the others take it for granted that Authority controls individuals. When they say, "a free country," they mean a country not conquered by foreigners; in that sense, Germany is a free country at this writing. When they speak of liberties, they mean what an American means when he asks, "May I take the liberty?" They mean a permission, granted to them, to do a certain act.

When mother says, "Yes, darling, put on your rubbers and you may go out to play," the child (having put on his rubbers)

148

The English Liberties

is free to play. That is, he has "a freedom." This means precisely that he is not free, but subject to Authority.

Mother may grant this freedom because she believes that every child has a right to play; this makes no difference whatever to the fact that she is responsible for the child and must restrain his acts, by force if necessary, to prevent his doing anything that she thinks harmful.

Of course, she commands the child for his own good. This makes no difference, either. *Especially when her only concern is his welfare,* she will keep him from doing anything that she thinks is not good for him.

The very fact that she grants him "a freedom" to play, means that neither she nor the child regard him as free. When she thinks that he should not play, she will say, "No, dear; it's bedtime," and he will not be free to play. The Authority that grants "a freedom" can always withdraw the grant.

Freedom is not a permission granted by any Authority. Freedom is a fact. Whether or not this fact is known, freedom is in the nature of every living person, as gravitation is in the nature of this planet. Life is energy; liberty is the individual control of human life-energy. It can not be separated from life. Liberty is *inalienable;* as I can not transfer my life to anyone else, I can not transfer my liberty, my control of my life-energy, to anyone else.

My exercise of self-controlling energy can be forbidden, restricted, prevented, by force, by putting me in jail or in chains. My spirit may be so weak, or I may be so ignorant of facts, that I try to behave as if I did not control my own acts. But my self-control, which is freedom, can be taken away from me only by killing me.

So long as I live, I am self-controlling and responsible for what I do. Ignorance is no escape from a fact. Rocks fell on men before an apple fell on Newton. Not knowing how fast you are driving is no escape from the fact of momentum. No one escapes from the fact of freedom, by lacking the brains or the nerve to face it and say, "I act like a coward only because

The Discovery of Freedom

I *am* a coward. If I act like a crook, I *am* a crook. No one and nothing but I, myself, can be responsible for what I do."

I can not crawl out from under, saying, "I have to do this, if I don't I'll lose my job," or, "We've *got* to, we can't afford to lose the contract," or, "I have a family to support," or, "We have a responsibility to the stockholders," or, "It's the Party Line; the end justifies the means."

Liberty is inalienable. I can not transfer my responsibility to anyone or anything.

This fact is not recognized when individuals submit to an Authority that grants them "freedoms." Implicit in that plural is the belief that individuals are not free, that adult men and women must be controlled and cared for, as children are, and that, like children, they are naturally dependent and naturally obedient to an Authority that is responsible for their acts and their welfare.

This is the pagan belief that has generally prevailed for six thousand years and that still prevails over the greater part of this earth. The English have modified it toward reality, as far as it can possibly be modified, but they have not rejected it.

And do not think that this distinction is unimportant.

The British colonists in America were granted "a freedom of speech," "a freedom of assembly," and other freedoms from aggressions of Government upon their liberty, long before they began the American Revolution. They were granted these freedoms because the English had fought and died to defend the human rights that were recognized in the feudal system.

The colonists were furious when the British Parliament withdraw from them some of these freedoms, which until then had not been granted to Englishmen in England. The English could not understand their fury. British Government had every right to act as it did; any Authority that can grant a freedom can withdraw it.

The English view was that every individual, in his class, has certain duties and certain rights. Men in the lower classes owed obedience, service, and rents to the upper classes; in re-

The English Liberties

turn, their superiors owed them guidance, justice, and protection.

The Squire had taken the communal land that his ancestors' serfs and peasants had tilled in the old feudal system. He held this land, not as his property, but as family property which he managed in trust for his descendants. The descendants of former serfs and peasants still lived on the land and worked it for the Squire.

He still had the feudal responsibility for them. He appointed their clergymen, he judged and punished their crimes, he gave them paternal advice and orders, and treats on holidays. He approved or forbade their marriages, placed their children in jobs, inspected their cottages; in short, if he were a good Squire, he took good care of them. Neither he nor they ever dreamed of any class-equality between them, nor imagined that either could leave the class into which he was born.

On the Continent, the Kings were regarded as semi-Divine. The English denied that a King had Divine Right. Their King shared Authority with his Privy Council and the two Houses of Parliament; and the English held Magna Carta as the Royal grant that prevented British Government from destroying the feudal rights of man.

Men of the English ruling classes sincerely felt, and still feel, the obligations of their superior status. Until recently, the aristocratic families owned the land of England. The aristocrat still has the privileges of his rank (whether inherited or bought), including the advantages of University education. His schooling, his conscience, and the expectations of all classes of Englishmen still exact from him the performance of the duties of his rank.

He can not properly go into business or manufacturing; those are middle class occupations. An aristocrat serves England, in the Government, the Army or Navy, or The Church. His duty is to protect the interests and the rights of Englishmen, the humblest cottager's as much as, or more than, his own.

151

The Discovery of Freedom

This is the English system that has stood the assaults of hundreds of years, and still stands today. It is a system, an admirable one. For centuries it was the only defence of human rights on earth.

Half a century after Americans began the Revolution that is now shaking the whole human world, the President of the United States, John Quincy Adams, made the official Independence Day speech in Washington. He described the British system:

"The people of Britain, through long ages of civil war, extorted from their rulers, not acknowledgements, but grants, of right. With this concession they had been content to stop. They received their freedom as a donation from their Sovereign; they appealed for their privileges to a sign manual and a seal; they held their title to liberty, like their title to lands, from the bounty of a man; and in their moral and political chronology, the great charter of Runnymead was the beginning of the world.

"Instead of solving civil society into its first elements in search of their rights, they looked only to conquest as the origin of their liberties, and claimed their rights but as donations from their Kings.

"This faltering assertion of freedom is not chargeable indeed upon the whole nation. There were spirits capable of tracing civil government to its foundation in the moral and physical nature of man; but conquest and servitude were so mingled up in every particle of the social existence of the nation, that these had become vitally necessary to them."

V. The Third Attempt

1. AMERICANS

THE third attempt has hardly begun. Men are living today whose grandfathers remembered its beginning.

It began when Living Gods governed nearly all the earth, as Living Gods governed Egypt and as a Son of Heaven governs the Japanese today. Semi-Divine Kings owned South America, Central America, and most of North America, including three-fourths of the area of these present United States.

The British King and Parliament governed about two and a half million men and women living in scattered settlements on the edge of this continent, from Labrador to Spanish Florida.

These people were of all races, colors, and creeds. French were in the north and in the Carolinas. Dutch had built the town on Manhattan island, and their patroons' estates in the Hudson valley; now they were building their own cabins in the Mohawk Indian country that is now New York State. Germans had settled in the Jerseys and in the far west, beyond Philadelphia. Germans and Scotch-Irish were climbing the Carolina mountains; Swedes were in Delaware, English and French and Dutch and Irish were settled in Massachusetts, the New Hampshire Grants, Connecticut, and Virginia. Mingled with all these were Italians, Portuguese, Finns, Arabs, Armenians, Russians, Greeks, and Africans from a dozen very different African peoples and cultures. Black, brown, yellow and white, all these peoples were some of them free and some of

The Discovery of Freedom

them slaves. Also they were intermarried with the American Indians.

The British had founded, or the British Government had seized, these thirteen colonies. Their ruling classes were therefore largely British. These colonies were then as old as this Republic is now. The Spanish and French colonies were older.

Land in America, as everywhere else, had always been free; that is, the Kings owned it, and gave it to their subjects.

Eager to build settlements in New France and New Spain, the French and Spanish Kings gave the land, in communal fields, to selected peasants of good character, sound morals, and industrious habits. The Governments gave them carefully detailed instructions for clearing and fencing the land, caring for the fence and the gate, and plowing and planting, cultivating, harvesting, and dividing the crops.

The Government allotted land for the village, to be built as in Europe, a compact mass of cottages. It protected the villagers by a detachment of soldiers, and a well-built fort. (By an unfortunate error made in Madrid, the fort at St. Louis was ordered to be built on a site which the Missouri river flooded at least eight feet deep every spring. Even the children in St. Louis knew that the battering ice would destroy the fort, but the orders were definite and must be obeyed. The fort was built; the river destroyed it; and St. Louis was unprotected when the British attacked. But such errors were few.)

In every settlement, a Commandant kept order and dispensed justice, usually with much human sympathy and wisdom. Typically, he addressed the settlers as "my children," and they were obedient, well cared for, and gay. They had no trouble with the Indians. They learned the Indians' ball games, and played ball, raced horses, fought cocks, feasted and danced and sang, and gambled a great deal. They enjoyed safety, leisure, and enough to eat, in the American wilderness.

During a century, the Kings of France established such snug little settlements from the Atlantic along the St. Lawrence, around the Great Lakes, down the Mississippi valley to Mobile

The Third Attempt

and New Orleans. Before Thomas Jefferson was born, there was a little Versailles in Illinois; ladies and gentlemen in silks and satins and jewels were riding in sedan chairs to the Twelfth Night balls, and Indians and happy villagers, fatter than any in Europe, crowded outside the ballroom to watch the gaiety.

The English Kings were never so efficient. They gave the land to traders.[1] A few gentlemen, who had political pull enough to get a grant, organized a trading company; their agents collected a ship-load or two of settlers and made an agreement with them which was usually broken on both sides.

Landed in America, the colonists were never sure of getting the promised supplies; if the company's directors did not send them, the colonists died. But the directors could not depend on the settlers; they didn't work, they didn't get the expected furs, and the bound servants, especially, were always skipping out to live with the Indians.

When Raleigh's promised supplies did not arrive, his whole colony vanished, and today you can talk with men from the Carolina foothills to the Osage mountains in Oklahoma, who swear that their ancestors were in Raleigh's "lost colony," and that they simply moved to the mainland and up into the mountains.

To the scandalized French, the people in the English colonies seemed like undisciplined children, wild, rude, wretched subjects of bad rulers. Their villages were unplanned, their houses were scattered, they did not cultivate the land in common (though the towns did have communal pastures); their harvests were not equally divided, and they were always quarreling with each other and with the Indians. Their settlements split into factions; rebels left them and made other settlements. From the Great Lakes to the Gulf, in 1750, "Bostonian" meant what "Bolshevik" meant in this country twenty years ago.

These unmanaged settlements all grew much more rapidly than the French and Spanish settlements. They grew so rapidly

---

[1] Pennsylvania and Georgia, of course, were later given to philanthropists.

that in a hundred and fifty years they numbered more than a
million persons, and the rate of population-growth was rapidly
increasing.

Then a conscientious King, the first in generations, came to
the British throne. With Germanic thoroughness, he worked
hard to establish a good social order in England and in the
colonies.

All the brilliant French intellectuals, then clamoring for the
Rights of Man, profoundly admired George the Third. They
praised his government as the best of all possible governments.
And anyone must agree that an economy could not be more
intelligently planned by any living Authority.

Consider for example the rapid growth of the colonies. The
statistical curve revealed that if American population continued
to increase at that rate for fifty years, not a single human being
would remain in the British Isles; London would be a deserted
city.

Here you have the dawn of modern times. Saul consulted
the witch of Endor; and the Kings sent hurriedly for Balaam;
but modern men consult the statistical curve. It shows what
has happened, and therefore what will happen. (For this is a
static universe; nothing in it changes.) Thus, only yesterday,
the statistical curve of the American birthrate revealed that in
1960 the great majority of Americans will be over sixty years
old; nurseries and schools will be empty and factories closed
for lack of workers; and a terrifying question confronts the
intellectual: Where will the Government get funds to support
a population almost entirely dependent upon old-age pensions?
See the serious American intellectual magazines of about 1936,
for grave discussions of this vital problem.

King George's Government wisely acted, to prevent the
catastrophe to England. It restricted emigration to the colonies,
and stopped any expansion of settlement in America by strictly
excluding the colonists from the Ohio country, which England
had just taken from France by the French and Indian wars.

This action also reserved the western Mississippi valley, for-

The Third Attempt

ever, to the Indians who supported the valuable fur trade. If that is not a wisely planned economy, what is? [2]

The British Government was acting consistently for the good of all its subjects. It balanced industry, agriculture, and shipping most admirably. Nobody today can make a better plan, based on facts as they were then. The colonies were to be permanently agricultural; industry was kept in the small, home island; and shipping was provided with the triangular voyage between England, the West Indies, and the American Atlantic ports. Improve on that if you can.

The planned economy's thoroughness included even the pine trees. The King's men went through the American forests, marking the best pines, reserved for the Royal navy and merchant marine. This reasonable action so infuriated the colonists that they not only stole the King's pines whenever they could, but they made the pine tree stand for liberty. The Pine Tree flag flew from the masts of America's fighting ships through all the years of the first war for the Revolution.

Europeans could not understand it. Why, for instance, should anyone object to the Stamp Tax? a small, suitable tax put upon every required legal document. Still, when the colonists violently refused to pay that tax, the Government repealed it.

Then who could explain the Boston Tea Party? There was an over-production of tea; it threatened to lower prices and injure the East India Company that produced tea, and the London tea-merchants who sold tea. A fall in prices must always be prevented, at all costs; low prices increase consumption, and trade, and production and jobs. To prevent this disaster, the British Government might have burned the surplus tea, as Brazil has been burning surplus coffee. Instead, it shipped the tea to America for sale at a controlled price, a little less than Americans had been paying for the same tea.

---

[2] Most American textbooks mention a decline of the fur trade about a century ago, as if that were the end of the fur trade. The Mississippi valley today produces six to ten times the valuable furs that the wilderness produced in the greatest days of the famous fur traders. St. Louis is normally the leading world-center of the fur trade.

The Discovery of Freedom

Did the colonists greet this good, cheaper tea with grateful cheers? No, they raided the ship and threw the tea into the harbor.

And when the King's troops moved in to restore order, a rabble rose in arms. The dregs of the lower classes stood up and fired on the British Regulars.

2. WITHOUT A LEADER

THE American Revolution had no leader. Hundreds of thousands of men and women who lived and died unknown to anyone but their neighbors, and now are completely forgotten, began the third attempt to create conditions in which human beings can use their natural freedom.

This is the great fact in history.

Abraham and the prophets after him knew that every human being is self-controlling and responsible. Christ knew it. Mohammed knew it. And eleven hundred years after Mohammed, some hundreds of thousands of ordinary men and women living on the coast of North America knew it.

This fact is the hope of the world. For only unknown individuals can create and maintain conditions in which men can act freely, conditions in which human energy can operate to improve the human world.

Only an individual who recognizes that his self-controlling responsibility is a condition of human life, and fully accepts the responsibility of a creator of the human world, can protect human rights in the infinite complexity of men's relationships with each other. Only this individual protection of all men's rights can keep their natural freedom operating on this earth.

Living men and women create the human world. Everyone is responsible for the stupidity, the cruelty, the injustice, the wrongs of which he complains. Let him take the beam from his own eye. Have I never been stupid, have I never committed a cruelty, an injustice, a wrong against another person?

The Third Attempt

I am a creator of this world as it is; I am responsible for what it is.

But because no man can control another, and twenty-two hundred million human beings are living on this planet, a great many—one by one—must stop believing in pagan gods, and know the real nature of human life-energy, before that energy can operate effectively to make a world fit for human beings to live in. The earth was never flat, but more than a few men had to know that it is not flat, before ships sailed around it.

So nothing in history, or on earth, is more valuable than an individual who knows that men are free. America began with a few hundred thousand of them. Only a few hundred thousand, then, but never before had individuals acted without a leader.

These first Americans did not need a Fuehrer. They had no use for a shepherd; every one of them knew he was not a sheep. He had learned what reality is, from experience.

As human material, they were nothing to brag about. (My ancestors were among the earliest of them.) Successful, important, admired men do not leave home to vanish in a remote wilderness. The colonists were the rag-tag and hobtail of Europe. No statue of Liberty stood in New York harbor, saying to Europe, "Send me the wretched refuse of your teeming shores," but that was precisely what Europe sent. Starving wretches lucky to escape debtors' prisons, vagrants from highways and slums who sold themselves to slavery for years to pay for their steerage passage across the Atlantic, peasants shipped like cattle, shiploads of hungry women and girls without dowries, auctioned in the ports to settlers who needed wives.

The Pilgrims and the Friends (called Quakers in contempt) were the Holy Rollers and Jehovah's Witnesses of the time. The Cavaliers and the Puritans were hounded out of their own countries, not because they wanted to be. The Royal Governors and their suites were greedy, unscrupulous grafters and

159

The Discovery of Freedom

partners of pirates; more than one of them openly shared the bloody loot with murderers whom it was his duty to hang. Excepting these, the aristocrats in the colonies were younger sons, poor relations, and black sheep of the European gentry, who were jolly well pleased to be rid of them. Americans have always been immigrants; America has always been Ellis Island.

In America these failures, outcasts and refugees came up against the actual human situation on this earth.

The gentlemen-directors of the trading companies had spent large sums of their money to collect the colonists and ship them to America. Expecting large profits, they promised the settlers ample supplies. Often they sent supplies next year, with letters confidently anticipating in return the first installment of profits.

Then, howling in increasing anguish for those large profits, for some profits, for at least a return of their investment, finally for even a little of it back, they lost it and the Company went broke. This left the colonist stranded between an empty sea and an unknown wilderness, both of them totally indifferent to his fate.

He could not help knowing that nothing whatever but human energy, attacking this earth, can keep any man alive. He could not afford the illusion that anyone or anything outside himself controlled him. He had to know that he was responsible for his own life; if he did not save it, nothing would.

In Virginia there were horrible decades when even an aristocrat had to work. Or starve; he could choose. He had not even a precedent to guide him, for no man of the ruling class had ever before had to make such a choice.

As to men of the middle and lower and lowest classes, their lives had always depended upon getting jobs. On this side of the earth, not a single job existed.

They had to attack bare earth with their hands. They learned that the only source of wealth is human energy attacking this earth. Each one of them, using his energy with all his might to save his life, knew who controlled his energy.

The Third Attempt

These colonists did not believe in the pagan gods. They did not imagine that Neptune ruled the sea or that a thunderstorm was angry Zeus, and when Captain Standish and John Alden saw that saucy little French girl, Priscilla Molines, neither of them believed that Eros had shot a poisoned arrow into his heart.

In a hundred and fifty years, five generations of colonists created towns more comfortable and farms more productive than any in Europe. They had the feudal class system now: Royal Governors with their resplendent small courts, King's Justices in gowns and wigs, respectable burghers, and beneath these the peasants, the bound servants and slaves, and the vagrant hunters and woodsmen.

But of all these, only a few aristocrats and such wild young radicals as those whom Benjamin Franklin knew in Boston, had so much as heard of the modern pagan gods.

The French intellectuals were then imagining the first of these.

No one could any longer deny that the earth is round, nor that it moves in space. But Old World thinkers had recovered from that shock, marvelously without disturbing, after all, their pagan belief that the universe is motionless and changeless. They now explained that the universe is mechanistic.

In this new pagan universe, the parts move. The Mechanistic Universe moves—as a watch does; that is, its wheels revolve. Nothing changes in it; nothing *is being created;* life is not in it, it is not energy. All its movement is absolutely controlled; its wheels just revolve forever, never changing, never going anywhere. It does not even need winding up; it has no mainspring; it has nothing to give it energy. It simply is; that's all. It *has been created;* it is now controlled.

What controls it? you may well ask. The answer is, Natural Law. (If that's an answer.)

This new idea of the ancient static universe was part of a great intellectual awakening of Europe. The French intellectuals then were as crazy about Science as American intellectuals recently were about psychoanalysis. (Remember psychoanalysis?) Galvani had captured something tingling in a jar, and Franklin had pulled the same thing down from the sky on a kite-string, and proved that it was lightning.

Typical of their kind through all the ages, the French intellectuals at once declared that there is no God, and made a god of Science.

Natural Law, they said, controls the universe and all things in it, of course including men. That is, Natural Law naturally controls Natural Man, but Civilization had somehow got control of actually living men. Civilization is an un-Natural control, causing all human miseries and crimes. Civilization depends upon Religion, and Science, the hope of mankind, is making war on Religion.

(These intellectuals saw war as the nature of things, because Mani had; and perhaps some Americans imagine there is war between Science and Religion, because the French intellectuals did. Of course there was never any conflict between religion and science. Facts disagree with fantasies, but not with other facts. No fact in the material world quarrels with a moral or spiritual fact. As Thomas Paine said, the study of science is a divine study because it is a study of the works of God in creation; men do not make the principles of astronomy or mathematics, nor give properties to the circle and the triangle; they discover these facts.)

The French intellectuals had faith in Science. Science would win the war, destroy Religion, and thus wipe out Civilization with all its evils. Science would then reveal Natural Law. An Enlightened Despot must be found, to issue a series of edicts based on Natural Law. These edicts would establish the Age of Reason. The Enlightened Despot would then wither away, for men living according to Natural Law no longer need despots. And Natural Man, at last living naturally, would be good and happy ever after.

I am not exaggerating, nor trying to be funny; this is pre-

The Third Attempt

cisely what the great European intellectual leaders sincerely believed in 1776.

Young Benjamin Franklin stopped his radical talking about the possibility of Progress; he went to Philadelphia and built up a progressive printing business. George Washington, in his teens, was carrying a musket and keeping a sharp lookout for Indians while he earned his living as a surveyor in the Virginia wilderness.

The French intellectuals lived on aristocrats, while writing books and plays to undermine the aristocrats, and looking for the Enlightened Despot who would establish the Age of Reason. They vastly admired George the Third; he was one possibility, but most of them were betting on Frederick the Great of Prussia, the most enlightened despot in Europe. He was the despot who suggested dividing up Poland; he was the one who—on a whim, as he said—started the Seven Years' War.

Voltaire spent a long time at Frederick's court—and on Frederick's pay-roll—talking brilliantly about Science and Natural Law and the Age of Reason and listening to Frederick's poems, which he could not admire as much as he admired his own. After a long evening of brilliant talk interrupted by Frederick's poetry, sometimes Voltaire could not help wondering how deeply Frederick cared about the Age of Reason. Of course Frederick could not impose Natural Law on the Prussians until Science revealed what Natural Law was, but still —Could it be that the King of Prussia was wasting his promising intellect in schemes for enlarging Prussia? Such doubts, combined with a strongly resisted but increasing realization that Frederick was easing him off the pay-roll, made Voltaire cynical.

All this intellectual world was far above the heads of most Americans. Educated men were reading Voltaire, Rousseau, Montesquieu, Chateaubriand, all along the Mississippi and the St. Lawrence and in all the British possessions, but the uncultured tradesmen, farmers, sailors, hunters, read practically nothing but almanacs, small-town papers, and the Bible.

The Discovery of Freedom

They were children of men and women who had risked their lives to read the Bible. They knew of men burned at the stake, wrenched joint from joint on the rack, broken on the wheel, for saying that men had a right to read the Bible. They heard about the stealthy meetings in the dark, to hear the Bible read in a whisper by the light of one shaded candle— the alarm, the terror, the frantic escapes from killers pursuing, with torches, through the alleys and over the rooftops. Or the meetings on the open moors under moonless skies, to read the Bible; the sudden halloo, and the charging horses, and the running, running before the galloping hunters, the troopers riding down men and women, slashing them down with swords. Then the long hiding while the troopers searched craftily and mothers that night widowed lay under water in the ditches, praying to God that the baby would not whimper and the hunt end before dawn.

So, in America, they read the Bible. They were happy to be safe in America, where in open daylight and fearlessly they could read the Bible.

In Genesis they read the nebular hypothesis of creation, and the evolutionary theory of life's development on earth. They read about adventures and crimes, hairsbreadth escapes, and wars and spies and business deals, and political intrigues, and stories of young lovers and of family life. They pondered the salty wisdom and the unsparing analysis of human motives and human nature. And when they read the words of Abraham and Moses and Gideon and Samuel and Christ, saying that every individual is self-controlling and responsible, these words checked with the fact they knew from experience.

So when British Government tried to control them, they ignored it. To them the King's mark on a tree was only a mark; if they needed the tree, they used it. When Government stopped weaving in the colonies, weaving did not stop; women went right on working at their looms. When the King controlled trade, he did not control it; the colonists went right on trading.

The Third Attempt

The American rebellion against England began in 1660, thirty-nine years after the first Pilgrim set foot on the stern and rockbound coast. And until Cornwallis surrendered at Yorktown one hundred and twenty-one years later, the American rebellion was one continuous revolt against, precisely, Authority pretending to control a planned economy.

In 1660, while England was a piece of land entirely surrounded by smugglers and ghouls were digging up the dead to get woolen cloth, Charles the Second turned back his lace cuffs and signed another Act to improve the industry of the realm. It provided that the American colonists could not ship wool, cotton, tobacco, sugar, and other articles desperately needed by the wretched English lower classes, to any country but England.

If Government were responsible for its subjects, this Act would be as sensible as a farmer who, when his cattle are hungry, does not sell his corn but carries it only from the corn-crib to the feeding troughs.

But human energy was working in America. The colonists were trading with the Spanish and French colonists. To stop this trade meant wretchedness in America. The Americans knew something about reality; they were fighting the sea and the earth for their lives, and a piece of parchment was not going to stop them.

Overnight, this piece of parchment made them criminals, but they went right on trading with the West Indies. And the truth is that Charles the Second was too negligent to control trade. His ships sunk a few traders' ships, but not a single colonist was broken on the wheel or burned alive for the crime of trading wool for sugar.

For seventy-three years, American business was partly smuggling. Running the blockades was an ordinary business hazard. The King's gunners killed a few sailors, wasted some goods, and kept prices higher than they would have been; that was all. The colonists, far from starving, prospered.

Then in 1733, the Government announced a Five Year Plan.

The Discovery of Freedom

The French Government was actually protecting French trade. The Sun King was reigning in France; that long, glorious reign was shining over Europe, an increasing brilliance that dazzled and civilized all Europeans (who mattered) and lightened even the barbarian darkness of Muscovy. This was the Eighteenth Century, the Age of Enlightenment, that dazzles Americans even yet. This was the century of French art and culture and intellectual leadership, the century of Versailles, which implanted in the minds of Parisians an imperishable belief in the imperishable glory of France.

The French people kept no feudal liberties; they kept the feudal class-structure and feudal duty. Ragged, hungry, starving, the French people as loyal as sunflowers dying in a drought, still turned their faces up to their glorious and Divine Sun King.

French Government absolutely did not permit its colonists to ship food to France, to lower prices there and ruin merchants. So the French colonists had no markets; that is, there was over-production in the West Indies. Desperately their needy people would sell the products of their canefields for anything they could get.

So, naturally, to protect its subjects from such ruinous competition, British Government prohibited its American colonists' buying cheap molasses and sugar and rum. But, a great part of the colonists' business depended upon the West Indies trade. Cutting it off meant wide-spread ruin in the British colonies. The colonists uttered an awful howl, and in 1735 the British Government soothingly replied, "This is only a Five Year Plan. It may hurt a little now, but it will soon be over."

A large number of business men in the colonies, therefore, were doing a little temporary smuggling. But in 1738 when the first Molasses Act expired, the British Government renewed it, saying, "This is the Second Five Year Plan." Smuggling now began to be very well organized. By 1743, repealing the Molasses Act would have caused a business crash in the

166

The Third Attempt

colonies. But the Government renewed it, saying, "This is the Third Five Year Plan."

By this time, conditions in America were just what they became again when the Federal Government stopped drinking in this Republic. Every jug of molasses, every lump of sugar, every rum-toddy from Florida to Maine was illegal, a defiance of Government. Anyone who dreamed of obeying the law was a crack-brained fanatic, and trying to enforce it was a farce.

In and out of the ports and along the coast and across the Caribbean the agile American ships showed their heels to His Majesty's Navy, or, cornered, stood and fought, cheered on by the folks back home. Trade was thriving like anything; traders were making fortunes. Every traveler to America marveled at the prosperity here. And in 1748, the reliable British Government renewed the Molasses Act, repeating an explanation to which no one any longer listened, "A Five Year Plan."

Then those two Authorities (that had to move their frontiers) turned their guns on each other. The French *and Indian* wars, the provincial colonists quaintly called that French war, because in America both Governments gave the Indians scalping knives and paid good prices for scalps. The cabins burned, the settlers were killed and scalped, or scalped and kept to be tortured and burned at the stake; the women were driven away to be Indian squaws, and the children to be adopted Indians.

But people must eat; trade must go on, and it did. Out of the war itself, the business men got a peaceful way of doing business. So long as the war with France lasted, trade prospered between the English colonists and the French; and a trading ship's captain no longer ran from the Royal navies, but stood to, waited for the King's officers to come on board and met them with a smile, and a paper.

For six thousand years under "planned" economies, a peaceful exchange of useful goods has survived by two means: smuggling, and graft. In the true spirit of an old tradition, the colonial business men had produced a bright idea: Governments at war have prisoners to exchange. Why can't a trader exchange the prisoners?

They bribed the French and British officers; they bribed the British and French port authorities. They got the prisoners, and official permits to sail to the West Indies to exchange the prisoners. Then so long as the war continued, the ship could sail back and forth, carrying goods, and the prisoners.

A lively business in permits and prisoners developed in every port. The permits were sold at public auction; prices went up and down, and speculators played the permit-market. Of course, nothing but force could have separated the prisoners from the permits; idle and well-fed, the captives, both French and English, went right along with those papers, and rode out the war in endless sea-voyages.

Trading was peaceful so long as the war lasted. But it ended; British Government once more renewed the Five Year Plan, and traders put the guns back on their ships.

Nine years later, the captain of a trader's (smuggler's) sloop tricked a pursuing British coast-guard schooner into running aground on the shore of Narragansett Bay. The people of Provincetown and Bristol were cheering him in their streets. But a second thought sobered them: The Government's ship would work its way free in the rising tide.

Eight rowboats from Provincetown and one from Bristol, full of men armed with knives and muskets, set out in broad daylight to attack an armed schooner of the King's Navy. Its captain ordered his men to the guns, and fired a broadside at the rowboats. The rowers went right on rowing. They swarmed up over the schooner's side, laid out the crew, wounded the captain, put them all on shore, and burned the King's ship. Its name was the Gaspee. The place where its ashes lay is still called Gaspee Point.

Not a British officer in the colony dared to make an arrest. The officers of His Majesty's navy, off shore, did not dare to land to arrest those men of Provincetown and Bristol. Everyone knew who they were. His Majesty's Government posted

The Third Attempt

offers of large rewards for information leading to their arrest, and there are Americans along that coast who are laughing yet.

Individuals began this Revolution. They began it in every colony. They fought against Government's pretended control for a hundred and twenty years. Men came out of the frontier cabins in Virginia, five hundred of them, disobeying the grafting Governor who was protecting the graft-paying fur-traders who sold whiskey and guns to the Indians; they fought the Indians, they cleared the frontier of those murdering raiders, and then they turned on Jamestown and drove out the Royal Governor and burned his house.

Individuals acted, in the Carolinas, in Pennsylvania, in Connecticut, in the New Hampshire Grants, in Massachusetts. For a hundred and fifteen years, their rebellion was continuous and increasing.

And when at last this rebellion compelled the British Government to use the only power that any Government has— force, used with general consent—and British troops moved into Boston to restore order, Americans did not consent. They stood up and fought the British Regulars.

One man began that war. And who knows his name?

He was a farmer, asleep in his bed, when someone pounded on his door and shouted in the night, "The troops are coming!"

What could he do against the King's troops? One man. If he had been the King, that would have been different; then he could have done great things. Then he could have set everything to rights, he could have made everyone good and prosperous and happy, he could have changed the course of history. But he was not a King, not a Royal Governor, not a rich man, not even prosperous, not important at all, not even known outside the neighborhood. What could he do? What was the use of his trying to do anything? One man, even a few men, can not stand against the King's troops. He had a wife and children to think of; what would become of them, if he acted like a fool?

Most men had better sense; most men knew they could do nothing and they stayed in bed, that night in Lexington. But one man got up. He put on his clothes and took his gun and went out to meet the King's troops. He was one man who did not consent to a control which he knew did not exist.

The fight on the road to Lexington did not defeat the British troops. What that man did was to fire a shot heard around the world, and still heard. One finger on one trigger began the war for the Revolution that is dropping bombs today from Hamburg to Tokyo.

That shot was the first sound of a common man's voice that the Old World ever heard. For the first time in all history, an individual spoke, an ordinary man, unknown, unimportant, disregarded, without rank, without power, without influence.

Not acting under orders, not led, but standing on his own feet, acting from his own will, responsible, self-controlling, he fired on the King's troops. He defied a world-empire.

The sound of that shot said: Government has no power but force; it can not control any man.

No one knows who began the American Revolution. Only his neighbors ever knew him, and no one now remembers any of them. He was an unknown man, an individual, the only force that can ever defend freedom.

3. The People's War

NO one can say when or where the first war for the Revolution began. Ten years before the fight at Lexington, Americans came out of their cabins in the valley of the Conocheague, and stormed and took Fort Louden. One by one, Americans walked the trails of the Green Mountains, and came down to the lake and took the King's fort at Ticonderoga.

They acted as individuals, each man with his own knowledge of reality. The respected and respectable men were

The Third Attempt

against him; the teachers, the thinkers, the writers of books, were against him; the important men, the rich men, all men in high places, stood with the King.

How and when each of these men chose between the conformity, the submission, that looked like safety, and the fight that looked hopeless, no one can know.

In 1838, a retired small-storekeeper named Ebenezer Fox, who had fought through the war as an ordinary seaman under the Pine Tree flag, wrote down his "simple narrative" for his grandchildren. He says:

"I was born in the East Parish of Roxbury, State of Massachusetts, January 20, 1763.

"Nothing out of the ordinary course of human events occurred, of which I have any recollection, until I arrived to the age of seven.

"My father, who was a tailor, being poor and having a large family, thought that my physical powers were adequate, at this time of life, to my own maintenance; and placed me under the care of a farmer named Pelham.[3]

"With him I continued five years, performing such services in the house and upon the farm as were adapted to my age and strength. I imagined however that I suffered many privations and endured much hardship; which was undoubtedly true, were my situation compared with that of many other boys of my age, at that time or in this more refined period.

"I made frequent complaints of a grievous nature to my father, but he paid no attention to them, supposing that they arose merely from a spirit of discontent which would soon subside.

"Expressions of exasperated feeling against the Government of Great Britain, which had for a long time been indulged in and pretty freely expressed, were now continually heard from the mouths of all classes; from father and son, from

[3] This was usual; boys seven years old were generally expected to be self-supporting by their own labor, at home or as servants. Eighty years ago the age was nine.

The Discovery of Freedom

mother and daughter, from master and slave. Almost all the talk that came to my ears related to the tyranny of Government.

"It is perfectly natural that the spirit that prevailed should spread among the younger members of the community. I, and other boys situated similarly to myself, thought we had wrongs to be redressed; rights to be maintained; and that it was our duty and our privilege to assert our own rights. We made a direct application of the doctrines we daily heard, to our own circumstances. I thought that I was doing myself great injustice by remaining in bondage, when I ought to go free; and that the time was come when I should liberate myself and set up a government of my own; or in other words, do what was right in my own eyes."

So he ran away from his master and got a job at $5 a month on a ship to San Domingo, which, returning with a bootleg cargo of molasses and coffee, was attacked by two war ships and a tender off Stonington, Connecticut, run ashore, and captured. The crew, including twelve-year-old Ebenezer, swam ashore under fire from the British ships; near drowning, he stripped off his clothes in the water, and so returned from his first voyage penniless and stark naked, "without injury, but nearly exhausted with fatigue and fear, not a little augmented by the sound of the bullets that whistled around my head while in the water. . . . My appearance [among the crew in a cornfield] in a state of entire nakedness excited not a little mirth. 'Holloa, my boy!' exclaimed one of them. 'You cut a pretty figure; not from the garden of Eden, I can swear to it, for you have not even an apron of fig leaves to cover you with; you were not born to be drowned, I see, you will live to be hanged.' But after a few jokes at my expense, the mate took off one of the two shirts with which he had taken the precaution to provide himself before he left the vessel, and gave it to me." [4]

> [4] *The Revolutionary Adventures of Ebenezer Fox of Roxbury, Massachusetts.* Boston, 1838.

The Third Attempt

Naturally he sought another job, diligently, and he had the good fortune to get one—on a ship sailing to the West Indies for molasses and coffee.

Ebenezer Fox volunteered to fight for independence. He fought to the end of the war. The guns he fired completely destroyed his hearing in one ear. He was wounded, captured, starved on the prison ship in Long Island Sound; he escaped, fought again. America's fighting seamen were left stranded in France when the war ended. Ebenezer Fox eventually worked his way home, and got a job ashore. His wages for those years of fighting were his common seaman's share of the prize money for a captured British ship. As an after-thought he mentions in a footnote that this money was worth-less, as it was paid "in the paper currency of the time."

Such men began the war for the Revolution, and fought it. For ten years and more they had been fighting British troops, storming and taking the King's forts. They stood and fought at Lexington. They fought at Bunker Hill. And that hilltop where in June they stood against wave after wave of the disciplined British Redcoats was white in next February's snow before they had a leader.

He was a workman, growing old, and a failure. Grandson of a farmer, son of a stay-maker, he went to work at his father's trade when he was thirteen. His parents were Quakers; they had cheerfully endured great privations to give him the advantage, rare for a boy of the English working class, of learning to read and write. He married the daughter of a tobacconist, and in time they inherited the tiny shop in Lewes, England. He also earned a shilling and nine pence half-penny a day in the tax-collector service; taxes were collected every two weeks in every market-town.

So he struggled along until he was nearly forty. Then the little shop was sold for debt, and he lost his job.

Friends lent him money to come to America. Benjamin Franklin most kindly encouraged him, and gave him a letter to a Philadelphia printer. This printer hired him, at the

The Discovery of Freedom

marvelous salary of $5 a week, to start a little magazine, *The Pennsylvanian*. A whole new life of affluence and opportunity must have opened before him.

The colonies were now blockaded in earnest, and the people could not get gunpowder. The new editor thought of a scheme for using saltpeter, and *The Pennsylvanian* came out with it, to sensational success. That summer quite a number of people adopted the saltpeter idea, and heard the name of its inventor, Thomas Paine.

He saved his money until he had enough to pay for printing a little pamphlet, 40 pages of honest common sense. He wrote the truth as he saw it. He said to the confused Americans: Fight for independence; cut loose from England; set up a government of your own and do what is right in your own eyes. "There hath not been such an opportunity since the time of Adam. We have it in our power to make a new world."

Not since the invention of printing had anyone dreamed of such a sale. There has not been such a success since then. Of a population of 2,500,000, more than a hundred thousand persons bought Thomas Paine's pamphlet, *Common Sense*. Everybody read it.

Thomas Paine gave the copyright to printers in every colony. "I must make no profit of my political writings," he said. "They are with me a matter of principle. I cannot desire to derive benefit from them or make them the subject to attain it."

He volunteered as a private in the Continental Army. He was in Washington's retreat, with the defeated troops falling back before the British advance, from Long Island to Manhattan, to Jersey, to Pennsylvania, and when Congress was running away and soldiers were deserting and panic terror was in every house, and sensible men were flocking to the British, Thomas Paine wrote, "These are the times that try men's souls. The summer soldier and the sunshine patriot will, in this crisis, shrink from the service of his country. Tyranny, like hell, is not easily conquered. What we obtain

The Third Attempt

too cheap, we esteem too lightly. It would be strange indeed, if so celestial an article as FREEDOM should not be highly rated."

The whole country flamed with courage to meet that challenge.

Thomas Paine was worth more than the whole army, Washington said. Congress took him out of the ranks and made him Foreign Secretary. He was too honest for that job. But he went to France and got money that saved the Revolution. To the whole world, for twenty years, Thomas Paine was the leader of the Revolution. From first to last, he spoke the truth as he knew it. His *Rights of Man* utterly demolished the British darling, that famous orator and sleek crook, Burke; the hangman burned the book and the King's Justices sentenced Thomas Paine to fine and imprisonment; and the book sold more than a hundred thousand copies in the British isles. Thomas Paine was the greatest political influence of his century.

A year and three months after the farmers fought at Lexington, more than a year after Bunker Hill, six months after Thomas Paine's *Common Sense* had gathered all the common men's voices into one roar for independence, a group of gentlemen met in Philadelphia. Jefferson had asked Thomas Paine for a draft of a declaration, and Paine had sent it to him.

These gentlemen were safe if they stood with the King; they had everything to lose, if they did not. Scattered guerilla bands and mobs could not defeat the full force of Great Britain. A declaration of independence would throw every colony into chaos. The King's troops were solidly advancing down the Hudson, the King's fleet was approaching New York. Every man at that meeting in Philadelphia had a large landed estate or a substantial business or professional position; he need only do nothing, and he would surely keep his money, his superior class-status, and his life.

(And he could always say to himself that, while he did

not agree with the Government's policies, still a good subject's duty is always to his King.)

The penalty for signing that Declaration was death. The men who signed it took a slim chance. Not only for themselves; for their families and their dependents. Their property would be seized, their families dispossessed and disgraced, their sons and their son's sons forever attainted.

Thomas Jefferson had written the plain fact: "We pledge our lives, our fortunes, and our sacred honor." That was what each man pledged to the weak, the losing side, when he signed a declaration of that ten-year-old war, and of its cause and his motive:

"We hold these truths to be self-evident, that all men are created equal, and endowed by their Creator with certain unalienable Rights, that among these are Life, Liberty, and the pursuit of Happiness."

4. Democracy

A compelling reason for the long hesitation of these men— Washington, Jefferson, Franklin, John Adams, Madison, Monroe—was their fear of democracy.

They were educated men. Excepting Franklin (self-educated), each one had the education of an English gentleman. That is, the philosophy and the history of the whole European past had been pounded into his head before he was twelve years old. Therefore, when he was old enough to think for himself, he had thousands of years of human experience with every form of Government, to think about.

This knowledge was then regarded as necessary to every man whose birth entitled him to take any part in the government of his country.

They also knew the meaning of every word they used; they knew its Greek, Latin, or Anglo-Saxon root. Until forty years ago, this knowledge was still considered of first importance in American schools. Every pupil, at thirteen and

The Third Attempt

fourteen, learned etymology as he had learned spelling since the age of six, by dogged repetition until the facts were fixed in his mind.

Today the confusion of the meaning of words in these United States is a danger to the whole world. Few American schools any longer require a pupil to dissect his words to their roots, and to know what he means when he speaks. And for twenty years the disciplined members of the Communist Party in these States have been deliberately following Lenin's instruction, "First confuse the vocabulary."

Thinking can be done only in words. Accurate thinking requires words of precise meaning. Communication between human beings is impossible without words whose precise meaning is generally understood.

Confuse the vocabulary, and people do not know what is happening; they can not communicate an alarm; they can not achieve any common purpose. Confuse the vocabulary, and millions are helpless against a small, disciplined number who know what they mean when they speak. Lenin had brains.

Today, when you hear the word "democracy," what does it mean?

These United States, of course; and England, the British Commonwealth, the British Empire, Norway, Sweden, Denmark and Belgium, part of France, Finland when Russians attack the Finns but not when Finns attack Russia; Russia when Russians fight Germans but not when Stalin signs a pact with Hitler; the kingdoms and dictatorships of the Balkans; and economic security and compulsory insurance and the check-off system of collecting labor union dues; and friendliness and neighborliness and the unique American sense of human equality, and a vote for everybody, and socialism and communism and the Spanish cause for which republicans, democrats, socialists, syndicalists, anarchists and Russian and American communists fought, and freedom and human rights and human dignity and common decency.

177

The Discovery of Freedom

That is, the word has no meaning. Its meaning has been destroyed.

It was once a sound word. It is a necessary word, because no other has its real meaning. Demo-cracy means, rule by The People; as precisely as mon-archy means, rule by one (person).

Demos, The People, was a fantasy imagined by the ancient Greeks, in their search for The Authority that (they imagined) controlled men. To this fantasy they attached the meaning of God, which always attaches to every form of Authority, and there are still persons who believe that "the voice of The People is the voice of God."

The People does not exist. Individual persons compose any group of persons.

So in practice, any attempt to establish democracy is an attempt to make a majority of persons in a group act as the ruler of that group.

Consider this for one moment, not in fantasy, but as applied to your own experience in groups of living persons whom you know, and you will understand why every attempt to establish democracy has failed.

Of course there is no reason to suppose that majority-rule would be desirable, even if it were possible. There is no morality or efficiency in mere numbers. Ninety-nine persons are no more likely to be right than one person is.

In the Federalist Papers, Madison stated the reason why every attempt to establish a democracy quickly creates a tyrant:

"A pure democracy can admit no cure for the mischiefs of faction. A common passion or interest will be felt by a majority, and there is nothing to check the inducements to sacrifice the weaker party. Hence it is, that democracies have ever been found incompatible with personal security or the rights of property; and have, in general, been as short in their lives as they have been violent in their deaths."

The gentlemen who took responsibility for saving the

The Third Attempt

American Revolution were fearful that democracy would end it. The unknown Americans, the Ebenezer Foxes, for years had been fighting Authority; each was determined "to do what was right in my own eyes." But they had no Latin or Greek, they knew nothing about all the previous efforts to make democracy work, and they were shouting for democracy.

On the other hand, the large landholders, bankers, rich merchants, and a thick-springing crop of rapacious grafters and land-speculators, led by Alexander Hamilton, the illegitimate adventurer from the West Indies who was also a genius, were demanding an American monarchy.

The real revolutionists, when they signed the Declaration of Independence and of individual freedom, were undertaking not only to win a war against impossible odds, but to create an entirely new kind of Government.

They faced the armed power of the British Empire, with thirteen disorganized, quarreling colonies at their backs, and two dangers threatening them: monarchy, and democracy.

They said nothing about The People. They repeated no nonsense about Science and Natural Law and the Age of Reason. They did not gush about the noble nature of Natural Man. They knew men. They were realists. They had no illusions about men, but they did know that all men are free.

They stood against both monarchy and democracy, because they knew that when men set up an imaginary Authority armed with force, they destroy all opportunity to exercise their natural freedom.

Educated men, they had studied the many attempts to establish democracy. The results were known twenty-five hundred years ago in Greece. Democracy does not work. It can not work, because every man is free. He can not transfer his inalienable life and liberty to anyone or anything outside himself. When he tries to do this, he tries to obey an Authority that does not exist.

It makes no difference what he imagines this Authority to

The Discovery of Freedom

be—Ra or Baal or Zeus or Jupiter; Cleopatra or the Mikado; or Economic Necessity or the Will of the Masses or the Voice of The People; the stubborn fact is that there is no Authority, of any kind, that controls individuals. They control themselves.

Anyone in a free group can decide to give up his own idea and go along with the majority. If he does not want to do this, he can get out of the group. This is a use of freedom, an exercise of self-controlling responsibility.

But when a large number of individuals falsely believe that the majority is an Authority that has a right to control individuals, they must let a majority choose one man (or a few men) to act as Government. They will believe that the majority has transferred to those men the Majority-Right to control all individuals living under that Government. But Government is not a controlling Authority; Government is a use of force, it is the police, the army; it can not control anyone, it can only hinder, restrict, or stop anyone's use of his energy.

As Madison says, some common passion or interest will sway a majority. And because a majority supports the ruler whom a majority chooses, nothing checks his use of force against the minority. So the ruler of a democracy quickly becomes a tyrant. And that is the swift and violent death of the democracy.

This always occurs, invariably. It is as certain as death and taxes. It occurred in Athens twenty-five centuries ago. It occurred in France in 1804, when an overwhelming majority elected the Emperor Napoleon. It occurred in Germany in 1932, when a majority of Germans—swayed by a common passion for food and social order—elected Hitler.

Madison stated the historic fact: in democracy there is nothing to check the inducements to sacrifice the weaker party. There is no protection for liberty. Hence it is, that democracies always destroy personal security (the Gestapo, the concentration camps) and the rights of property (what rights of property ownership are there in Europe, now?) and are as short in their lives as they are violent in their deaths.

The Third Attempt

5. The Rights of Property

WHEN Madison wrote, "the rights of property," everyone knew what he meant. The right of property was the essence of the Revolution; it was a right that Americans were fighting to establish.

The fantastic notion that property rights can be opposed to human rights had never entered anyone's head. That notion today is part of the confusion of American vocabulary and American thinking.

Of course, property can not possibly have any rights. Property is a legal human right.

An undiscovered island is not property. It is land and timber and metals, but it is not property. It becomes property only when someone owns it. That is, when someone has a legal ownership of it.

When Eric the Red landed on this continent, not an acre of it was property. The American Indians were communists; they owned no property.

When Spaniards were exploring this continent, every acre of it and all its resources were the property of the Spanish Crown, by legal right which the Pope conferred.

Later, by legal right of conquest and by legal transfer, the Kings of France and Spain and England owned this continent. In 1776, George the Third owned every tree that grew in British property here. The Pine Tree flag meant that Americans asserted a right to own private property.

This right had never existed.

No individual owns property in communism. No one owned property under the ancient absolute monarchs. No one owned property in Athenian democracy, where everyone's property and life were at the mercy of the majority's whim.

The Church maintained the theory of private property as Church doctrine, as it maintained the equality of souls; for a right to own property is essential to individual freedom, and

181

The Discovery of Freedom

The Church recognized the freedom (the self-controlling responsibility) of souls, in abstract theory.

But no one owned actual property in the feudal system. Serfs were tied to the land, they did not own it. Peasants held land as communists. Barons held castles and land and villages in fief from the King, who could take the property from them if they failed in feudal duty. The King's holdings in property were controlled by the Barons who used it. The Church held property in *family* ownership; Churchmen used Church property but no individual Churchman owned the property.

The Divine Right Kings owned all property in their realms. Actually they could not take property away from any noble who commanded men enough to fight for it, but in theory the Kings owned the property. They controlled the property of the lower classes, as Louis XIV "controlled" the weavers' use of their looms. The King could take anyone's property (if he had the strength) and he could always forbid anyone's possession of any *kind* of property. For instance, in 1776, no Frenchman who was not a noble could own a pigeon.

Americans were fighting for a right to own property.

Individual ownership of property was a daring aim of the Revolution. American Tories vigorously opposed it. Jefferson fought them for years, to get individual ownership of land recognized legally in Virginia.

The Revolution for the individual's right to own property has hardly begun on this earth. This right does not exist in Asia or in Africa, nor in continental Europe at this moment.

The right to own property is not an inalienable natural right, as life and liberty are. It is a legal right, absolutely essential to an individual's exercise of his natural rights.

Nothing can take his natural rights from any living person. But without legal protection of those rights, no one can exercise them. Europeans today have no legal protection from seizure, torture, or execution. Helpless in the hands of torturers, a man still controls his thoughts and speech; but he can not act or speak freely.

The Third Attempt

Legal rights, when they exist, protect the individual's *exercise* of natural rights. The Revolution protected every American's exercise of his natural freedom, by the revolutionary method, new in history, of forbidding American Government to seize or search an American's person without due process of law; to imprison him without trial; to try him in secret or without letting him call witness in his defence; to try him twice on the same charge; to punish him for a crime that someone else committed; to refuse him a jury trial or to deny his right of appeal; to torture him; or to deny his right of assembly, or his right to petition the Government, or his right to bear arms, or his right to own property.

Every one of these legal rights is necessary to protect any individual's use of his natural liberty. Let anyone who doubts this, look at Germany.

The right to own property is the newest of these rights. American revolutionists were the first to see the simple fact that no man can use his natural freedom, if he has no right to stand upon this earth. No one can act freely, if by merely living he is a trespasser upon property that Government—the King, the Squire, or the Commune—owns.

This is the reason why the counter-revolutionists who are attacking man's inalienable right to freedom, first attack his legal right to own property. Private property is the first individual right that Lenin, Stalin, Mussolini and Hitler abolish.

Today the world is full of innumerable new kinds of property. In one century, this Revolution has released such terrific human energy that it has created an entirely new world.

Americans using human rights protected by Constitutional law, Englishmen protected by their defence of feudal human rights, and a few Europeans getting a little leeway for free action, in fifty years have created unforeseen and totally new forms of ownership of all kinds of property that never before existed.

No one yet understands these. There has not been time. There are no historical precedents. Nor even any historical

The Discovery of Freedom

parallels. Nothing of this *kind* has ever been known before. This is a completely new world. Human energy is creating so many new methods of producing such tremendous quantities of goods, and of attacking poverty and disease and space and time, that no one knows what is happening.

So it is easy to confuse the thinking about property. It is possible to attack the Revolution at its newest, and therefore weakest, point: the individual's right to own property. Therefore we have this preposterous suggestion that "property rights" are the enemy of human rights.

This new world is not yet fifty years old. Strangely enough, it is not perfect. Unjust men, believe it or not, still act unjustly. Stupid men still act stupidly. And Diogenes himself, with the wisdom of Socrates, can not know in advance how all these unprecedented forms of individual ownership of totally new kinds of property are going to work. Not all of them can be expected to work perfectly.

The right to a jury trial does not work perfectly, either. I have known juries to convict innocent men, and acquit guilty ones. I knew a man who was sentenced to imprisonment for life, convicted of accepting, as a bribe, from the hands of another man, a certain box containing $100,000 in bills. The man who (according to this verdict) handed him the box, was tried for the bribery, and on the identical evidence, a jury decided that he had not handed the other man this box, and acquitted him. Fifteen years later the prisoner, dying of tuberculosis, applied for parole and appeared before the Parole Board. The chairman of the Board was the man who had been acquitted of bribing him.

All politicians, all journalists, almost all Americans, know many such instances. Then why do we hear no passionate voices declaring that "jury rights" must not be permitted to interfere with human rights?

I will tell you why. Such an attack upon every American's legal right to trial by jury would sound like the nonsense it is. The same nonsensical attack upon every American's right to

The Third Attempt

own so much as his own house, sounds like an attack upon the rich. If this attack can confuse American minds, it can destroy an essential safeguard of every American's personal security and his exercise of his human rights.

And let no one imagine that tender sympathy for the poor inspires this attack. These men and women who weep for Americans who own so much less than the rich (and so much more than the poor ever owned in history before) are proposing to take away from them and their children the right ever to own any property.

When Madison wrote that "democracies have ever been found incompatible with personal security and the rights of property," all Americans knew that he was saying that majority-rule has always been the enemy of human rights, and that he was stating the reason why this Republic is not a democracy.

6. The Constitutions

FOR a dozen years the rebellious Americans had been stripping their Government to its naked reality: force. Then the Declaration of Independence abolished all Government in the colonies.

The Royal Governors had governed by the authority of charters. A charter was a written statement of the Authority that British Government granted to the Governor of a colony, and the liberties it granted to his subjects.

Because these charters were grants of freedoms, the Americans at first had struggled to keep them. British Government of course had a right to withdraw its grants, and sometimes it did so. The people of Connecticut, when their charter was revoked, stole the charter and hid it in a tree—to keep their liberties!

Now they saw how absurd it is to believe that a Government can give anyone liberty. The Declaration of Independence was also a statement that men are naturally free.

185

The Discovery of Freedom

This declaration abolished Government. But here was war, in a chaos. The King's troops were advancing from the north. The King's fleet was sailing into New York harbor. The time was past when individuals could attack Great Britain. This was war. (Or it was a punitive expedition to "pacify" the colonies, with military reprisals, martial law, and the body of every signer of the Declaration hanging by the neck from a gallows.)

Only a Government can make war. The revolutionists must have authority to mobilize, arm, command and feed troops and to pay them if possible, and to collect taxes to pay the bills.

From all the colonies, messengers galloped post haste to the Continental Congress, with letters asking for instructions and a grant of authority. Post haste they galloped back, with letters or news to the effect that the politicians hardly knew what to do, could not agree upon what measures to adopt, had no money and no power to get any, and that the essential thing to do was to fight, somehow, above all, to fight. The King's troops were landing on Long Island.

In every colony a few men had thought "to the foundation of civil government in the moral and physical nature of man." Since every individual is self-governing, the men in public office have no natural authority over anyone but themselves. Any authority that they exercise over any other man must be granted to them by that man.

So, while issuing orders with no authority whatever but the direct consent of any person who obeyed them, the Revolution's leaders called for a general grant of authority from all the men in their State.

Time and space did not permit all of them to meet in one place; they must meet in many places, and each group must send someone to represent all the individuals in that group. Thus the circumstances led Americans to invent a new and unique device—the convention of delegates.

Generation after generation of colonists in their scattered

The Third Attempt

and unprotected settlements had naturally got together in any time of danger, and had sent one man to get help, to bargain for it if necessary and make contract-agreements for them. So they were used to delegating to one man their natural right of free speech and free contract. Now they sent him off on horseback through the woods to find out what was happening and to see to it that no one made a Government that they would not agree to. Often before he reached the meeting place, the King's troops were there, and someone told him that the delegates intended to meet later, somewhere else.

Amidst alarms, defeats, retreats, most of the delegates met. A few of them took quills in hand and wrote out substitutes for the Royal charters. They were used to charters, and there must be some document to show to the folks back home. The American Revolutionists did not attempt to govern, as all Old World rulers had always governed and still do, with no written authority of any kind.

The Royal charters had been grants of freedoms, from Government to its subjects. They rested on the old pagan belief that Authority controls individuals, that this Authority is Government, and that no individual can do anything without permission from that controlling Authority.

But Americans knew, and the Declaration stated, that there is no such superior Authority. All men are born equally of the same human kind and equally endowed with inalienable liberty. Therefore, it is the men in Government who can do nothing without permission from the individuals whom they govern.

This meant turning all past Old World experience upside down. There was no precedent in known history, for a Government that was not (believed to be) a controlling Authority.

But there were the Royal charters. It was necessary only to turn them upside-down. So the delegates wrote documents that were grants of certain freedoms, from the folks back home to the men in public office.

The Discovery of Freedom

These documents were the first Constitutions in the history of the world.

The next job was to get the delegates (or most of them) to consent to granting these freedoms to this new kind of Government. And the next job was to get the folks back home to agree to their delegates' actions.

But the folks back home were fed up with Government; they didn't want any part of it. They thought of Government (as we all do) as the kind of Government they knew. They thought of an imaginary Authority, which they knew didn't exist, and of men who pretended to use Authority, and actually used force, to prevent free individual action—to keep traders from trading where they wanted to trade, and sailors from sailing where they wanted to go, and farmers from cutting the trees on their own land.

The folks back home were out with their muskets, fighting Government; they did not intend to let a new Government grow up (like the hated forests always sprouting up again from the stumps in their fields) as fast as they cut the old one down.

So in every colony (now a State, for "these United Colonies are, and of Right ought to be, Free and Independent States") the ordinary people resisted and refused these new Constitutions. It was two years before any State had a government. And for twelve years, while the Revolution's leaders tried to evade the King's troops, and to hold an army together somehow, and to get food and shoes and powder and bullets for the soldiers from petty politicians and grafting contractors who stuffed their own pockets and let the soldiers die; and while they tried to get French help against the British, and to borrow money from France, and then to negotiate the peace treaty in Paris and to hold the Continental Congress together and to keep The States from starting wars with each other, and to settle their boundary disputes and to figure some way of paying something on the debt to France before a French army came in to collect it, while they were doing all this they were trying to persuade the folks back home to agree to the Constitutions.

Grudgingly and most suspiciously, Americans did at last accept this new kind of Government. But only on condition that every Constitution, while it granted certain limited permissions to men in Government, also definitely prohibited their using force as Governments always had used force.

These prohibitions are called the Bills of Rights.

The name is not a good one, because it is not accurate. It confuses a careless mind.

The name, "Bill of Rights," is English. It is accurate in England. The English Bill of Rights is a statement of certain freedoms which British Government permits to its subjects.

An American Bill of Rights is the exact reverse of the English one. The "Bill of Rights" in American Constitutions is a statement of the uses of force which American citizens do *not* permit to men in American Government.

This difference is of the utmost importance. It is the essence of this World Revolution. This difference is the whole difference between American revolutionary Government and all other Governments in past history or on earth now.

This is the point upon which the future of the whole world depends today. And on this point, precisely, depends every American's own personal safety, his liberty, his life.

If Americans ever forget that American Government is not permitted to restrain or coerce any peaceful individual without his free consent, if Americans ever regard their use of their natural liberty as granted to them by the men in Washington or in the capitals of the States, then this third attempt to establish the exercise of human rights on earth is ended.

This curbing of Government is our defence against the ancient tyranny that reigns in Europe today. This is the protection of every American's life; it is his safety from the Gestapo, the Ogpu, the torturers, the firing squad, the revolver at the back of his neck in the cellar.

The counter-revolution that now threatens every American

The Discovery of Freedom

is not merely a matter of submarines and bombers. In this country, in American minds, in every American's mind and spirit, liberty on this earth must be defended.

Everything that an American values, his property, his home, his life, his children's future, depends upon his keeping clear in his mind the revolutionary basis of this Republic.

This revolutionary basis is recognition of the fact that human rights are natural rights, born in every human being with his life, and inseparable from his life; *not rights and freedoms that can be granted by any power on earth.*

Americans hold this truth. This knowledge attacks, and for a hundred and sixty years has been attacking, the very foundation of the Old World. This is the knowledge that the Old World's defenders are now determined to destroy utterly.

American Government is not an Authority; it has no control over individuals and no responsibility for their affairs. American Government is a permission which free individuals grant to certain men to use force in certain necessary and strictly limited ways; a permission which Americans can always withdraw from American Government.

The American Constitutions are statements of the permissions which Americans in the past have granted to men in public office. And every Constitution contains a statement of the uses of force which Americans prohibit to this Government.

An American "Bill of Rights" is in fact a Bill of Prohibitions. It prohibits the men in public office here, to do acts customary everywhere else when these Bills were written, and today either continuing or revived nearly everywhere on this earth.

The true revolutionary course which must be followed toward a free world is a cautious, experimental process of further decreasing the uses of force which individuals permit to Government; of increasing the prohibitions of Government's action, and thus decreasing the use of brute force in human affairs.

This is the only course toward a richer world. For the only

The Third Attempt

energy creating wealth is human energy. A man is able to use his self-controlling energy effectively toward its natural aim of improving living conditions, precisely to the extent that no use of force restrains him.

During the first century of the Revolution, Americans made, tried, rejected and replaced Constitutions, to the number of a hundred and three. On into this second century, Americans have been making and remaking Constitutions.

Never before on earth, never anywhere in six thousand years, has there been anything like this—a multitude of human beings constantly creating their own Government.

The two instruments which American revolutionists created, the convention of delegates and the Constitution, never before existed.

The Constitution grants and limits the power of men in Government. The convention of delegates is the tool that Americans use to change their Constitutions.

Americans can always peacefully and legally diminish or withdraw any power that Americans in the past have granted to politicians. Americans can always increase, to any extent, the curbs on Government that are called the Bills of Rights.

So no American can justly complain of anything that men in public office do, so long as he is not using or trying to use the instruments that the leaders of this Revolution created and gave him for the purpose of restraining the men whom he permits to govern him, and carrying on this Revolution into the future.

For example: Recently there was protest about the increasing public debt. Now I shall not discuss finances. But, the only American who can honestly object to the size of the national debt, no matter how large it is or how dangerous, is a Nebraskan.

Nebraskans do not permit their politicians to put them into debt.

A Nebraskan controls his money. Any Nebraskan who is

in debt, put himself there. The Constitution of Nebraska does not permit the politicians in Lincoln to contract a debt for other Nebraskans.

Nebraska has fine roads, fine schools, every public institution that anyone can desire. They are paid for. Nebraska has the most beautiful State capitol in this country; it cost ten million dollars, paid down, cash on the barrel head. Every penny of ten million dollars is right there, transformed into beauty and utility in metal and marble and glass. When Nebraskans spend ten million dollars for their State, they get ten million dollars' worth; they do not get six million dollars' worth and let the balance evaporate in interest paid to creditors. Nebraska has no public debt.

The citizens of every State have the same means of getting out of debt. If they do not want to mortgage their children's lives, they need only amend their Constitutions.

What a spectacle is this. After six thousand years of abject human misery, slavery and hunger, a few people on the edge of a wilderness see that the whole pagan view of human life is false. They begin a Revolution against the whole world. They fight, and starve and freeze and die, for the opportunity to begin this Revolution. They create a new kind of Government, which has no power that individuals do not grant to it. They create the instruments that will forever serve future generations as tools to control and to withdraw the power granted then.

The release of human energy is terrific. It makes the great-grandchildren of these revolutionary leaders the richest and most powerful people on earth; it begins to change human life on the whole earth. And these great-grandchildren, heirs of the Revolution, inheritors of this new knowledge of individual freedom and responsibility, and of this unprecedented wealth and this world-power, having in their hands these unique revolutionary tools by which individuals limit and check and withdraw the authority they grant to Government —in every one of these States they sit howling that Govern-

The Third Attempt

ment is spending too much of their money and that *Government* should do something *to curb itself*.

And what a strange spectacle is Nebraska. Nebraskans are not only Nebraskans; they are citizens of the Republic. If, as Nebraskans, they object to public debt, why do they not object as Americans?

They have in their hands, and they are well accustomed to using, the means of checking their debt as Americans. Why do they not add to their Constitution a prohibition of the spending of borrowed Federal money in Nebraska as charity to Nebraska's citizens? The Federal Constitution does not permit the men in Federal office to use force to compel the citizens of any State to accept money from the Federal Government.

I am not speaking of public debt. Public debt is a new problem for Americans; a century ago, no one imagined it. Congress then did not know what to do with all the surplus money in the Treasury, and finally returned it to the States.

The Americans who began this Revolution could not imagine any of today's problems. Even thirty years ago, most of them were unimaginable.

But responsibility for whatever the men in American Government do, is the individual citizen's responsibility. The men who began the Revolution created and bequeathed to every future American the tools for progressively reducing the use of force in human affairs. Every American inherits these unique tools: the Constitution that checks the acts of men in public office, and the convention of delegates which is the peaceful means of changing the Constitution.

The American who leaves Government to the politicians, permitting or urging the men of his party, when they are in office, to increase their power and use it upon other Americans for his benefit, and howling when men of the other party are in office increasing their power and squeezing him for the benefit of other Americans, is trying to evade his responsibility.

He will not evade it; he can not. His natural liberty *is* re-

193

sponsibility. He is born free; he controls his life and his affairs; he is responsible for them. In trying to make any other person responsible for his welfare, he must try to transfer his control of himself to that other man, for control and responsibility can not be separated.

In demanding that men in Government be responsible for his welfare, a citizen is demanding control of his affairs by men whose only power is the use of force.

If men in public office accept that controlling responsibility, they must use force; they have nothing else to use. Then the citizen must lose the use of his natural human rights; his exercise of free action and free speech, his legal right to own property, must be checked and curbed and prevented, by force.

This use of force against the natural uses of human energy must reduce the production and the distribution of wealth—of the material goods that nothing but productive uses of human energy can create. If men believe that Government is responsible for their welfare, the increasing poverty increases their demand that men in public office control the individual's affairs. This demand increases the use of force against productive energy. This use of force must progressively destroy all the protections of an American citizen's natural human rights, and eventually—if at last he protests—his life.

The men in public office can no more prevent this result of their assuming, or accepting, responsibility for the citizen's welfare, than they can prevent water from seeking its own level.

Responsibility-evading citizens in this Republic, if they become numerous enough, can wreck the Republic, the Revolution, and the whole modern world. But not one of them can evade responsibility. Each one will be responsible.

American Government is not an Old World Government; it is not the use of force in an attempt to control subjects who try to submit because they believe the ancient superstition that Authority controls them. American Government is a limited

The Third Attempt

use of force, permitted by free men who are leading a world revolution.

American Government is unique in two ways. It is a kind of Government that is not superior to an individual, but permitted by the individual; and it is neither Government by superhuman Authority nor by living Authority, but Government by Law.

(This was the incredible apparition that horrified the French people under the American occupation, when this Government crossed the Mississippi, 138 years ago. The French said, "These Americans are barbarians; they have no Government; nobody governs them." The Americans, equally horrified, said, "These Frenchmen are barbarians; they have no Government; they have no laws.")

Government by Law is a daring experiment, not yet two centuries old. No one knows yet whether it can be permanently established.

Superstition, that deep darkness in human minds, supports all other kinds of Government. The awe and dread and desire for the supernatural creates the belief that Authority controls individuals. In communism, this Authority is believed to be superhuman, a Great Spirit of some kind, a Law of Lycurgus or a Will of the Masses. In all forms of Government by living rulers, a superhuman quality is supposed to be in the ruler; he is a living God (the Pharaoh, the Roman Emperor, the Mikado) or he is God's personally appointed agent on earth (The Czar, the Divine Right Kings), or God has made him a superior *kind* of human being (the Hapsburgs, the Hohenzollerns) or he is himself a mystic pagan Power (Hitler).

This general superstition supports a living ruler's use of force. He commands the police and the army. So long as a majority of his subjects believe that he is Authority, the police and the soldiers obey him and he can always use them to terrify, imprison, torture and kill any rebellious individuals or minorities.

195

The Discovery of Freedom

The power of superstition in human minds always made it unnecessary for rulers to have any written authority. Until this Revolution began, Government always rested on superstitious belief.

But no superstition supports an American Constitution. It is intangible, but no one believes that it is a pagan god. Nor does it give orders to the police or the army. Law is nothing but words on paper. Its only power is in the free will of individuals —of the public officials who swear to obey it, and of the citizens who insist that they obey it.

What holds the public official to his oath? Nothing but his conscience, and the vigilance of multitudes of citizens.

Consider the actual situation of an American politician elected to office. The Constitution limits the time that he holds the office, and fixes his salary. He will get that much money, whether he earns it or not; he will get no more, though he earn it twice over.

He has sworn to obey the Constitution that limits his power. His honor and—if he is intelligent—his patriotism, hold him to that oath. All the other incentives that human beings feel, impel him to break it.

If he wants to do good (as he sees good) to the citizens, he needs more power. If he wants to be re-elected, he needs more power to use for his party. If he wants money, he needs more power; he can always sell it to some eager buyer. If he wants publicity, flattery, more self-importance, he needs more power, to satisfy clamoring reformers who can give him flattering publicity.

And what prevents him from using more power?

Constitutional law, words on paper. Its only force is moral.

One thing protects a busy American's exercise of his human rights, his free action and free speech, his home, his business, his money, his life, from such tyrannical violence as Governments have always used, and as Hitler, Stalin, Mussolini, Franco, the Mikado, are using upon their subjects now—and that is the American politician's conscience.

The Third Attempt

The only support his conscience has, against the whole weight of his material and personal-political interests, is each American's vigilant defence of every American's human rights.

That is a plain statement of the actual situation.

The men who first led this Revolution understood this risk. They had not begun the Revolution; they were more cautious. They preferred to continue the very slow process of modifying British Government. But the unknown Americans, the farmers, sailors, craftsmen, frontiersmen, who were driven by the necessity to live on this bare earth, broke loose from the economic "controls" that restricted their energies; they fought the feudal social order until they brought the British Regulars to America to subdue them.

Then the American gentlemen—workers, themselves, who knew reality—accepted the destruction of social order here, and pledged their lives for the Revolution.

After six years of dragging out a war that was ended at last by foreign help, and six more years of confusion and discouragement, when Washington no longer had even as much hope as he had felt at Valley Forge, they made one last effort to save the Revolution, and wrote the Federal Constitution.

With sound common sense, they did not debate it publicly. They opened the convention by shutting its doors and pledging their honor to keep their discussion secret. That handful of veterans, and the assembly of young men in their thirties, were hard-headed realists. They knew that nothing but rock-bottom honesty and plain speaking could save the existence of the Revolution and no public man but Thomas Paine had ever risked telling the truth in public.

They had no fantastic faith in The People; no more notion of consulting or obeying public opinion than Wilbur Wright had when he was trying to invent an airplane. They knew that every man's real responsibility is to his own moral standard. As Washington realistically said, "If, to please the people, we offer what we ourselves disapprove, how can we afterward

197

defend it? Let us raise a standard to which the wise and just can repair. The event is in the hand of God."

For weeks they struggled, with argument and compromise and bargain, to construct a new kind of Government. They disagreed so profoundly that the job seemed impossible; they adjourned for three days, agreeing to spend that time not with their supporters, but in the company of their opponents.

The Constitution was not their ideal; it was the practical best that they could get. It was a compromise, it was an effort. It was a desperate hope.

Then they went out and fought, for two years more, with every political weapon they had, against the powerful pressure-group that was demanding the one-man responsibility of monarchy. They fought, with argument, with speeches, with appeals to logic and justice and common sense, with pamphlets and newspapers and books, and political deals, with every weapon they had they fought against the rioting mobs that were demanding democracy, the majority-rule that always creates an irresponsible tyrant.

And when they won, when they got nine States to accept the Constitution as amended with ten additional prohibitions of Government, when at least they had saved the existence of the Revolution through that crisis, Jefferson could only say that they had done the best they could do.

The future, he said, must show the results. Whatever the results might be, they depended upon individuals, since every individual *is* self-governing.

American Constitutional Government is now the oldest existing Government. It is the only form of Government now on earth that has been flexible enough, well enough adjusted to reality, to survive the strains of one century and a half.

All other Governments have been shattered during that time, either by war or by the conflict between human energy and the Government's coercive force.

The men who invented this kind of Government were not

The Third Attempt

enthusiasts. They worked out no plan for a better world; they had no illusions and no dreams of any Utopia. You can see their realism in the Constitutions they wrote. They designed the Federal Constitution with the firm intention of preventing any man in public office from using Government's monopoly of force, to seize, torture and arbitrarily kill ordinary Americans.

They knew that the purpose of all revolts, through the Old World's sixty centuries of revolts, had been to give an imaginary control and a real monopoly of force to men who would not use force atrociously. After each revolt, sooner or later the men in Government had used force atrociously.

The results of six thousand years of experimenting along that line had convinced such men as Madison that so long as an opportunity to use unrestrained force exists, some man will use it atrociously. As Aristotle said, A wild beast leaps into a despot's throne.

Governments had always had the simple governing function that every parent has. Every mother makes laws, enforces laws, judges and punishes law-breaking. She could hardly say precisely when she is a legislator, and when she is a policeman or a judge. She simply thinks and acts to take care of the child. So had all living rulers always governed their subjects.

The English civil wars were like quarrels between parents, one saying that the other treats the children unjustly. The result is that they share the responsibility of governing. The King and the Parliament govern the English, and custom and conscience and prudence limit their use of force. English Government, so to speak, does not believe in spanking and never loses its temper. Its power, however, is still the same whole power, a simple power to govern.

The men who wrote the Constitutions destroyed, here, that *kind* of power. They divided it into three parts, legislative, executive, and judicial. This is the first attack ever made upon Government's *use of force,* itself.

Let any mother of a three-year-old imagine that one person

The Discovery of Freedom

can make a general statement that children should not pull cats' tails; that a second person can see that this child is pulling a cat's tail; and that a third person can act to separate the child and the cat; but that no one person exists who can have the general idea *and* see this particular situation *and* act.

In that case the child and the cat will take care of themselves, and learn from experience how to take care of themselves.

That was the result intended by the Americans who divided governing power into three parts. They did not regard adult human beings as helpless children. They knew that all men are, by their nature, free. Weakening the Government, hampering the use of force in human affairs, is the only way to permit individuals to use their natural freedom.

It is tough on the child and the cat. Perhaps it is tough on human beings, that no Authority exists to take care of them. But no such Authority does exist, or can exist. In the human world there is nothing but individual persons, born free. That's the brutal fact. It is a tough job to be free. But six thousand years of trying to escape from freedom were tougher.

Having divided Government into three parts, the revolutionists limited each one of the parts. The Federal Constitution, for example, forbids men in office to increase their own salaries. It forbids the President to adjourn Congress. It forbids him to make treaties, or even to appoint his own assistants, without the advice of the Congressmen and their consent. It forbids both the President and the Congressmen to interfere with the courts. It forbids the President and the Senators to appropriate money from the Federal Treasury. It forbids them to impose, collect, or spend taxes; only the members of the House of Representatives are permitted to do that, and they are subject to recall every two years. In short, a Constitution forbids. It exists to limit and restrain and check and hinder American Government.

The Federal Constitution also uses the Federal and State Governments as checks upon each other. An American has

The Third Attempt

two Governments, or three, or more, including his county and his town. He should always aid the weaker to check the stronger, for this divided sovereignty is the protection of his freedom.

These divisions and prohibitions made the weakest Government that could possibly exist at that time. They prevented monarchy.

The revolutionists then went on to prevent democracy.

Consider for a moment what this problem is. Every individual is naturally self-governing; but because men must combine their energies in order to live, and in any large number of men there are some who use force to injure others, there is a necessity for a use of force to stop them; that is, there is a necessity for Government.

Government is a group of men who have the monopoly of the use of force. But since, as individuals, they are no stronger than anyone else, they hold their monopoly of force only by general consent. All Government derives its power from the consent of the governed. (This fact, though always true, had seldom been known. The majority's grant of power had actually appeared in history, as a rule, only when the majority did *not* consent; then it caused rebellions and civil wars.)

The American revolutionists knew these facts. So their problem was to devise some method by which a majority of citizens could peacefully give, or deny, their consent to the men in Government. But here was the danger of majority-rule. Democracy had been tried before, again and again. It always destroys personal safety, and ownership of property, and it always quickly creates a tyrant, who oppresses the majority until they revolt in civil war.

That is the problem. The Greeks could not solve it. The early Romans could not solve it. No one ever had been able to solve it.

The American revolutionists solved it. They prevented tyranny, not only by dividing and checking the Government's use of force, but also by dividing and checking the majority.

The Discovery of Freedom

The original Federal Constitution permits only one exercise of majority rule. It gives a majority the power to elect, and quickly recall, the members of the House of Representatives, who assess and spend the taxes that a majority must always pay.

A majority was not permitted to have any other direct action upon Government. The Senators did not represent citizens, and citizens did not elect them. A Senator represented his State in its relations to other States; the men in his State Government appointed him.

Neither the States nor the citizens elected the President. His duty within the Republic was only to execute the laws made by Congress. But in world affairs he was the Republic's substitute for a King. He commanded the Army and the Navy and (subject to the advice of the citizens' representatives and the states' representatives; and with their approval) he directed the Republic's course in world affairs.

So that he might be completely free to do this, the President was not to be elected by (and therefore dependent upon) either the citizens or the States. Temporary popular motions or changing public opinion were not to touch him. Local interests were not to be able to bring pressure upon him.

The President of the United States was to represent no group of Americans, no section of the Union; he represented The Republic.

Representative Americans, not in politics, but men of outstanding achievements in other fields, were to elect the President. They were required to vote for men who were not citizens of their own States. These Electors were to be brought from the American public into Government probably only once in their lives, to serve the Republic by choosing its world representative. They were expected to choose, from all Americans, a man whose achievements were widely known and respected, and proved his ability to guard the Republic's interests in a hostile world. He was to be able to take the long view, to act with complete freedom and with no possible self-interest, for the permanent welfare of the Republic in world affairs.

This was representative government. Ordinary citizens, whose contact with Government is paying taxes, were directly represented by the men who assessed the taxes, and had the power to recall them every two years.

Citizens of States elected the men in their State Governments. These men appointed the State's representative in the Federal Government.

The President represented all Americans. No group had any claim upon him.

And many a President in a time of crisis, since that freedom was taken away from his high office, must have silently cursed the Amendment that plunges him to the neck in a mob of short-sighted, local-minded, clamoring men, clutching and pulling at him with a thousand hands. Today that Amendment does not let the captain of this ship of State make one clear decision unhampered by the ignorance and prejudices and fears of all the passengers on all the decks and all the men playing poker in the ship's bar. An ocean liner could not be navigated for a day under such conditions.

7. THE RIGHT TO VOTE

WHEN American politicians took the election of the President of the United States into their hands, they had no idea that this would be the result. No one then imagined that everyone should vote, or ever would vote. In all the States, voting was restricted.

Today, voting is an American superstition. Hardly anyone ever thinks about it. Americans take it for granted that every human being has a natural right to vote.

Of course this is not true. No one has a natural right to vote. Everyone is born with inalienable liberty, but nobody is born with an inalienable ballot.

Voting is a legal right, like the right to own property.

The Discovery of Freedom

A legal right is a general belief (prevailing among people at any place and time) according to which the police act (or should act). For instance, people in the Roman empire generally believed that a Roman citizen was entitled not to be arbitrarily tortured and killed. They also believed that everyone should worship pagan gods. So St. Paul had a legal right to be tortured and killed only according to law. He prized that legal right most highly, but what was its value?

The only actual value of a legal right is in its actually protecting the individual's use of his natural human rights, his freedom.

A man alone, on an island or in the mountains, has no use whatever for legal rights. Nothing interferes with his freedom; he uses his own energy to protect himself from the hostile non-human energies around him.

Put him among other men, and a few of them will attack him. In civilization he does not use his own energy against them, because civilized men delegate their use of brute force to Government. Government is a monopoly of the use of force. So Government, the police, will act against the criminals.

The peaceful person's actual protection in civilization is the respect for his natural rights which most people feel. This general attitude is expressed in law, in legal rights; these are supposed to protect him, and Government is supposed to enforce them. Actually, the men in Government can not protect anyone; they can only punish and kill those who have injured him. The police can not prevent crime; they punish criminals. An American's legal right to property does not keep him from being cheated or robbed; it is Government's authority for punishing crooks and robbers. A man's legal right to life does not save him from being murdered; it is Government's authority for hanging the person who has murdered him. No American is any safer now than Americans were on the frontier where there was no Government and no legal rights.

Government can not prevent crimes because men in Government have no control over anyone but themselves. Their

The Third Attempt

function is the use of force, normally against criminals, and in war against the common enemy.

But what prevents the men in Government from stopping any man's use of his natural freedom, by force?

His legal rights. A general belief, or knowledge, definitely stated in writing, and constantly backed by a majority of living persons—a legal right—protects the individual from an arbitrary use of force by men in Government. (Through most of history, and today wherever Government acts as absolute Authority, individuals have no legal rights. Hitler only yesterday abolished legal rights in Germany.)

The value of a legal right is wholly in its protecting individuals from Government's use of force.

Legally restricting Government's action to its smallest possible minimum reduces (to the smallest possible minimum) the use of force in human affairs, and thus permits the great majority of individuals to speak and act with the greatest possible freedom. Precisely by restricting Government, American Constitutional law permits Americans to act more freely than any other people on earth.

Then what is the actual value of an American's legal right to vote?

The Constitutions restrict this Government. Voting can restrict it further, but only when voters elect delegates to conventions to make their Constitutions stronger.

Or, when voters have an opportunity to elect men who will repeal laws and reduce Government's area of activities.

Voting for Congressmen can not repeal laws. Voting can never *control* Government. Men in public office are individuals, and nothing outside an individual can control him. The Constitutions limit the time that a man may stay in office, but during that time he controls himself.

At the end of that time, a majority of voters can put him out of office. So an American's legal right to vote can be used as a threat to office-holders who want to be re-elected.

But a majority of voters can never use that threat. A ma-

The Discovery of Freedom

jority can not even know what their Congressmen are doing. Human beings must use their energies in productive work, and they want to, and they do. The more freely they can act, the more energetically they improve their living conditions, and the less attention they give to anything else. The fact is that Americans pay no attention to Government so long as it does not interfere with them. Normally they never think of it except at election time. Americans are busy; not half of them even know the names of their Congressmen. Ask the next forty persons you meet, if you doubt it.

So the threat of the vote does not operate to restrict Government and protect human rights. The fact is that pressure groups use it to increase Government and restrict the use of natural human rights.

Every American politician is constantly assailed by small groups fiercely determined to make the men in this Government exceed the Constitutional limits of their use of force.

Stupid men believe that force can improve other men's morals; they want force to stop men's drinking, or smoking, or gambling. Superstition clouds their minds; they imagine that force can produce economic results; they demand that police clubs *control* the growth of crops, and the making of goods, and wages and prices and trade. They dream that because a law can make any action a crime, it can stop that action. (Though they know nothing of the history of smuggling and graft, they should be able to remember the law that stopped drinking in these States.)

To these ardent reformers who want to do good (as they see good) by using force upon the greatest number of their inferiors, add the groups of those who want to rob others by force without risking going to jail. Since Government has the only legal use of force, all these groups try to persuade and compel the men in Government to use force as these reformers and these thieves want it used. Their weapon is a threat to use the vote, at the next election, to put out of office the politicians who resist them.

The Third Attempt

And whenever they succeed, and do increase the Government's use of force, they reduce the area of every American's free action. They decrease the productive use of energy in this country. And they weaken the only legal protection of every American's property and liberty and life.

Groups have been trying to do this ever since the first Congress met. The Constitutions, and the morality and patriotism of a few politicians—who are almost never thanked—have all this time protected the natural human rights of Americans, from these pressure-groups who use the threat of the vote.

The majority of Americans can not use that threat. They haven't time, they are too busy, they are making their livings and supporting the Government; they can not spend their time in Washington or in their State capitals, watching Congressmen.

Now and then, in a crisis, they can send up a roar from this whole country, and they do. But their voting can not undo anything that Congressmen have done.

If there is a candidate who promises to repeal laws and to reverse a course of action begun by men in Government, then voting can elect him. But electing him is no guarantee that he will keep his promise. He may not be able to keep it. He may be one of those politicians who make promises only to get votes. An average citizen has no means of knowing a candidate personally; no means of knowing how honorable he is.

In any case, while he is in office he controls himself; the voters have no control over him.

On the whole, of course, this is fortunate. For why does anyone suppose that a majority of citizens *should* control their Government?

No one imagines that a majority of passengers should control a plane. No one assumes that, by majority vote, the patients, nurses, elevator boys and cooks and ambulance drivers and internes and telephone operators and students and scrubwomen in a hospital should control the hospital. Would you ever ride on a train if all passengers stepped into booths in

The Discovery of Freedom

the waiting-room and elected the train crews by majority vote, as intelligently as you elect the men whose names appear in lists before you in a voting booth?

Then why is it taken for granted that every person is endowed on his twenty-first birthday with a God-given right and ability to elect the men who decide questions of political philosophy and international diplomacy?

This fantastic belief is no part of the American Revolution. Thomas Paine, Madison, Monroe, Jefferson, Washington, Franklin, did not entertain it for a moment. When this belief first affected American Government, it broke John Quincy Adams' heart; to him it meant the end of freedom on earth; it made him doubt the goodness of his God.

The superstition that all men have a right to vote is a triumph of Old World reasoning.

It is all but impossible to root the ancient pagan superstitions out of Old World minds. When they must admit a fact, they twist it to fit the superstition. For example: They believe there is no energy in the universe. So when they had to admit that this earth spins in space, they imagined the Mechanistic Universe, in which motion is motionless, and energy itself is static.

Just as doggedly, they believe that Authority, Government, controls all men. If they do not flatly deny that men are free, they reason this way: To control himself, an individual must *control the Government that controls him.*

Isn't that bright?

Here are the two points of view:

The revolutionist says that every human being is naturally self-controlling. Therefore, the best conditions for human life are those that least interfere with any individual's exercise of his natural freedom. He can act most freely when no other man uses force to prevent his acting. Government is a group of men who have the use of force; Government is necessary to stop criminals. But any use of force by men upon men is evil, because force has no moral value or effect. Therefore, the best conditions are those in which Government is restricted to the smallest possible minimum; and further progress toward greater use of freedom is in further reducing and restricting Government.

The Old World belief is this: Individuals are cells in a greater organism. All men are naturally dependent, obedient, controlled by Authority. (Communists, Fascists and Nazis say this in a cliché, "The individual is nothing.") Government is Authority, controlling the masses and responsible for their welfare. Therefore, the stronger the Government, the better for the masses. Liberty is the right of the masses to choose the men who control the masses. It is doubtful whether it is advisable to grant the masses this liberty; but, if it is granted, it is a right to vote.

There are the two points of view. They can not be reconciled; they can not be combined. The reason why the American revolution is world revolution, is precisely the fundamental antagonism between these points of view.

A century and a half ago, Americans recognized the fact that all men are free. The Revolution restricts Government. Restricting American Government permits every individual in these States to exercise his natural freedom to a greater extent than freedom can be exercised anywhere else on earth.

One effect of the Revolution is that some Europeans adopted the belief that liberty should be permitted; that is, that all men should vote. During the past forty years this belief has been increasing in these United States.

It gets such thinkers into practical difficulties, for the Mechanistic Universe can stay in the realms of fantasy, but human beings are real. So these Old World thinkers must struggle with the question: How can all individuals control the Government that controls them?

Obviously, it is not possible for *each* person to control himself by controlling someone else who controls him.

So they say that every individual has a right to vote, and a majority of votes must control the Government that controls all citizens. Thus, the largest possible number of persons will control the Government that controls them.

Then what becomes of the exercise of freedom by the individuals in the minority? Why, they must submit to control by the majority. Everyone should be happy to sacrifice himself (the Greeks did) to the pagan god Demos, The Greatest Number. The voice of the Greatest Number is the voice of God. If anyone is not willing to obey the Greatest Number; why, this is outrageous, this is anti-social; make him submit and obey.

And how can you make him submit? Why, by force, of course; the police. Oh yeah, Mr. Hitler?

This is not the reasoning of the Americans who wrote the Constitutions that protect individual freedom. It is not the reasoning of many Americans now. But it is the reasoning that has been extending the vote in these States for half a century.

Small groups of reformers, fiercely determined to do good to others, have made these extensions by using the threat of the vote upon office-holders. A few crooked politicians and ward-heelers have aided them. They have worked against the vast indifference of most Americans. For instance: American women did not want to vote; Miss Alice Paul forced woman's suffrage through Congress and the State legislatures.

These extensions of the vote are in two directions; they take in increasing numbers of the population, and they throw more office-holders to the wolves of "a common passion or interest felt by the majority."

American common sense does not attach much importance to voting. In normal past elections, not half the qualified voters took the trouble to cast a ballot. The typical American reaction to voting is, "What's the use?"

In the first place, no one can possibly vote intelligently, unless he gives his whole time to politics and knows, personally, each of the candidates of both parties. Most Americans are

The Third Attempt

too busy, using their energy to raise the American standard of living.

In the second place, the vote does not control men in office. The protection of an American's liberty is not in voting, it is in the Constitutional restriction of the office-holder's interference with individuals; and in every American's vigilant defence of human rights—his own, and every other person's—by individual and mutual action, in all human relationships.

In the third place, the very idea of a majority is a delusion. Wherever this idea is applied, the actual result is that the decision is made by a few. All votes are ties, so to speak, and the Chairman casts the deciding vote. A few hundred thousand votes have decided elections in which millions of Americans cast ballots. In 1916, Mr. Hughes was congratulated as the President-elect for almost twenty-four hours, before a last little dribble of votes from California re-elected Mr. Wilson.

Average Americans have common sense. They know that there are always enough stupid, ignorant, dishonest voters to carry any election; they know that demagogues, liars, hillbilly bands, popular actors and orators, free picnics and vote-buying can always corral enough voters. They know that these extensions of the franchise have broken down the moral standards of American politics, and have so overcome the moral character of American politicians that both parties use these methods of getting votes. And that therefore an election is merely a sporting event, like a ball game, its outcome depending on luck as well as on skill, and its object being no more than to get ballots into boxes, and men into office.

Unquestionably, these extensions of the franchise are dangerous to individual liberty and human rights.

They are dangerous because, by amending the Constitutions, they destroy representative government and increase the danger of democracy—*which always creates an irresponsible tyrant.* And they are dangerous because they are made in the superstitious belief that individuals can control a Government that can control individuals, and therefore they tend to in-

211

The Discovery of Freedom

crease the false, counter-revolutionary belief that Government is an Authority controlling men and responsible for their welfare.

More and more, the multitudes who vote are believing this, and demanding that Government be responsible for their living conditions.

The fact is that nothing but human energy working productively can produce any of the necessities of human life, any human living conditions.

Men in Government can not be responsible for activities which they do not control, and never can control. Police can no more control any man's working than they can control his drinking or his breathing. The whole of history proves this, if common sense does not. Government regulation, government "control," slows down production, hinders it, prevents it, reduces it, and can not possibly control it.

The more the men in American government are dependent upon satisfying popular demands, and the more Americans believe that Government is a controlling authority, the more this Government is compelled to use force to hinder and restrict the exercise of natural individual freedom; that is, to prevent human energy's working under its natural control and for its natural productive purpose.

Constitutional law, and the American politician's conscience, still resist this attack upon the exercise of natural human rights in this Republic.

But in this increasing democracy there is, as Madison said, nothing to check the inducements to sacrifice the weaker minority; there is no protection for any man's property or personal safety.

The increasing belief that everyone has a natural right to vote because *voting is mass-control of a Government that controls individuals,* is counter-revolutionary in these States. It is a revival of the ancient Old World superstition. It threatens every American's home and liberty and life; it threatens the existence of the Republic and the survival of the Revolution.

The Third Attempt

Originally, the use of majority-vote in American government was only as a check on Government. Constitutional law gave a majority of tax-payers a quick recall of the men who assessed and spent their taxes.

This principle is worth thinking about.

Using this principle today would alter the structure of State governments, for the people of each State determine the qualifications of voters. But the unique characteristic of American Government is its flexibility. Americans are always adapting the structure of their Government to the new conditions that American energy constantly creates. A State legislature or a convention of delegates can always make a new Constitution.

Apply the principle of using the vote, not as an imaginary and impossible *control* of men in office, but realistically in the American revolutionary way, as a check on men in office. The effects today would be innumerable.

For example: No one but automobile owners would vote for members of Highway Commissions or pay for highways. They would elect the Commissioners by direct vote, pay taxes directly to them for building and maintaining highways, and re-elect (or not re-elect) the Commissioners frequently. (Of course, American Government never should have interfered with highways. Americans had created a free, *mutual* association, the American Automobile Association, which was dealing competently with all the new questions arising from the invention of automobiles. Private enterprise originated and built the first trans-Continental American highway; free manufacturers and car-owners would have covered this country with highways, as free Americans covered it with wagon-roads. Americans wanted cars and highways; no police force was needed to take their money from them and spend it for highways. And it is injustice to the Americans who do not own cars, to compel them to pay for highways.)

In general, using the vote on its genuine American basis would make it possible for voters to vote intelligently, concerning their own personal affairs with which Government is dealing, and for a few men whom they would naturally watch. It would give tax-payers a direct check on the spending of their tax-money, and on the men who assess and spend it.

And it would certainly be a welcome relief and help to every honest American politician in office, and an inducement to able and honest Americans to go into politics.

8. REPUBLICANISM

"THIS republic is born a pigmy. It has required the support of two such powerful States as France and Spain to obtain its independence, but the time will come when it will be a giant, a colossus formidable even to those countries.

"The liberty of conscience, the facility of establishing a large population upon an immense territory, will attract agriculturists and mechanics of all nations, for men ever run after profit.

"In a few years we shall see the tyrannical existence of this colossus of which I speak. *These fears are well founded.* They must be realized in a few years, if some greater revolution even more fatal does not sooner occur in our Americas."

Count Aranda, saying this, was hopelessly trying to arouse the Old World to its danger. He was the distinguished European statesman of the time. Like Charles the Second, he had the misfortune to be Spanish; his country was still the plaything of Europe because Spaniards were still abjectly submissive, and had no energy. But Count Aranda was truly intelligent; he saw beneath surfaces to principles of human nature and human action. So he spoke in vain to the "practical" men.

He spoke a century and a half ago, thirteen years after the Declaration that all men are free. Europeans did not understand this Declaration. They heard of republicanism, far away in England's rebellious colonies, as Americans in 1917 heard of bolshevism in Russia. They asked each other, "What are republicans? What is republicanism; what does it mean?"

When they heard that the rabble in America had lived some

The Third Attempt

two years (and more, in some States) with no Government whatever, and that now they were trying to substitute a Constitution for a King, they could not take the spectacle seriously. European intellectuals went wild with enthusiasm, believing that the fabled Age of Reason had suddenly appeared in America. But not the practical men.

By all reports, conditions in America were rapidly going from bad to worse. Naturally; for republicanism was anarchy, there was no social order, no Authority. The lower classes were entirely out of hand. Disorder was increasing daily; affairs were in utter chaos at last report; the rebel colonies were doubtless fighting each other by this time. The next ship will bring news that the whole mad scheme has collapsed. Americans will gladly welcome England and Spain when they move in to restore order.

Europeans used the new word, republican, to mean a ridiculous, detestable fanatic, a "bolshevik." Anyone who, like Count Aranda, took republicanism seriously, must be half in sympathy with the crazy scoundrels.

Look at the actual situation. True, the rebels are out of British control, but the French did that, as a war-measure to weaken England. French finances are in such a deplorable state that France can hardly afford to resume the war and take the colonies, so England will get them back. England holds the Atlantic, Canada, and the northwest; British troops are in Ohio and their loyal Indians kill any American who ventures north of the Ohio river.

Spain holds the Floridas, from the Atlantic to the Mississippi, and the great river and the whole continent west of it. Look at the map. These republicans are penned in, surrounded. They have no outlets for trade, they have no money, no resources, no ally but doubtful France, and they are hopelessly in debt to France; they can not pay their French debt, they can not even pay their rag-tag army, and the unpaid troops are revolting. This pigmy Republic survive? Don't be fantastic; it's collapsing now.

The Discovery of Freedom

The immediate question, as no one knew better than Count Aranda, was whether England or Spain would take western Virginia (Kentucky). A rabble of ungoverned Americans was fighting the Indians in that wedge of country between England and Spain. They could not live with no trade-outlet to the sea. Spain closed the Mississippi to them, and Major-General Wilkinson, commanding the United States Army, went down to New Orleans and sold Kentucky to Spain. The Spanish Government was generously paying him for it in advance.

The British still regarded American ships as British property. British naval captains, needing seamen, commandeered them from American ships, and laughed at protests that these men were not British subjects, but American citizens. Nonsense; a few rebels do not change facts by signing a piece of paper. "Citizen," indeed! These men are proper British subjects, trying to act above their station; a dose of the cat-o'-nine-tails will teach them better. This upstart "republic" is a little incident of the French war. Time will remedy that.

"This republic will be a colossus," said Count Aranda. "The liberty of conscience . . . men ever run after profit . . . These fears are well founded. They must be realized *in a few years.*"

Thirteen years after the Declaration of Independence and of freedom, the ox-wagons and the roving hogs that were the city's scavengers were cleared from New York's main street for the inauguration of His Excellency General Washington, first President of the United States. Two months later, the members of the States-General in France declared themselves a National Assembly, and announced their intention to make a French Constitution. This was republicanism. The American Revolution was erupting in Europe.

Too many young French aristocrats had fought with the Americans for freedom. Too many had felt, as the captured Hessian soldier said to Thomas Paine, "America is a fine, free country! It is worth the people's fighting for. I know the difference by knowing my own; in my country, if the Prince says, Eat straw; we eat straw."

Too many believed, as the Marquis de la Fayette ("American," the French now called him) believed: "For a nation to love liberty, it is sufficient that she knows it." Jefferson had advised Lafayette to call a National Assembly; Lafayette stood up in the Assembly of Notables and demanded that they call a national assembly.

The assembly was called. When the Court moved quietly to dissolve it and whiff away this preposterous idea of a Constitution, the people of Paris stormed the Bastille. "Why, this is a revolt," said the surprised King. He was answered, "No, sire; it is a revolution."

The Revolution's colors, red, white and blue, rose over all France. Under the American flag and the French tri-color, under the portraits of Washington and Franklin, the revolutionists debated their policies. They raised in Europe the standard of the American Revolution; to dramatize their accepting American leadership, they made the Revolution's leader, General George Washington, a citizen of the French Republic—first citizen of the two Republics that foreshadowed the future World Republic. They sent for Thomas Paine; they gave him French citizenship; three French provinces elected him to represent them; he sat in the inner councils of the National Convention.

So quickly, Count Aranda's fears were realized. Republicanism was in Europe. Every army in Europe attacked it. This war lasted twenty years; it was the first war ever fought to extinguish a political idea.

"An army of principles will penetrate where an army of soldiers cannot," Thomas Paine wrote. "It will succeed where diplomatic management would fail; neither the Rhine, the Channel, nor the ocean can arrest its progress; it will march on the horizon of the world, and it will conquer."

The French revolution lasted twelve years; it ended when French democracy elected the Emperor Napoleon.

The Discovery of Freedom

9. THE REPUBLIC SURVIVES

THE bewildered, struggling, unfortunate French people, however, perhaps saved the Revolution. So long as their energy kept the Napoleonic spectre of republicanism stalking across Europe, the desperate Kings paid little attention to the distant Republic in America.

Russia simply refused to recognize the United States. England kept troops on their soil as a bulwark against Spain, and still treated American sailors as rebellious British subjects. France had recognized the Republic, but Napoleon disregarded it in his plan to take North America from both Spain and England.

Indeed, why should anyone take it seriously? In six years of fighting, the Americans had not been able to win their own independence; in thirteen years they were barely able to say that they had a Government, and by what a narrow margin —3 votes in New York, 9 in Massachusetts. And what a Government, that did not even pretend to govern. Without unity, without money, without an army, without any social order or any ruling Authority, surrounded on all sides by the Great Powers and as helpless as Poland had been, how long would these rebels keep their shadowy independence?

Based on all past European history, that was sound reasoning.

It did not apply here, precisely because American Government was weak. The opportunity to exercise human rights released a terrific human energy. No one expected what happened; no one could possibly have planned it.

When individuals are not prevented from acting freely, they create the unprecedented. Americans acted in ways that good subjects never dreamed of. Americans still seem to Europeans the most lawless of peoples.

While the precarious Government was carefully not offending England, in the western wilderness Mad Anthony Wayne, grossly exceeding his orders, followed up his victory over the

The Third Attempt

British Indians by threateningly backing the British troops out of Ohio.

When Major-General Wilkinson, commander of the armed forces of the United States, had sold Kentucky to Spain and been paid for it, in Paris two Americans, without authority, without even communicating with their Government, bought half this continent from under the feet of Spain.

They paid fifteen million dollars, which they had no authority to spend, and bought Louisiana from Napoleon, who had no right to sell it. (But Napoleon was an Emperor.)

They had instructions to buy, if possible, a port on the Gulf, to pacify the lawless Kentuckians who were threatening both to secede to Spain and to fight Spain in order to get an outlet for their bear-fat and furs.

Already Napoleon was feeling baffled at times by the strange way in which his planning did not work. His invasion of England, planned perfectly again and again, somehow never came off. His plan for conquering North America receded, again and again. Asked if he would sell a port in Louisiana, he had a brain-storm. He replied, No. He would sell all Louisiana, or nothing.

This reply staggered Talleyrand. It reversed Napoleon's whole world-policy. Asked why, Napoleon said simply, "I need the money." He added that, since he could not get Louisiana, he would make the Americans strong enough to keep England from ever getting it. "Perhaps it will also be objected to me that the Americans may be found too powerful for Europe in two or three centuries, but my foresight does not embrace such remote affairs. Besides we may expect rivalries between the members of the Union. The Confederations that are called perpetual only last until one of the confederating parties finds it to its interest to break them." [5]

He demanded an answer immediately; yes or no, and be quick about it. So right now, without authority, acting on

[5] Louis Houck, *History of Missouri*, Vol. 2, p. 349. R. R. Donnelly & Son Co., Chicago, 1908.

The Discovery of Freedom

their own responsibility, Robert Livingston and James Monroe bought Louisiana. No one knew its boundaries.

And anarchy poured from Kentucky across the Mississippi. Sixty thousand Americans in ten years. One hundred years of planned and encouraged settlement had done just one-tenth as much.

When Captain Stoddard raised the Stars and Stripes above the heads of the silently weeping crowd in St. Louis, he ended free land west of the Mississippi. Land had been free until then; the French and Spanish governments had given the settlers not only free land, but free tools and free seeds, and free provisions until crops could be raised.

American Government gave no one anything. It sold land, to the highest bidder. Five million acres, unmapped, sold in one day's frenzied bidding in Franklin, Missouri; and that one day's bidding ran the price of land sight unseen to $50 an acre. (When wages were twenty-five cents for a twelve-hour day.) American Government took no care whatever of the buyers, most of whom were speculators and lost their shirts.

Ten years later, Americans had fought and won a second war for recognition of the Republic's independence. Napoleon was in St. Helena; and Divine Right monarchy was triumphantly restored everywhere in Europe. (Triumphant, but—a little shaky, a little apprehensive, listening now and then; surely not to a small crackling sound in the foundations?)

Five years more, and in all these States the wild bull-market in western lands suddenly collapsed. All banks failed; all trade stopped. Families on the frontier were starving; men could not buy powder and lead to kill game. Moses Austin was wiped out.

In those fifteen years since the American occupation, Moses Austin had made his third fortune, into the millions of dollars. His trade ran from St. Louis to the West Indies, to the Atlantic coast and Europe. His mines and his foundries and shot-towers supplied munitions to Napoleon, and to Andy

The Third Attempt

Jackson's men who licked the British at New Orleans. Moses Austin founded a bank in St. Louis; his young son, Stephen, back from college in Connecticut, represented the Austin interests in the Territory's legislature.

One week's crash ended all that. Nothing was left, nothing. Moses Austin owed $300,000 to creditors in Kentucky, for the one little item of rented slave-labor. The old man, nearing sixty, did not even own a horse. He walked two hundred and fifty miles to Little Rock, Arkansas, where young Stephen sat in a log-cabin, defeated candidate for a seat in the Arkansas legislature. Stephen had a mule and one slave. His father insisted on giving him a $90-promissory note for them, and the old man and the slave took turns riding the mule seven hundred and fifty miles to San Antonio. There Don Moses Austin asked again for free land in New Spain. He got it, and died of exhaustion from the trip, with his last words urging Stephen to develop the free land and pay the debts.

Desperate westerners were walking a thousand miles through hostile Indian country to get the Santa Fe trade that revived the west. Young Stephen found hundreds of families eager to travel a thousand miles for a barrel of corn, three pounds of lead, and a chance to work ten years to pay for a farm.

Stephen Austin, the college boy, the millionaire's son, grew old in the next twenty years. He never married, he never owned a roof; a horse and saddle were his only possessions. He worked day and night, trying to get the settlers established on that raw land, trying to keep peace between them, and peace between them and the Mexican Government. Every cent he got from the settlers he applied to paying his father's debts. He paid the last one of them, and lay down in a settler's house, ill from exposure and exhaustion.

For several days he rested, intending to get up next day. Then all one day he was unconscious. Suddenly he woke and sat up, radiant. "Have you seen the papers!" he exclaimed. "The United States have annexed Texas!"

The Discovery of Freedom

It was not true, but he never knew that it was not. He fell back on the corn-shuck mattress and died.

In his old age Jefferson, considering the future, could not be sure that the Revolution would succeed. Eternal vigilance, he said, is the price of liberty. Would Americans in the unknown future remember that? Who could say? Only the ordinary, unknown individual could defend freedom on earth, for not by any use of force can men in Government maintain any man's use of his natural human rights.

In two centuries or so, he thought—say about the year 2000 —the Mississippi valley would be settled. Then there would be the danger of cities growing up. Men lose touch with reality in cities. If Americans would stay on the land, making their living with their own energy from the earth; and if they could all learn to read, so that future American thinkers and writers could educate them constantly in the principles and meaning of the Revolution, then Americans would make a new world.

10. The Industrial Revolution

HERE it is: the New World.

No one expected anything like this. No one could imagine it. A hundred years ago, fifty years ago, thirty years ago, no one could imagine such a world as this.

For six thousand years men and women lived and died young in hunger, filth, and disease. Believing that Authority controlled them, in six thousand years they contrived to build pig-sty shelters (and pyramids, and marble palaces) and to sow grain and cook meat, to saddle horses and yoke oxen and chain slaves to mills and to oars.

For a hundred and fifty years, Europeans of all races, creeds, and cultures lived here in America, rebelliously subject to Authority, and by disobedience to Authority they improved their living conditions; they built houses, sowed seed, cooked meat, rode horses, goaded oxen and owned slaves.

The Third Attempt

The Revolution began here, in living conditions hardly changed since Nebuchadnezzar reigned. A little more than a century ago, here in this country, men carried men on their shoulders, as coolies still carry men in China.

American women still cooked over open fires, as women had cooked since before history began, and as more than two-thirds of the women on this earth are still cooking.

Eighty years ago in New York State, every woman made her household's soap and candles. Oil was always in this earth; men discovered it when Babylon was young; Romans knew it and saw it burning; no European had ever made kerosene.

American women still spun thread and wove cloth, with the spindle and the loom that were older than Egypt. Older than Egypt, the water-wheel and the millstones still ground the grain that American farmers still cut with the knife and threshed with the flail that are older than history.

In one century, three generations, human energy has created an entirely new world, a dynamic world, constantly changing under the drive of terrific, incalculable energy.

What explains this? What explains the effectiveness of any kind of energy? Nothing but the existence of conditions which permit that energy to operate naturally, under its own natural control. A gasoline engine works effectively because men have created the cylinder, piston, and spark plug, which permit gasoline vapor to transform itself into force by the laws of its own nature.

Then what are the conditions that permit human energy to work effectively to satisfy human needs and desires?

Look at what has happened. Where has this terrific effectiveness of human energy appeared on this earth? Only in this Republic, in England, and on the western rim of Europe; only on this small part of the earth, among this minority of the earth's population, during this one century.

Where is the greatest effectiveness of human energy? Here in this Republic, where a seventh of the earth's population creates more material wealth than all the rest of the twenty-

223

two hundred millions of human beings, and distributes that wealth more equally than wealth has ever been distributed anywhere else. Next most effectively, among the people of the British Commonwealth. And a little effectively, in western Europe.

Human energy works to supply human needs and satisfy human desires, only when, and where, and precisely to the extent that men know they are free. It works effectively only to the extent that Government is weak, so that individuals are least prevented from acting freely, from using their energy of body and mind under their own individual control.

All history shows this fact. Every detail of common experience today proves it. The electric light proves it; the car in the garage proves it. How did Edison create the electric light? How did Americans create the millions of American cars?

They used free thought, free speech, free action and freehold property. The unhindered use of natural human rights creates this whole modern world. Nothing else makes it possible for men to create new things, and improve them and keep on improving them.

And what stops this dynamic creation of the constantly changing New World?

Precisely the same thing that for six thousand years prevented its creation: submission to Authority, to Government.

The "control" of trade by Governments stopped it, in this country, in 1929. The denial of human rights in Europe and Asia stops it, now, here, in this Republic.

Americans at this moment are suspending their exercise of individual freedom; and what is happening to their transportation, their shopping, their normal building, their housekeeping?

Certainly, Americans are submitting to Government's "control" willingly, more than willingly; because tyranny makes war, and only tyranny can fight a war; and in the New World that freedom has created, tyranny on the other side of the

The Third Attempt

earth compels Americans to fight a world war for the Revolution against the tyranny that denies human rights.

But energy works by its own natural laws, or it does not work. Submission to Authority is always and everywhere voluntary, because individuals control what they do. Submission is voluntary now in Japan and in Germany. An Egyptian obeyed the Pharaoh because he believed that the Pharaoh was God. A Nazi obeys Hitler because he believes that German Authority can make the kind of world he wants, or because he believes that he must obey. An American obeys an order from this Republic's leaders in Washington, because he *knows* that nothing but his obedience to Authority can win this war.

The practical effect in all cases is the same: Obedience to Authority stops the effective working of human energy to satisfy normal human needs.

This submission to Authority has always been permanent in the Old World. Americans will turn their terrific energy, the energy of free men, temporarily into war, as Spaniards turned their energy into the conquest of the American hemisphere and of all Europe. Nothing on earth can stand against this American energy in war. But if ever Americans believe that the effectiveness of human energy comes from submission to Authority, they will win this war and lose the New World.

The free exercise of natural human rights creates this New World. Stop this exercise of human rights, shed individual responsibility and individual freedom, submit to "control" of ordinary human affairs, and this whole new world of economic abundance, this unprecedented wealth of food, shelter, health, knowledge, comforts, luxuries, pleasures, this young world of swift transportation, swift communication, this dynamic complex of productive human energies encircling the whole planet, can no longer be improved, then no longer be created, then no longer exist.

Do you assume that this new world can not vanish? This world that your grandfather could not imagine, and that your children now take for granted, do you think that your grand-children must surely inherit it?

Do you imagine that the planes can not be grounded, the factories close, the radio be silent and the telephone dead and the cars rust and the trains stop? Do you suppose that darkness and cold and hunger and disease, that have never before been so defeated and that now are defeated only on this small part of the earth, can never again break in upon all human beings? Do not be so short-sighted.

The energies of living individuals must constantly create these defences of human life and these extensions of human powers.

Relinquish the free use of individual energies, and these defences must vanish as the Roman galleys vanished. This whole modern world must disappear as completely as the Saracens' swift, clean, healthy and luxurious world disappeared. Every effect ceases when its cause no longer operates.

This whole modern civilization, that is not fifty years old, that is not yet established on any large part of the earth, can cease to exist.

It must cease to exist, if individual Americans forget the fact of individual liberty, and abandon the exercise of individual self-control and individual responsibility that creates this civilization.

Young Americans who have known nothing but this new world, naturally take it for granted. They see a great deal that is wrong in it; they can very easily imagine a better world. So can any honest person. The eternal hope of humankind is in the eternal human desire to make this world better than it is.

But when they imagine that a control exists, or can exist, which can be used over individuals, to make a better world according to any plan, they are falling into the ancient delusion that Hitler now has. They are listening to European-minded Americans who never have awakened from that delusion.

The Third Attempt

This new world is an exercise of free, self-controlling individual human energy, precisely as a plant is an exercise of the natural life-energy in a seed.

The exercise of human rights creates this whole new world, this dynamic interplay of productive energies around this whole planet, that must constantly be created or it cannot exist. Nothing but individual human energy, working freely under its natural, individual control, can keep on creating this new world and keep it existing.

The industrial revolution is only the material part of the American World Revolution. This is Revolution in the whole of human life, because it is a recognition of the real nature of human energy.

This Revolution has actually changed every aspect of everyone's life, in health, hygiene, sanitation, diet, clothing, in knowledge, culture, art; it changes all human relationships, in families, neighborhoods, politics, work and play.

The material changes are called the industrial revolution; they are changes in methods of producing from this earth the material things that human beings need and want; that is, wealth.

The industrial revolution did not "rise"; it is not pagan Aphrodite rising from the foam. It didn't just happen; nothing happens without a cause, and in the human world nothing is done that is not done by living persons. There is no inevitable Progress controlling human beings; Tennyson was quite wrong when he said that the thoughts of men are widened with the process of the sun. Time is completely indifferent to human beings. The year 1000 did not make a single Englishman's thoughts as wide as Aristotle's had been, and there is no guarantee that the year 2000 will.

"The growth of Science," that pagan god of the French intellectuals, did not "create the Industrial Revolution and produce Capitalism." Science does not grow; it does not exist; the word is a name for whatever knowledge of the material world may be in the heads of living persons at a given time.

The Discovery of Freedom

Individual energies, free to work—Edison's, for one—create this totally new human world, and pagan-minded men have made a god of the sum of their successful efforts (forgetting their far more numerous failures) and called it the Industrial Revolution.

It is time that Americans stopped thinking carelessly in these pagan terms, and got down to brass-tack facts.

Any young man who wants to make America over, has within himself the energy that will do it. He lives in his country; it is all around him; his energy is acting upon it now. His daily use of his energy is making America.

The generation that made America what it is now, is dying now; his parents made America over, and so will he.

Forty years ago nobody imagined this America. (There was a $40-a-month mechanic, working ten hours a day, six days a week at his job, and tinkering nights and Sundays in the woodshed behind his little rented house—no bathtub, no running water, no light but a kerosene lamp—in a far, cheap suburb of Detroit; even he did not imagine this America.)

There were no cars, no highways, no radios or planes, no movies, no tall buildings, no electric lights, no toothpaste, not many toothbrushes, no soda fountains, no bottled soft drinks, no hot-dog stands, no High Schools, no low shoes, no safety razors or shaving cream, no green vegetables in the wintertime and none in cans, no bakers' bread or cakes or doughnuts, no dime stores, no super-markets. An orange was a Christmas treat, in prosperous families. There was no central heating, and only the very prosperous had bathtubs; they were tin or zinc, encased in mahogany in the homes of the very rich. The rich, too, had gas-lights. Some streets in the largest cities were lighted, with gas-lamps. Spring came to American children when mama let them go barefoot. No moderately prosperous parents thought of letting children wear out good shoe-leather in the summertime. Stockings were cotton. Sheets were made at home, of muslin seamed down the center, for looms had never made muslin as wide as a

228

The Third Attempt

bed. Mother made all the family's clothes, except Father's best suit, and sometimes she still made that. Forty years ago, a journey of ten miles to the next town (by buggy or mail-hack or train) was planned and prepared for, at least some weeks in advance. America has been made over. Making America over is a continuous process, now almost a hundred years old.

When Americans began the Revolution, no one expected this. Thomas Paine and the other revolutionists of his time were not thinking of changing living conditions. They were thinking of moral values.

What actually occurred, when men could act freely, was a terrific outburst of human energy, changing all life-values, and utterly transforming the material world.

One little incident among hundreds of thousands will illustrate what happened:

Some three thousand years ago, the Greeks knew the principle of the steam engine. Two and a half centuries ago—in 1704, to be exact—a steamboat was running successfully on the river Elbe in Germany. It threatened technological unemployment of boatmen. The steamboat was burned; its inventor barely escaped with his life and died, starving, in exile.

Englishmen were not so well governed as that. About fifty years later, they began to put glass in their windows. They began to take the rotting and leaking thatched roofs from their houses, and use roofs of split slate. They began to use coal and smelt iron. When Washington was President here, some Englishmen were making steam engines.

All these activities, of course, were more or less under Government "control." British Government protected, encouraged, subsidized and controlled the manufacture and sale of steam engines.

Three years after Cornwallis surrendered at Yorktown, an uneducated American, a wandering tinkerer, watch-repairer and surveyor, invented a steamboat; he made a little model of it in a wheelwright's shop in Bucks County, Pennsylvania, and

229

tried it on a nearby stream. It ran. This man saw that steamboats would transform the world; he dreamed of trans-Atlantic steamers.

Acting as men had always been obliged to act (or be criminals) he got a letter of introduction to a politician, and through this politician's favor he submitted a petition to the American Government:

August 30, 1785

Sir:

The subscriber begs to lay at the feet of Congress, an attempt he has made to facilitate the internal navigation of the United States, adapted especially to the Waters of the Mississippi. The machine he has invented for the purpose has been examined by several Gentlemen of Learning and Ingenuity, who have given it their approbation. Being thus encouraged, he is desirous to solicit the attention of Congress to a rough model of it now with him, that, after examining into the principles upon which it operates, they may be enabled to judge whether it deserves encouragement. And he, as in duty bound, shall ever pray.[6]

John Fitch

To His Excellency, The President of Congress.

This letter was read, and referred to a committee. The committee never reported upon it.

John Fitch proceeded patiently in the time-honored manner, from politician to politician. A habit of mind, thousands of years old, assumed that men whose interest is in political principles and political power are naturally the men to decide all industrial and economic questions.

He was a common man with no connections in high places, but the times were simple. He reached Washington, Madison, Monroe, Patrick Henry, Franklin. Each of these gentlemen

---

[6] "For Your Excellency's health, fortune" etc., is understood.

listened to him courteously, and kindly gave him introductions to other politicians.

For five years, in increasing poverty and mounting frenzy, John Fitch petitioned Congress, again and again, and again. Also, every year, he petitioned the legislatures of Virginia, Maryland, Delaware, New Jersey, and Pennsylvania.

He was trying to give his invention to the Government. The Spanish Minister offered to buy it for Spain, but John Fitch refused to sell it to a foreign country. He wrote in his petition to Congress in 1787, "I do not desire at this time to receive emoluments for my own private use, but to lay it out for the benefit of my country. I do not wish any premiums to make a monopoly to myself."

The New Jersey legislature, however—perhaps to get rid of him—and perhaps as a joke—gave him a monopoly of steamboat transportation in New Jersey. This was rather like giving a man today a monopoly of transportation to the moon. But John Fitch was in earnest. A Government grant of monopoly suggested profit, and in six weeks John Fitch found forty men willing to put up some money to build a steamboat.

In the summer of 1790, his steamboat was running in regular service on the Delaware river. Twice a week it carried passengers between Philadelphia and Trenton, at the unheard-of speed of eight miles an hour.

Success was assured. New York State granted John Fitch a monopoly of steamboat transportation, so did Maryland and Delaware and Virginia. But profits eluded the stockholders. The engine and the paddles constantly needed repairs and changes. John Fitch was experimenting and improving. The boat had not even begun to pay for itself, when a storm wrecked it. The Virginia monopoly expired, the stockholders had lost every cent they invested. They would not risk any more money on steamboats.

For eight years John Fitch tried to raise capital. Laughed at, jeered, pitied as a poor crack-brain, finally he went back to the wilderness. He built a remote and isolated cabin in Kentucky,

The Discovery of Freedom

and there, alone, he made a beautifully finished brass model, three feet long, of a railroad engine, with four flanged wheels running on iron rails. Then he killed himself.

Two years later, Chancellor Robert Livingston—who with Monroe had bought Louisiana—got the New York legislature to transfer John Fitch's monopoly to Robert Fulton and extend it for twenty years, provided that within two years Fulton run a steamboat on the Hudson river at a speed of four miles an hour.

Robert Livingston and Nicholas Roosevelt, rich Americans with powerful political influence, were backing Fulton. Fulton had tried to run a steamboat on the Seine in Paris; his engine sunk it. Now he intended to use an English engine.

For four solid years, these politically powerful men brought every possible political influence to bear upon the members of the King's Privy Council.

Chancellor Livingston had been too confident of his power at the British Court. The two years passed; he had to get the New York legislature to renew Fulton's hold on the twenty-year monopoly.

The difficulty, of course, was that men in Government must use economic authority for political purposes. Their function is to use force, in their countries to stop actions that a majority does not approve or does not defend, and in relations with other countries to stop actions that threaten their own countries. Politics deals with questions of the proper uses of force. International diplomacy is a use of the threat of war. (A Great Power is a country strong enough to be dreaded in war.) Men in Government are politicians; their interests are political; their proper and necessary job is politics. If their interests and their proper job were in making steamboats, they would not be in Government offices.

The British Government had no political reason to permit an English manufacturer to sell a steam engine to an American. At the time they were making a diplomatic deal with the Government of Holland, offering a steam engine for a war-

The Third Attempt

alliance. What did the Government of the United States offer His Majesty's Government for a steam engine?

Not a thing. Chancellor Livingston was a politician to be reckoned with. But James Monroe, Minister of the United States to the Court of St. James, nevertheless replied firmly to the Chancellor's request that the Minister request that the King's Privy Council permit the sale of a steam engine to Robert Fulton; he said that the diplomatic situation at the moment did not make such a request advisable from the Government of the United States to the Government of Great Britain.

Bribery is the next recourse. Bribery of Government officials was usual, and expected. (Americans think that graft in American politics is new; actually it is a dying-out survival from pre-Revolutionary days. The old Chinese official's "squeeze," and the Turk's "backsheeh" were customary in Colonial America. The Royal Governors publicly complained when their income from graft was low, and officially petitioned the King to make up the deficit. An income from bribes belonged to any European official, as naturally as the franking privilege belongs to an American Congressman.)

I know no record of the means by which Chancellor Livingston and Nicholas Roosevelt finally got His Majesty's Government's permission to buy a steam engine. They got it, and in 1807 the steamboat ran, at four miles an hour, from New York City to Chancellor Livingston's country estate, Clermont, on the Hudson, and on to Albany.

New Englanders immediately saw the stupendous possibilities of steamboats. They applied at once to their legislatures for protection. Fortunes, and workingmen were in peril. Steamboats would ruin the river sloops, the packet-lines, all New England's sailing-ship industries. They would throw out of jobs all the rivermen, sailors, ships' carpenters, rope-makers; they would wreck all New England.

The Connecticut Legislature excluded steamboats from Connecticut's waters. The Senate of Rhode Island taxed all steam-

The Discovery of Freedom

boat passengers, and restricted by quotas the numbers of them permitted to disembark in Rhode Island's ports.

Governments had always protected their subjects in precisely this way. This is the only way in which Government's use of force can protect any man's economic welfare—by preventing other men's economic activities; that is, by stopping economic progress.

But such laws could not be enforced here. They were un-Constitutional. The sailing-ship men must have felt the solid ground give way beneath them.

Twelve years after Fulton's Clermont steamed on the Hudson, steamboats were scaring the Indians in distant Nebraska, and the first steamship crossed the Atlantic—from the New World to Europe.

Three thousand years before, men had known the principle of the steam engine. One hundred and fifteen years before, a steamboat had run successfully on European waters. For fifty years, British Government had been encouraging, protecting, subsidizing and "controlling" the making of steam-engines.

In twelve years, Americans—not encouraged, not protected, not helped and not "controlled"—covered the Western Waters with steamboats, and launched the first steamer that ever crossed an ocean; the first challenge from the dynamic New World to the static Old World.

Speed was created again. Free men were attacking time and space again, as only the Saracens had ever done before.

For the second time in history, men were eagerly seizing upon scientific knowledge and using it, vigorously, to attack the material handicaps and the enemies of human life on earth.

The difference between the motionless Old World and the dynamic New World is not a difference in natural human energy, nor in human desires. It is not a difference in available materials; this whole earth is rich in raw materials. In the beginning, it was not a difference in knowledge.

It is a difference in the vigor, the *effectiveness*, of human energy in subduing this non-human earth to human needs and

The Third Attempt

human wishes. This effectiveness is possible only where individuals can exercise their natural freedom. Its result is the industrial revolution.

Where are the sailing ships now?

Where are the fortunes invested in them? Where are the jobs of the sailmakers and rope-makers, the ships' carpenters, the brass workers, the sailors and captains and pilots? Where are the fields of flax and hemp that used to blossom blue in New England, and the farmers' markets for hemp and flax?

They were older than history. These investments for money, these markets, these jobs, existed before the Trojan wars. Where are they now?

They are in the Old World. Full-rigged four masters still beat down the Black Sea to harbor by Istanbul, and the round-eyed Chinese junks sail like schools of fishes over the Sulu Sea to Borneo. Lateen sails still move traffic on the Nile, and fleets of fishermen (how picturesque!) go out under colored sails from every port of the Mediterranean.

Only on one ocean, between these States and England, the sailing ships have vanished, utterly wiped out in half a century.

The industrial revolution destroys. It is a stream of living human energy as ruthless as Nature itself, destroying to create and creating to destroy. It makes all forms of wealth as impermanent as life. Rome, Paris, Vienna, Nuremberg, are solid rock; decade after decade, century after century those buildings stand. Every American city is a fountain of energy.

How they rise, (and fall) the incredible sky-reaching buildings, more tremendous, more beautiful, loftier and more living than any Acropolis, pyramid or castle ever imagined.

Consider how the sailing ships vanished.

The unprotected sailing-ship men fought tooth and nail for their fortunes and their jobs, but they were doomed. Americans took to steamboats with a whoop and a holler. Lucky was the steamboat that lasted on the inland waters long enough to pay

235

for itself. Americans wanted speed. Rival captains, racing each other and wildly cheered on by their passengers, piled on the cordwood and tar and poured steam into her; they got speed and blew up the boilers, sank the boat. Steamboat traveling was high sport in those days. Many passengers lived to tell of it, but rarely a boat survived two years.

Steamboats had the rivers and the Great Lakes. Steamboats were taking the coast-wise traffic. Another steamer and another crossed the Atlantic from America to Europe. Scores of Americans were improving steam-engines; logically, there was no limit to steam-power. Sailing-ship men could never increase the power of the winds.

For thirty years they hung on, doggedly fighting the steamboat competition and losing, losing year by year. Steam was speed; Americans wanted speed; the passion for speed was ruining the sailing-ship men. They could not change the winds. They must change their ships.

John W. Griffiths, American ship designer, did it. He turned the bow of the sailing-ship inside out.

When his new design, the Rainbow, slid into the North River, New Yorkers gazed at it with the horror that New Yorkers would feel today if they saw the Empire State building standing upside down.

The bows of ships had always been bowls. They floated, they rose to the tops of waves; they stayed on the surface of water. They were safe. The Rainbow's bow curved *inward;* the prow was as sharp as a knife. It would cut into the water; with wind in the sails it would drive headlong to the bottom of the sea. Sailors looked, and backed away. Sail, on a thing like that? straight to Davy Jones's locker?

Griffiths did not intend this ship to rise on the waves. Every rise and fall was a loss of speed. He designed the Rainbow to slice straight through the waves and keep going, fast.

A crew of reckless men, hell-bent, took her out through the Narrows, bound for Canton, China. It was a year's round trip.

The Third Attempt

Six months and fourteen days later, the Rainbow came clipping into New York harbor, from Canton.

She was a wet ship, she took every sea over her decks, but never since God made the seas had there been such speed. Six months and fourteen days, to Canton and back!

American clipper ships took the world's sea-trade. Thin slivers of deck cutting through the waves under acres of canvas towering fifteen stories high, they reeled off the miles, four hundred, five hundred miles a day.

The English were aghast. Snugly protected as they still were in the planned economy that had made Americans into smugglers and rebels, the British sea-traders were losing their trade. In every port that was not British, the unprotected American clipper ships were nipping in under their noses and away with the cargoes.

It was not only that the clipper ships were faster, the British ships now second-rate and slow; the Yankee captains were quicker in a bargain. They had no rules and regulations; no red tape. Every Yankee captain sized up a situation, figured in his head, made his price—and loaded the cargo. In all the world's ports (except the British) the clipper ships came in and went out while British ships lay empty and British traders glumly saw the cargoes snatched away.

The City, the business men of London, were desperate. There was, of course, only one remedy: war. British trade must be protected. British police, the British army, were its only protection; it was safe now, only in British ports. If only the whole world's ports were British.

But the men in British Government thought of the Navy, the British Navy upon which the Empire's existence depended. The incredible Yankee clipper ships were filling the seas. Since the last war (which England had not won) American sea-power had increased enormously. In the next war, this new American marine might mop up the British Navy, the very life of the little island's world empire.

Parliament debated long and earnestly. Desperate situations

require desperate remedies. Englishmen boldly advanced and defended new ideas, for which they would have been transported to penal colonies twenty years before. The first reaction to the American Revolution had been The Terror in England; free speech and semi-free press suppressed; habeas corpus suspended; books burned, men jailed for being suspected of republican opinions; the death penalty for being in an assembly of more than twelve persons, even in a private house. But The Terror was over now. Thomas Paine's (suppressed) *Rights of Man* had sold more than a hundred thousand copies in the British isles. Adam Smith had published *The Wealth of Nations*. Many Englishmen had "traced civil government to its foundation in the physical and moral nature of man."

They stood up in Parliament and pointed to the American facts. What had created the clipper ships? Not the American Government. Not protection, but lack of protection. What made the British marine second-rate? Safety, shelter, protection under the British Navigation Acts.

In 1849, the British Government threw British trade to the wolves. It repealed the Navigation Acts, and opened British ports to the world.

The result was catastrophe. American clipper ships ran away with the Indian trade. They ran away with the trade in England's own home ports. While the now unprotected British ships waited for weeks on the China coast and their skippers begged for cargoes to England, the American clippers from California on their way home to New England dropped into Hongkong, snapped up a full cargo of tea at twice the freight rates that the British were asking, and *ninety-seven days* later they unloaded it in London.

All appeals to the British tea-merchants' patriotism failed. Tea-leaves are loyal to no flag; ninety-seven days from Hongkong they are more fragrant in the cup than they will be two months later, for any Empire's sake.

Desperation spurred the ship builders on the Clyde. In a very few years, the Aberdeen clippers were racing those Yan-

The Third Attempt

kees on the tea-trade routes. Now and then an Aberdeen clipper came in at the finish, minutes or hours ahead.

American clipper ships opened the British ports to free trade. Half a century of American smuggling and rebellion and costly ineffectual blockades; seven years of war in America, and the loss of the thirteen colonies; and all the sound and sensible arguments of English liberals and economists, could not break down the British planned economy. American clipper ships did it.

They were the final blow that brought down that whole planned structure. The great English reform movement of the 19th century consisted wholly in repealing laws. There was nothing constructive in it; it was wholly destructive. It was a destruction of Government's interference with human affairs, a destruction of the so-called "protection" that is actually a restriction of the exercise of natural human rights.

In that mid-19th-century period of the greatest individual freedom that Englishmen have ever known, they made the prosperity and power of the British Empire during Victoria's long and peaceful reign.

And to that freedom, and prosperity and power and peace, the American clipper ship contributed more than any other one thing.

The industrial revolution, which is part of the American Revolution, is a liberating power in human life. By its nature, it sets men free. By its nature, it combats and eliminates the use of force upon individuals.

Slaves who were chained to oars, under the lash, propelled the Roman galleys. Engineers *must* be individually self-controlling, self-reliant, personally responsible, to take a modern liner across an ocean. Did you ever see the engine-room of a modern liner? clean as a laboratory, white-painted, air-cooled?

Hessian peasants, when they fought Americans here, were sold and bought like cattle. They moved in ranks like automatons; every man (in fear of whipping and death) with precisely the same movements obeyed some sixteen orders

239

The Discovery of Freedom

when the ranks loaded, aimed, fired a volley. When their Prince said, Eat straw; they ate straw.

But today, Japanese soldiers are in Formosa *in training* to act self-reliantly, independently; and Hitler's system must *teach* the individual German private to be self-controlling, self-reliant, and responsible, because now the tyrants must use the tools that free men created—the motorcycles, tanks, and planes that oblige men to act as free men.

Any slavery in this world today is a surviving remnant of the ancient slavery. The use of man's natural freedom creates the industrial revolution and makes this New World in which individuals *must* use their natural freedom.

Chancellor Livingston had (in Robert Fulton's name) a twenty-year monopoly of steamboats in New York State. Nicholas Roosevelt apparently held a patent that gave him a monopoly of the side-paddle wheel.

What was the effect of this capitalist monopoly upon the development of steamboats?

Americans immediately objected to monopoly. In Albany a few men formed a company to build steamboats and run them on the Hudson, regardless of Fulton's monopoly. Fulton applied to the New York courts for an injunction to stop them.

Chancellor Livingston also impelled Fulton to get a steamboat patent from the Federal Government. Fulton really had not invented anything. He got the patent, but there was a hidden weakness there; for to get it he had to swear that he had invented the side-paddle wheel.

On the whole, it seemed best to get a stronger law. Chancellor Livingston got it from the New York legislature. This law gave Fulton the right to seize any rival steamboat as if it belonged to him and were stolen property; it compelled the New York courts to grant Fulton an injunction against any rival company whenever he asked for one; and it fixed the punishment of a rival steamboat owner at a $2,000 fine and one year's imprisonment.

The Third Attempt

The Albany owners launched their steamboats on the Hudson. Another man ran a steamboat on Lake Champlain. They pointed to the Federal Constitution, which forbids American Government to make an ex-post-facto law. They had built their boats before the New York legislature passed this new law.

And Americans declared that Government had no right to grant monopolies. In all the taverns they denounced the Chancellor and Fulton and their pet legislature. And worse than denouncing, they would not ride on Fulton's steamboats.

Mr. Cadwallader Colton of New York City, a most respectable gentleman who viewed with abhorrence the low rabble's disrespect for the Chancellor, saw with his own eyes their behavior.

In the summer of 1811, he says, "I was a passenger on board the Paragon, then new and recently established, confessedly, in every respect, and particularly as to accommodation and speed, the superior of the Albany boats. Chancellor Livingston was himself on board; and I recollect that Mr. Jacob Barker and his wife, and I think Mr. Walter Browne, who is now a senator, were also among the passengers, who in the whole were eighteen.

"We started a few minutes before one of the Albany boats. Something happened to our machinery, which stopped us, and enabled the Albany boat to go ahead. She must have had upwards of a hundred passengers on board; her decks were absolutely crowded. I wish you could at that moment have seen the Chancellor, and heard his reflections." [7]

The police and the courts were succeeding, however, in hindering the building of steamboats in the eastern States. Few men could afford the long and costly battles that the Albany men fought in the courts. The higher court stood firm for Chancellor Livingston, and Chief Justice Kent thundered from the bench:

---

[7] Seymour Dunbar, *A History of Travel in America*, Vol. 2, p. 383. Bobbs-Merrill, Indianapolis.

The Discovery of Freedom

"It is asked, can the entry of them [steamboats] into this State, or the use of them within it, be prohibited? I answer, yes; equally as we may prohibit the entry or use of slaves, or of pernicious animals, or an obscene book, or infectious goods, or anything else that the legislature shall deem noxious or inconvenient."

Meanwhile the Chancellor was thinking of a monopoly on the Mississippi. Governor Claiborne of Louisiana, visiting New York, had an interesting conversation with the Chancellor and Fulton, and when he returned, the legislature of the Territory of Orleans granted Fulton's company an exclusive monopoly of steamboats on the lower Mississippi.

As soon as this news arrived, Fulton built a steamboat in Pittsburgh. In 1811, Nicholas Roosevelt and his family, with a crew of six, embarked on it for New Orleans. This was the first steamboat on the Western Waters, and when the captain let its steam roar through the exhaust pipe, the settlers along the river banks heard Gabriel's horn and prepared to meet their Maker, now.

Next year the prodigy reached New Orleans, to that city's intoxication. Twelve months later a competitor was on the Ohio, not yet covered by any Fulton monopoly (except the Federal patent). Four years later, Henry Shreve of Virginia was on the Mississippi in the Washington, a double-decker driven by high-pressure engines. He made the round trip between Louisville and New Orleans—the round trip, mind you —in *forty-one* days!

All Louisville cheered itself hoarse. Louisville's ladies and gentlemen gave Henry Shreve a glittering reception and a dinner at which, pardonably affected by the occasion and wine, Henry Shreve replied to a toast with a prediction that someday a man would travel from Louisville to New Orleans *in ten days*. Everyone indulgently let it pass. The sheriff seized the Washington; Fulton's attorneys were in court, demanding an injunction to stop the boat's operation.

Twenty men along the western rivers cautiously began to

build steamboats, and stopped. Nicholas Roosevelt was warning them, by advertisements in the eastern papers:

"No other person in the United States has any patent, but myself, for the invention of Vertical Wheels. Having obtained a legal title to the sole use of steamboats with such wheels, I hereby forewarn all persons from using them hereafter without licence from me. Individuals or companies who use such wheels without my licence after this, will be prosecuted under the Law of Congress, for damages amounting to the profits of the boat. Licences will be sold by me at moderate rate, and warranted.

"Nicholas J. Roosevelt."

Evidently the partners had fallen out. Who knew what the courts would decide? And what chance did an ordinary man stand in a battle between those giants, Chancellor Livingston and Nicholas Roosevelt?

Two years passed in doubt. Then, Oh glorious news! The Louisiana courts release the Washington! A State monopoly is not Constitutional. Only the Federal Government can grant monopolies on inter-State waters.

Five years later, steamboats were running from Pittsburgh to New Orleans, from St. Louis to the western prairies beyond the settlements.

The struggle in the courts went on for years, but westerners take a chance. Sure, I'll try anything once! Hell, this is a free country! a man can't any more than lose.

Nicholas Roosevelt gave up. How can you chase a steamboat over two thousand miles? The police and the courts cost more than the licence is worth. Chancellor Livingston had lost the New York State monopoly; it was un-Constitutional. And he never made an effort to prosecute under Fulton's Federal patent on Nicholas Roosevelt's side-wheel.

These facts are a parable, too. Government maintains any monopoly.

An economic or financial monopoly today is a fragmentary

remnant of the ancient, absolute and complete Government monopoly. In this New World, every surviving monopoly is a Government grant, protected by the police. Without that protection, no monopoly could exist.

To demand that Government dissolve the monopolies that it maintains, is an absurdity on the face of it. American Government creates the Trusts; and American Government tries to enforce an anti-Trust law. Any Administration that wants to prevent and destroy Trusts has only to abolish the Office of Patents.

Let Government stop protecting the Trusts by police force, and there will be no restraint of trade.

Nothing but force obstructs the free action, creative and destructive, of human energies. And in civilization, Government is the monopoly of force.

The way to increase the power of any economic, industrial, commercial, financial monopoly, and to make it so impregnable that no peaceful means can destroy it, is to make it a Government monopoly. (No American can start a competitive postal service in this country.) The way to return to the ancient totalitarian monopoly of all industry and all commerce and finance, is to return to the planned economy, the Government ownership of all means of production and distribution.

Human beings want free, unprotected monopolies, or they would not create them. Individual Americans created the one telephone service in many cities in this country, by deserting many telephone companies. At the same time, Americans support some sixty thousand independent telephone companies in these States, for American Government is the only Government that does not hold a monopoly of telephone service.

Free Americans created the dime stores and the supermarkets, by deserting the flyspecked little Boston Racket stores and the old general merchandise emporium with its cracker barrels and plows. And Americans tomorrow will desert and destroy the chain-stores' so-called monopolies, if anyone invents a better method of satisfying an individual's needs.

The Third Attempt

During this revolutionary century, the monopolies that men have built in these States have been less protected by Government than any monopolies in the past or elsewhere. Generally speaking, this revolutionary Government has not tried to control (and actually restricted) anyone's buying and selling. And being able to act freely, Americans have destroyed monopolies as rapidly as they created them.

Americans can destroy the whole automotive industry tomorrow, simply by buying planes; just as, simply by buying cars, they destroyed yesterday that looming monster, that Shame of the Cities, the Street Car Monopoly; and as free Americans destroyed the stage-coach-and-tavern monopolies by using steamboats, and the river steamboat and the Pilots' Union monopolies, by using railroads.

In a free economy, that free individuals plan and control, no monopoly can exist that does not anxiously serve and please the largest number of individuals; no monopoly can survive if it ceases to serve and please them.

This fact is one great discovery, made during this past century. When the police do not interfere with the natural uses of human energy, no economic monopoly is safe.

This is the reason why the counter-revolutionists, the communists, fascists, nazis, who do not believe that men are free and who do not trust human nature, are trying to restore the ancient Government monopoly, which is protected and enforced by the police so that no individual can attack it and no inventive genius can destroy it.

And this is the reason why in every country today, "Big Business" and "Labor"—that is to say, the greedy and unscrupulous or ignorant among men of great wealth, and the ignorant or criminal men among labor-union leaders—welcome the Government that gives police protection to their monopolies of wealth and of labor.

When free men improved steamships so that not even the

clipper ships could any longer compete with them, Americans lost the American mastery of the seven seas.

They lost it because the British had free trade (which American clipper ships had given them), but Americans were still "protected" by the Protective tariff.

This semi-blockade of trade, maintained by American police at the frontiers of these United States, raised American prices and wages so high in the artificial terms of dollars, that an American steamship made of American metals by American workers could not carry passengers or freight in world trade as cheaply as the British metal ships. Therefore, Britannia rules the waves.

And therefore, when the Republic needs ships, this Government must take billions of dollars from these "protected" Americans and spend the money for Government building of ships—and lacks American seamen to man them.

Held inside the Protective wall, Americans stopped building ships. Instead, they built automobiles and planes. So no one can ever know what advance, as incredible as the clipper ships, free competition would have impelled Americans (and English) to create in steamships.

The high prices and high wages that the police can maintain by blockading trade, at a frontier or within a country, really mean nothing at all. It makes no actual difference whether a man earns $2 a day or $25. The real measure of the cost of goods is the amount of human energy that is used in creating these goods from the earth's materials.

Forty years ago, a man worked twelve hours for a dollar; butter cost ten cents a pound. Now a man works seven or eight hours for $10; butter does not cost a dollar, but perhaps fifty cents a pound. He can raise the price of butter by raising his wages, or lower the price by lowering his wages, and all this figuring in dollars is playing with illusions. The real cost of butter is the amount of energy used in producing the butter.

Forty years ago, a pound of butter cost an hour's churning in a pottery churn with a wooden splasher, by hand; not to mention all the straining of milk twice a day, and skimming the cream from the pans with a wooden ladle, and washing the strainers and pans and ladle, and running up and down cellar with the cream jar; and this does not mention the chores at the barn.

Today the milk flows by thousands of gallons through separators and creameries; machines do the churning and mould the butter and cut it into quarter-pounds and wrap it in paper and put it into waxed and lithographed boxes; it travels in refrigerated trucks to porcelain electric-refrigerators. And a pound of butter used to cost ten cents and now costs fifty, and actually its cost has been cut in half.

The obstruction of trade at this Republic's frontiers turned American energy away from building ships (so that now more energy is needed to build needed ships in great haste) but American producers—both owners and wage-earners—were mistaken in believing that the obstruction of trade increased American prosperity.

Americans are the richest people on earth, not because an exchange of useful goods is hindered at the frontiers, but because Americans are more able to use their natural freedom than any other people on earth.

Human energy is the only thing that produces goods. In one century, Americans have so increased the effectiveness of human energy, that an American worker produces an enormously greater amount of goods, in less time, with less human energy, than any worker ever did before in history or can do now anywhere else on earth where industry has not been "Americanized."

All goods are produced for use. There is no production that is not for use. The so-called "profit system" ceases to exist (as every American knows who can remember 1929) when people are hindered from consuming all the goods they are producing.

If no Government anywhere obstructs the free working of human energies, men distribute and consume goods as fast as they produce them. That is the purpose and object of production. No man can possibly have any other object in producing goods. Mr. Ford does not make profits by piling cars one upon another in Michigan; if Americans ever stop consuming his cars, Mr. Ford will go broke. All his past profits will vanish utterly with his vanishing plants, as all the stage-coach companies' profits vanished when the stage-coaches rotted.

Because all goods produced must be consumed, and human energy in America produces more goods than anywhere else, all Americans consume more. This is the reason why the American standard of living is the highest ever reached yet. This is the reason why, for the first time in six thousand years, men have begun to believe that poverty can be abolished.

It can be. It will be. The Revolution is only beginning. When all living men know that men are born free, the energy of twenty-two hundred million human beings will be released upon this earth.

A hundred million have made America. What will twenty-two hundred millions do?

11. THE WORLD REVOLUTION

FEWER than three million men and women began the Revolution, not two centuries ago. On a very small area of this earth, a small percentage of its population have been able to use their natural freedom;—to the greatest extent in these States, to a lesser extent in the British Commonwealth, and a little on the western rim of continental Europe.

For little more than a century, human energy has been effectively attacking the enemies of human life—most effectively in these States, a little less effectively in the British Commonwealth,[8] and somewhat on the western rim of Europe.

---

[8] Cross the world's only unfortified frontier, to Mexico or Canada, and see the difference. The Mexican revolution is not established yet. How slowly the Canadians penetrate their western forests; how few are their cars and their highways; how almost static their population. Their garage signs say, "Cold patches. Hot patches here!" as American garage signs said thirty years ago.

The Third Attempt

Americans have been most vigorously creating the industrial revolution: steamships, railroads, telegraph, trans-oceanic cables, telephones, farm machinery, elevators, skyscrapers, subways, bridges, dams, hydro-electric plants, radios, airplanes—the New World.

Americans created the machine age; mass production, and mass distribution of the produced wealth. (For wealth produced *must* be consumed.) Americans created modern medicine, modern hygiene, modern sanitation, modern dietetics.

Americans are now creating the power age; they are gathering the power of gravitation that keeps the stars in their places, and transforming it into streams of power flowing through the machines and driving the stream-lined trains and the hyrocompasses and the radio beams, and lighting the cities and the farmers' barns and toasting the bread for breakfast.

Americans are creating the chemical age; new chemicals, new metals, new fabrics, synthetics, plastics, innumerable ways of subduing to human uses the infinitesimal tininess within the invisible electron, that is totally imperceptible to any human sense or any instrument—a root of power that only human imagination can grasp.

Three generations—grandfather to grandson—have created wonders surpassing the utmost imaginings of all previous time.

Never before in their long history have Europeans lived ninety-five years without a famine. In the Americas, in the British Commonwealth, and in western Europe (but nowhere else) no mass-population has starved utterly to death (until this war) since the year 1848.

The free use of human energy in these States has completely transformed living for every American. Twenty years ago, American energy began transforming the whole human world for everyone living on this planet.

Since 1920, American energy, American techniques, Americans in person, have been building the New World around the earth. Americans industrialized Russia (a man from Connecticut built Dnieperstroy dam, that the retreating Russians

The Discovery of Freedom

have just destroyed). Americans rationalized German industries. Americans modernized China, Japan, Persia, Arabia, Africa.

All Europeans and Asiatics have one word for this creation of the New World in their countries. It is, "Americanization." (Their intellectuals hate it; it attacks the very basis of their Old World thinking.)

Only once before in known history has there been anything resembling this New World in character. That was the Saracens' world, that stretched across three continents, from the Atlantic to China and the Ganges, and lasted for eight hundred years.

This New World embraces the whole planet. It reaches the most remote islands, it includes the Eskimos beyond the Arctic circle and the naked savages in equatorial jungles. And it is not yet fifty years old.

Nothing like this was ever before dreamed of. This is a totally new world. This is a world that has nothing to do with races, creeds, classes or nations. It abolishes all barriers between human beings. Railroads pushed through frontiers; telephones pierced them. Planes fly over them. Radio knows nothing of any frontiers.

This new world is an intricate interplaying of dynamic energies, a living network enclosing the whole earth and linking all human beings in one common effort, one common fate. A Greek ate bread because an American smoked cigarettes. Americans ate pineapples ripened in Hawaii because the Burmese mined tin. A Japanese mother's baby grew fat and laughing because an American schoolgirl wore silk stockings. Americans sped on whirling rubber because the Malays tapped rubber trees. This is the brotherly human world that human beings naturally want to create; it is the world they begin to create when no false belief and no use of force prevents them.

But men's minds change more slowly than their acts. An old habit of thinking persists when the thinker's own acts contradict it; the men who made the first horseless carriages, the motor cars, equipped the dashboards with whip-sockets and whips.

Riders on the western prairies, where there is nothing to tie a horse to, throw the reins over his head. In mid-gallop, he halts when they touch the ground. He stands; hungry, thirsty, within sight of food and drink, he does not stir until those reins are lifted. He is not tied; he is free. A false belief holds him more firmly than ropes can.

The ancient world is more than six thousand years old. Americans began this revolutionary attack upon it not two centuries ago. And in every American there are remnants of pagan superstitions and of unquestioned old assumptions, and a taking-for-granted of barriers of race and class and creed and color and nationality between human beings. Americans must learn how to be free.

Of the twenty-two hundred million men and women living on this earth, only a few have ever understood the Revolution. Not even all Americans understand the fact that individuals control the only energy that makes the human world.

The discovery of this fact, here in America, has shaken and confused men's minds everywhere.

Its first world-effect was the French Revolution. For four years in France, a few men who understood freedom tried to establish the Revolution there, among a vast majority that unquestioningly believed in Authority. Then those few were overwhelmed in The Terror; they died on the guillotine.

Such as it was, and including The Terror, the first French effort lasted twelve years. Its life was as short as its death was violent. It ended when French democracy, by an overwhelming vote—3,500,000 to some (counted) 2,500—elected the Emperor Napoleon.

Shouting the battle cry of freedom, without knowing what it meant, conscripted Frenchmen marched out to conquer all Europe (and to attack Russia) for the glory of France and the hereditary Empire of Napoleon. They went willingly, eagerly, believing they were free because they had voted for

The Discovery of Freedom

the tyrant they obeyed, and their energy carried the French flag from the Atlantic to the Black Sea and from Gibraltar to Moscow. They wiped out frontiers and overturned thrones, and set up those thrones again with Napoleon's puppets upon them.

Napoleon's effort was what Hitler's is now. It was the Old World reaction to the American Revolution. Napoleon was trying to make (by force) a united Europe in which all Europeans would be controlled in a planned-by-Napoleon economy, enforced by French police and serving, not Hitler's Germany, but Napoleon's France. Napoleon's Continental System loomed over Europe as Hitler's New Order does now. His effort to establish it and to make it work went on until the human energy of France was utterly exhausted. Then Napoleon fell. As Victor Hugo said, God had grown tired of Napoleon.

That first French effort to join the Revolution had created modern Germany.

But the Revolution has never ceased in France. Since the French joined it, they have created three Republics, one Commune, and three Empires. All that, in less than ninety years. The Third French Republic ends now in two ways; in the dictatorship of Marshall Pétain, and the Fighting France of General de Gaulle.

Of course this is not the end of the Revolution in France. Writing about it less than a century ago, Carlyle said, "And from this present date, if one might prophesy, some two centuries of it still to fight! Two centuries; hardly less."

Meanwhile, the Revolution was spreading rapidly in Count Aranda's "our Americas."

1810-12: Uprisings in Mexico, Venezuela, Argentine, Chile, Paraguay, Uruguay. (Napoleon's Grand Army is invading Russia.)

1813: Mexico declares its independence. Bolivar, the liberator, drives the Spanish Monarchy from Venezuela.

1818: Constitutional Republic of Chile.

1819: Constitutional Republic of Colombia.

The Third Attempt

1820: Italians rise and fight for Italian liberty and unity.
And in the Balkans, and in Africa, the Revolution inspired men with a hope of liberty.

1815: The Serbians rise and fight for free Serbia.

1821: The Greek Declaration of Independence. Lord Byron, England's rebel poet, tried to lead the Greek revolution and died in Greece.

1821: The Constitutional Republic of Peru. The Constitutional Republic of Guatamala.

All over the Americas and all over Europe, the hope of liberty led countless unknown men to risk their lives, and lose them, or lose the hope. In a century of wars, they helped to tear Serbia, Greece, Egypt, Bosnia, Herzogovina, Croatia, Dalmatia, Roumania, Bulgaria, from the Turkish empire. The Austrian Empire got the western Balkans; the British empire took Egypt and dominated Greece.

Everywhere in Central and South America, liberators rose and fought and freed their countries from the Old World. From the Rio Grande to Cape Hope they established struggling constitutional Republics. And the President of these United States, as leader of the Revolution, announced to the Old World that Americans will fight to protect the existence of any or all of these younger Republics. That is the Monroe Doctrine.

In the 1840's, the American Revolution was causing confused rebellions in every European country. Tens of thousands of defeated revolutionists, especially from Germany, fled for refuge to these States.

In the 1850's, Garibaldi, the Italian liberator, returned from fighting for the Revolution in South America, to fight for it in Italy. Italian revolutionists still want both freedom and unity. To date, they have got Mussolini.

In 1860, the Czar of Russia freed the Russian people, serfs, from their feudal bondage to the land. And Russians began to try to establish a Constitutional Monarchy.

In the Americas, the revolts continued until 1898, when

253

The Discovery of Freedom

Americans first went out from the Republic to fight for the Revolution. United States troops helped Cuban revolutionists to free Cuba from Spain. At the same time, Filipino revolutionists won their long fight to drive the Spanish from their islands.

(But this is real World Revolution; it is not a dream; it will not proceed smoothly to Utopia. This Revolution is real, and up against realities. It has a world to conquer, a real world that resists it.)

Counter-revolution was in this Republic. Instead of freeing the Cubans, the Federal Government seized Cuba. When the victorious, happy Filipino revolutionists had welcomed American troops as allies and friends, the Americans attacked them and fought them for four bloody years (singing, "Civilize 'em with a Krag!") and took their islands; the Federal Government paid the Spanish Government for them.

Americans later repudiated this relapse into Old World imperialism. The Federal Government gave the Cubans their independence, and arranged to give the Filipinos independence in 1946.

In 1911, the American Revolution appeared in China. Chinese revolutionists, educated in these States and helped by Americans in China, dethroned the Dowager Empress and began their effort to establish a Chinese Republic.

At the same time, Kurds, Arabs, Turks, Armenians, were joining the Revolution. The frightened Sultan of Turkey granted them a Constitution; then, more frightened by the popular enthusiasm, he revoked it. Turkish revolutionists dethroned him, and after years of confused and bewildered efforts they have now got a dictator instead of a Sultan.

In 1912, the Revolution inspired even Albanian feudal lords. They came out of the Middle Ages to declare the independence of the Albanian Republic, and they modeled their Constitution of Lushnija upon the American Constitutions. The Five Powers (France, England, Germany, Russia, Italy) put a German King on a throne in Albania, and protected him from his sub-

The Third Attempt

jects with their gunboats in Durazzo harbor—but only until they turned their guns upon each other in 1914.

In 1917, Americans fought in Europe for the Revolution. First results: revolution in Russia, revolution in Germany; a brief essay at a Russian Republic, a longer-struggling German Republic; then communist counter-revolutionists seized Russia, Fascist counter-revolutionists seized Italy, and German democracy elected National Socialist counter-revolutionists.

So much for a rapid glance at the first century of World Revolution. Not one generation, nor one century, conquers the real world.

Ever since Count Aranda spoke, the enemies of the American Revolution have known that this is World Revolution. Until fifty years ago, every American school child knew that this Republic is a revolution against the whole world, and that its first enemies are the European despots. Every Fourth of July speaker until 1888 said so.

John Quincy Adams was merely referring to the general American expectation when he said:

"When the day shall come for your representatives to determine whether the territories of Ceylon and Madagascar, of Corsica and Cuba, shall be governed by rules and regulations emanating from your Congress; whether the inhabitants of those territories shall be governed for a discretionary time by such persons and in such manner as the President of the United States shall direct, and whether their people shall ultimately be constituted into States represented upon the floor of your national legislative assemblies, then will be the time for discovering in distant perspective the full import and final consequence of that second section of the Act for taking possession of Louisiana." [9]

_____

[9] *The Writings of John Quincy Adams,* Vol. 7, pp. 337-41, 1822. Mr. Adams opposed the Act of Congress which authorized the President to administer the ceded territory of Louisiana. He said that this Act exceeded the Constitutional power of Congress; and that, because of the inalienable rights of men, not Congress nor the President but the people of the ceded territory

255

The Discovery of Freedom

The World Revolution has been going on for only a little more than a hundred years. Americans lead it. Americans have already determined the freedom of Cuba. The time is near when Americans will determine the freedom of Madagascar and Ceylon and Corsica.

World Revolution is a revolutionary change in men's minds, in their view of the nature of this universe and the nature of man. The Revolution is a struggle of knowledge against blind superstition; it is the American revolutionary recognition of the fact that individuals are free, pitted against the ancient pagan superstition that Authority controls individuals.

The strongest counter-revolution comes naturally from Germany. Not because a German is naturally different from any other human being; he is not. Germans are naturally no more barbarous, no more cruel, no less brotherly to all human-kind than Americans are. (The American record is not blameless.) But the people who live on that part of the earth called Germany do not inherit from their ancestors any knowledge of freedom.

Those peoples have always been outside Europe. Rome did not conquer them; they knew nothing of the equality of Roman citizens in Roman law. The Church did not hold them strongly enough to teach them the feudal idea of human rights. They were too far away from the Saracens' world; its influence did not reach them as it reached Italy and England. In 1776, when their Prince said, Eat straw; they ate straw.

Suddenly Napoleon's imperialism overpowered them, as Hitler's tyranny overwhelms Poland now. Napoleon's armies compelled their Princes, at the bayonet's point, to join in the German Confederation that was part of Napoleon's Continental System.

---

must determine their form of Government. (Thomas Paine did not agree with him. He contended that the people of Louisiana had not fought for their freedom nor won it, and did not know what freedom is; that therefore they did not know how to exercise it and would not do so if they had the opportunity; that they must learn from experience in Constitutional Government that all men are free.)

The Third Attempt

When God grew tired of Napoleon, the German Confederation was left in the ruins of his Continental System. Bismarck took charge of it. He socialized Germany, under the Kaiser's Authority. (The Germans did not question Authority; they never had.) Bismarck regulated, regimented, disciplined the Germans, and treated them very well. Bismarck's Government established compulsory workmen's compensation; compulsory workmen's insurance (taken from wages) for old age and for unemployment; compulsory labor-union membership; compulsory socialization of farmers; old age pensions and mother's pensions, and compulsory State education for children.

For the first time in German history, the Prince did not say, Eat straw. Very kindly he said, Give me your money and I will give you back some of it when I think you need it.

This was a vast improvement. Naturally the Germans liked it. Anyone would, who knew no better.

Fifty years ago, all Europeans profoundly admired the German socialist-autocrat system. Forty years ago, the fashionable phrase that all fashionable American intellectuals were constantly repeating was, "Germany is fifty years ahead of us in social legislation."

Thirty years ago, Theodore Roosevelt, the most adored American President, for whom every American child's toy bear was named Teddy, climaxed his whole career (in popular American opinion) when, as ex-President, he was received as an honored guest by the Kaiser of Germany.

Since 1860, there has been coming out of Germany a world-current of counter-revolutionary thinking. Marx was German; he led world socialism, that became international communism; and, in Italy, Mussolini's (Fascist) dictatorship; and in Russia, Lenin's and Stalin's (Proletarian) dictatorship; and, in Germany, Hitler's (National Socialist) dictatorship. The basis of all these is belief that Authority can control individuals for their own good, in a better social order than individuals can create for themselves.

In these States, Americans sincerely desiring to do good to

The Discovery of Freedom

the masses or the working classes have been laboring for forty years to improve the condition of their (alleged) inferiors by Bismarck's methods. So Americans now have compulsory workmen's compensation, compulsory workmen's insurance (taken from wages) for old age; compulsory unemployment insurance; general taxation (in some States) for old age pensions; compulsory labor-union membership (dues, as in Bismarck's Germany, taken from wages); and some compulsory socialization of farmers.

It is not to be expected that World Revolution will not be affected by reactions. Forty years after this Revolution began, the English people were enduring what their historians call The Terror; all their liberties were taken from them. Yet forty years later, the English Reform Movement had repealed hundreds of restrictive laws, had thrown British ports open to free world trade, and had given Englishmen more liberties than any people in the Old World had ever before enjoyed.

Individuals control human energy; they make all forms of human association, according to their individual beliefs. No law and no force that exists in Government has ever stood, or ever can stand, against the belief or the knowledge that is in individual minds.

For this reason, the only dangerous change that the German reaction in this country has made, is the substitution of compulsory State education for the former American free education.

Forty years ago, American children went to school because they wanted to go, or because their parents sent them. Children knew the fact that schooling is a great opportunity which the Revolution had opened here to all American children alike. They made every effort to go to school; they walked miles through deep snow on winter mornings to reach school. They studied eagerly, to learn. They controlled their behavior in school, for improper behavior might be punished by their being sent home from school; deprived of half-a-day's schooling. The worst of all possible punishments was being expelled from school. That punishment, far worse than whipping, was held in reserve for rare instances of some pupil's utter lack of self-discipline.

The only schools supported by (compulsory) taxes were grammar schools. The belief was that a community should offer every young child an opportunity to learn. After grammar school age, a boy or girl was able to get his own education if he wanted one. Everyone did want one, who was capable of learning at all, for the years in grammar school only whetted an appetite for learning.

All over this country were Academies, private schools, privately owned and managed as the Saracens' schools were; they offered the equivalent (for those times) of the present High School curriculum; they offered it at various costs, suited to every circumstance. When Mark Twain was a boy in Missouri, graduating students of Missouri's Academies read their essays and delivered their orations in five languages (Latin, Greek, French, German, and English), to audiences that knew these languages well enough to appreciate fine points of style. There were bookshops where Kansas City is, before Kansas City was there; and by camp fires in ox-wagon stockades on the Santa Fe trail, the traders read Greek poets in Greek and European history in French. Any student could work his way through the Academies and the colleges. And many of America's most valuable citizens today, did it.

This American method of education never fully developed; it was stopped about forty years ago, by the eager German-minded reformers, who believed that the State can spend an American's money for his, or his children's, education, much more wisely than he can. American schooling is now compulsory, enforced by the police and controlled by the State (that is, by the politicians in office) and paid for by compulsory taxes.

The inevitable result is to postpone a child's growing-up. He passes from the authority of his parents to the authority of the police. He has no control of his time and no responsibility

The Discovery of Freedom

for its use until he is sixteen years old. His actual situation does not require him to develop self-reliance, self-discipline and responsibility; that is, he has no actual experience of freedom in his youth.

This is ideal education for the German State, whose subjects are not expected ever to know freedom. The discipline in German schools is strict; it tends to train the young into the obedient submission that men in German Government demand from their subjects.

But it does not work that way in this country, because American educators naturally try to compensate for the counter-revolutionary compulsion in this school system. They do not subject American children to rigid German discipline. On the contrary, they try to make schools so enjoyable that the children will not realize that the police compel them to be there. (But the children know it.) The teachers try to make learning easy, a game. But real learning is not easy; it requires self-discipline and hard work. The attempt to make learning effortless actually keeps a child from discovering the pleasure of self-discipline and of the mental effort that overcomes difficulties and does a thoroughly good job.

This is cruel treatment of the new generations of Americans who must come out of this compulsory and yet too softly pampering schooling to face the realities of a world in which human beings are free and living is not easy. And it is not the best preparation for inheriting the leadership of the World Revolution for freedom.

The Revolution has been causing upheavals in almost every country on earth, for a hundred years. Now the counter-revolutionists come out of Germany, determined to end it.

New tyrants, defending the ancient tyranny, intend to destroy utterly this new idea that men are free. They do not believe it. As firmly as Lycurgus or Nebuchadnezzar, they believe that all men are naturally subject to Authority (all but themselves.) Government, they believe, is Authority; they are Government. They accept that responsibility. They believe that

260

The Third Attempt

they should, and that they do, control the inferior masses. And by the use of the real power, force (permitted by the false beliefs of their wretched subjects) they intend to make their imaginary static world orderly, as it was before the Revolution began.

Mussolini will bring back the grandeur that was ancient Rome. Hitler will resurrect the Holy Roman Empire of the 16th century and establish it with pagan gods older than Rome, to endure for a thousand years. The Japanese will have all Asia for the Asiatics, as it was before Mohammed was born.

Fanatic reactionaries, counter-revolutionists, defenders of a tyranny older than history, they imagine that they can go back to the past before America was discovered. And they dare to claim that *they* are creating a new world!

And now they are armed. The Revolution has armed them as tyrants never were armed before.

The caterpillar tractor that Americans invented to plow the peaceful fields and multiply the farmer's productive energy as if by magic, now armored and armed it charges in battalions of tanks over the bodies of men. The submarine, that an American invented to rescue a broken man from imprisonment on St. Helena, now it lurks hidden under all the seas to kill men. The machine that two brothers invented in their bicycle shop, to give all men wings, now it makes the moonlit sky a terror that drives men underground. This is what Authority does with the tools of the Revolution.

Blind, ignorant, bestially unable to understand this New World, these counter-revolutionists use free men's discoveries, their inventions, their techniques and their tools, to tear this earth-encircling network of dynamic, productive energies to pieces and to destroy the freedom that creates it. Idiots who would kill the living thing they want, by clutching it.

This is war around the whole earth *because* human energy, working under its natural individual control and therefore working naturally and effectively to satisfy human needs, has created this New World encircling the whole earth.

261

The Discovery of Freedom

This is war in the air and war under all the seas, because for the first time in all known history, individuals have used their energy freely to explore the depths of the sea and to rise to the farthest heights of air.

Americans are fighting a World War now because the Revolution is World Revolution. Freedom creates this new world, that cannot exist half slave and half free. It will be free.

"Ignorance is of a peculiar nature; once dispelled, it is impossible to re-establish it. It is not originally a thing of itself, but is only the absence of knowledge; and though man may be *kept* ignorant, he cannot be *made* ignorant.

"There does not exist in the compass of language an arrangement of words to express so much as the means of effecting a counter-revolution. The means must be an obliteration of knowledge; and it has never yet been discovered how to make a man *unknow* his knowledge." [10]

Americans know that all men are free. All over this world there are men who know it now. The pigmy Republic has become a colossus. And too late and too little, the Old World tyrants attack this Revolution with its own tools.

Win this war? Of course Americans will win this war. This is only a war; there is more than that. Five generations of Americans have led the Revolution, and the time is coming when Americans will set this whole world free.

---

[10] *The Writings of Thomas Paine,* Vol. 1, "The Rights of Man," p. 151. Vincent Parke & Co., New York, 1915.

Fox & Wilkes

Charles James Fox (1749–1806) inherited wealth and guidance from his father, who tutored him in gambling and who advised, "Never do today what you can put off 'till tomorrow." In 1786, just nineteen, the roguish Charles Fox took his seat in Parliament and quickly earned the esteem of his colleagues, Edmund Burke among them. The two joined forces on many causes, including that of the American Revolution, until Burke's horror over the French Revolution occasioned a permanent break. Fox fought for religious toleration, called for abolishing the slave trade, and advocated electoral reform. In defending his views he was a powerful orator, acknowledged as the ablest debater of his day. Neither party nor crown could dissuade him from following his own path. Above all things Fox hated oppression and intolerance, and in his passion for liberty transcended the conventional party politics of his day.

Like Fox, **John Wilkes** (1727–1797), too, could be extravagant in his passions. He married into his money and was an active member of the proudly blasphemous Hellfire Club. A few years after joining Parliament in 1757, he began a weekly journal, *The North Briton*, that became notorious for its wit and wickedness. In the famous issue #45 Wilkes assailed a speech given in the King's name; he was jailed for his temerity. His *Essay On Woman*, an obscene parody of Pope's *Essay On Man*, along with a reprinting of #45, led to further imprisonment and expulsion from Parliament. But the public rioted for his release and kept voting him back into office. Wilkes eventually won substantial damages and set important precedents regarding Parliamentary privilege and seizure of personal papers. After finally being allowed to rejoin Parliament in 1774 as Lord Mayor of London, he introduced libel legislation ensuring rights to jury trial, and continued to fight for religious tolerance and judicial and parliamentary reform. The monument on his grave aptly describes him as a friend of liberty.

Both Fox and Wilkes could be self-indulgent, even reckless in pursuit of their own liberty, but they never let personal foibles hinder them in championing the rights of the individual.